D1367658

HUMAN COMMUNICATION
An
Interpersonal
Perspective

Stewart L. Tubbs
General Motors Institute

Sylvia Moss

Random House · New York

First Edition
987654321
Copyright © 1974 by Random House, Inc.

Library of Congress Cataloging in Publication Data

Tubbs, Stewart L. 1943–
HUMAN COMMUNICATION.
Includes bibliographical references.
1. Communication—Psychological aspects.
I. Moss, Sylvia, 1937– joint author. II. Title.
BF637.C45T8   153   73–13941

ISBN 0-394-31634-7
Manufactured in the United States of America. Composed by Cherry
Hill Composition, Pennsauken, N.J. Printed and bound by the
Kingsport Press, Kingsport, Tenn.

Cover: Jeheber & Peace
Design: Arthur Ritter

Acknowledgments

Grateful acknowledgment is made to the following illustrators and agencies for permission to reprint illustrations from copyright material:

Drawings by Charles M. Schulz. © 1970 United Feature Syndicate, Inc. Reprinted by permission.

Drawing by Art Sansom. Reprinted by permission of Newspaper Enterprise Association.

Drawing by James Thurber. Copr. © 1957 by James Thurber. From *Alarms and Diversions*, published by Harper & Row. Originally printed in *The New Yorker*. Reprinted by permission.

Drawing by Handelsman; © 1972 The New Yorker Magazine, Inc. Reprinted by permission.

Grateful acknowledgment is made to the following authors and publishers for permission to reprint selections from copyright material:

From Dean C. Barnlund, "Toward a Meaning-Centered Philosophy of Communication," *Journal of Communication,* 11 (1962), p. 199. Copyright © 1962 by the International Communication Association, and reproduced by permission.

From Harriet Rheingold, Jacob Gewirtz, and Helen Ross, "Social Conditioning of Vocalizations in Infants," *Journal of Comparative and Physiological Psychology,* 52 (1959), p. 69. Copyright © 1959 by the American Psychological Association and reproduced by permission.

From David Jenkins, "Prediction in Interpersonal Communication," *Journal of Communication,* 11 (1961), p. 134. Copyright © 1961 by the International Communication Association. Reprinted by permission of the publisher.

Excerpted from "To Know Why Men Do What They Do," by David McClelland in *Psychology Today* Magazine (January 1971). Copyright © 1971 Communications/Research/Machines, Inc. Reprinted by permission of the publisher.

From C. M. Mooney and G. A. Ferguson, "A New Closure Test," *Canadian Journal of Psychology,* 5 (1951), pp. 129–133. Copyright 1951 by the Canadian Psychological Association. Reprinted by permission of the publisher.

From Magda B. Arnold, "A Demonstrational Analysis of the TAT in a Clinical Setting," *Journal of Abnormal and Social Psychology,* 44 (1949), p. 100. Copyright 1949 by the American Psychological Association and reproduced by permission.

From Abraham S. Luchins, "Primacy-Recency in Impression Formation," in *The Order of Presentation in Persuasion,* edited by Carl I. Hovland *et al.,* pp. 34–35. Copyright © 1957 by Yale University Press. Reprinted by permission of the publisher.

ACKNOWLEDGMENTS

vi

From Solomon E. Asch, "Forming Impressions of Personality," *Journal of Abnormal and Social Psychology*, 41 (1946), p. 261. Copyright 1946 by the American Psychological Association and reproduced by permission.

From Clairol Incorporated; advertising slogan property of Clairol Incorporated and used herein with its permission.

From *Attitude and Attitude Change*, by Harry C. Triandis, p. 53. Copyright © 1971 by John Wiley & Sons, Inc. Reprinted by permission of the publisher.

From David Smith and Clark Sturges, "The Semantics of the San Francisco Drug Scene," *ETC.: A Review of General Semantics*, 26, no. 2 (1969), pp. 168–175. Copyright © 1969 by the International Society for General Semantics. Reprinted by permission of the International Society for General Semantics.

From Sam Glucksberg, Robert M. Krauss, and Robert Weisberg, "Referential Communication in Nursery School Children: Method and Some Preliminary Findings," *Journal of Experimental Child Psychology*, 3 (1966), p. 335. Copyright © 1966 by Academic Press, Inc. Reprinted by permission of the publisher.

From John Haller, "The Semantics of Color," *ETC.: A Review of General Semantics*, 26, no. 2 (1969), p. 203. Copyright © 1969 by the International Society for General Semantics. Reprinted by permission of the International Society for General Semantics.

From Dominick Barbara, "Nonverbal Communication," *Journal of Communication*, 13 (1953), p. 167. Copyright 1953 by the International Communication Association. Reprinted by permission of the author and the publisher.

From Randall Harrison, "Nonverbal Communication: Explorations into Time, Space, Action, and Object," in *Dimensions in Communication*, edited by Jim Campbell and Hal Hepler, p. 165. Copyright © 1965 by Wadsworth Publishing Company, Inc. Reprinted by permission of the publisher.

From Weston La Barre, "The Cultural Basis of Emotion and Gestures," *Journal of Personality*, 16 (1947), pp. 49–68. Copyright 1947 by the American Psychological Association, and reproduced with permission.

From *My Fair Lady* by Alan Jay Lerner and Frederick Loewe. Copyright © 1956 by Alan Jay Lerner and Frederick Loewe. Reprinted by permission.

From Donald Hebb, *A Textbook of Psychology*, 3rd ed., p. 235. Copyright © 1972 by W. B. Saunders Company. Reprinted by permission of the publisher.

From David W. Johnson, *Reaching Out: Interpersonal Effectiveness and Self-Actualization*, p. 35. Copyright © 1972 by Prentice-Hall, Inc. Reprinted by permission of Prentice-Hall, Inc.

Adapted from Cal Downs and Wil Linkugel, "A Content Analysis of Twenty Selection Interviews." Paper presented to the annual conference of the International Communication Association, April 1971, in Phoenix, Arizona, and later published in *Personnel Administration/Public Personnel Review*, September-October 1972. Reprinted by permission of the authors.

From Edgar H. Schein, "The Chinese Indoctrination Program for Prisoners of War," *Psychiatry*, 19 (1956), pp. 159–160. Copyright © 1956 by William Alanson White Foundation, Inc. Reprinted by permission of the publisher.

From Michael A. Wallach, Nathan Kogan, and Daryl J. Bem, "Group Influence on Individual Risk-Taking," *Journal of Abnormal and Social Psychology*, 65 (1962), p. 77. Copyright © 1962 by the American Psychological Association and reproduced by permission.

From *Personality and Interpersonal Behavior* by Robert Freed Bales. Copyright © 1970 by Holt, Rinehart and Winston, Inc. Reprinted by permission of Holt, Rinehart and Winston, Inc.

From *Up the Organization,* by Robert Townsend. Copyright © 1970 by Robert Townsend. Reprinted by permission of Alfred A. Knopf, Inc.

From Carl Larson, "Forms of Analysis and Small Group Problem Solving," *Speech Monographs,* 36 (1969), pp. 452–455. Reprinted by permission of the author.

From Robert Blake and Jane Mouton, "The Fifth Achievement," *Journal of Applied Behavioral Science,* 6 (1970), p. 418. Copyright © 1970 by the *Journal of Applied Behavioral Science.* Reprinted by permission of the publisher.

Excerpted from "Community: The Group Comes of Age," by Carl Rogers in *Psychology Today* Magazine (December 1969). Copyright © 1969 Communications/Research/Machines, Inc. Reprinted by permission of the publisher.

Excerpted from "Group Therapy: Let the Buyer Beware," by Everett L. Shostrom in *Psychology Today* Magazine (May 1969). Copyright © 1969 Communications/Research/Machines, Inc. Reprinted by permission of the publisher.

From Warren G. Bennis, "Interpersonal Communication," in *The Planning of Change,* by Warren G. Bennis, Kenneth Benne, and R. Chin, p. 409. Copyright © 1961 by Holt, Rinehart and Winston, Inc. Reprinted by permission of Holt, Rinehart and Winston, Inc.

From Roger Harrison, "Defenses and the Need to Know," *NTL Human Relations Training News,* 6 (1962), pp. 1–4. Copyright © 1962 by *NTL Human Relations Training News.* Reprinted by permission of the publisher.

From *The Decline of Radicalism,* by Daniel J. Boorstin. Copyright © 1969 by Daniel J. Boorstin. Reprinted by permission of Random House, Inc.

From Franklyn S. Haiman, "The Rhetoric of 1968: A Farewell to Rational Discourse," in *Contemporary American Speeches,* 2nd ed., edited by W. Linkugel, R. Allen, and R. Johannesen. Published by Wadsworth Publishing Company, Inc. Copyright © 1969 by Franklyn S. Haiman. Reprinted by permission of the author.

From Evelyn Sieburg and Carl Larson, "Dimensions of Interpersonal Response." Paper presented to the annual conference of the International Communication Association, April 1971, in Phoenix, Arizona. Reprinted by permission of the authors.

From *Prisoner's Dilemma: A Study in Conflict and Cooperation,* by Anatol Rapoport and Albert Chammah, pp. 24–25. Copyright © 1965 by The University of Michigan Press. Reprinted by permission of the publisher.

From *Of Human Interaction* by Joseph Luft by permission of National Press Books. Copyright © 1969 by National Press Books.

From *Self-Disclosure: An Experimental Analysis of the Transparent Self,* by S. Jourard. Copyright © 1971 by John Wiley & Sons, Inc. Reprinted by permission of John Wiley & Sons, Inc.

To
    Gail and Brian,
Harry and Michael

Preface

When Anna Freud discovered that infants in foundling homes were literally dying for lack of human contact and affection, the scientific community began to attach new importance to the old dictum that, in a very basic way, people need people. Today it is recognized that the mechanism for establishing, maintaining, and improving our human contacts is interpersonal communication, and much useful work on this process has been undertaken by a variety of disciplines. The result is a newly emerging view of a man as communicator and as social being. We offer the present text as a means of exploring the traditional concerns of speech communication from the broader perspective of interpersonal communication.

From this point of view, public speaking is placed within the total context of human communication—which, in turn, must also include two-person and small-group communication as well as the social-psychological make-up of the individual participants.

Our dozen chapters represent both an interpretation of the current state of knowledge in interpersonal communication and an effort to synthesize and clarify material which, though pertinent, has heretofore remained disjointed, fragmented, or little noted. Thus we have drawn upon existing knowledge from several sources including anthropology, linguistics, psychology, sociology, and organizational theory. Our dual focus, however, is on speech communication and on social psychology, as the book's organization makes clear.

Part One lays out a working definition of our field, with special emphasis on communication outcomes. Moreover, it presents a process model of communication, plus a discussion of the uses and limitations of models. Part Two explores the social psychology of the communicator: the acquisition of social behaviors including communication behaviors, the effects of personality and motivation upon communication style, the perception of other human beings, the bases of interpersonal choice. Part Three isolates components of verbal and nonverbal messages and studies the manner in which the communicator encodes and interprets them. Part Four is devoted to various communication contexts. A chapter on two-person communication unfolds the basics of all human interaction. Two further chapters detail the dynamics of small groups, after which the unique character of public, or person-to-group, communication is viewed within this social-xii contextual framework. Part Five highlights the relationship aspects of communication.

Throughout, we have sought to relate significant points in our text to the wealth of firsthand experience in interpersonal communication that every student brings to the course in speech communication. In some instances we have offered suggestions as to alternative ways that one might act in a particular situation. And the chapter-end Exercises and the Appendix provide additional devices through which students can assimilate the insights and develop the interpersonal skills introduced in the text. It should be noted, of course, that all such "real world" applications are possibilities, rather than ironclad formulations.

We have also tried to keep before the reader some sense of the dynamic nature of modern communication study. Where research appears inconclusive, or contradictory, we have preferred to note this rather than force a point. It has been our aim in this way to better present the current state-of-the-art to today's introductory student, whom we have found to be intensely concerned about communication and whom we hope to interest in our field.

We wish to thank those who encouraged and aided us in our writing. The Behavioral Objectives preceding each chapter were prepared by Dr. Donald Cegala of Ohio State University, who also gave us the benefit of his advice on the Review Questions and Exercises. Dr. Philip Shaver of Columbia University, Dr. Ronald L. Smith of the University of Nebraska, Dr. Robin Widgery and Professor Roger P. Wilcox of General Motors Institute offered advice and support throughout. Richard Kennedy initiated the project, and Nancy Tiedemann offered editorial guidance. Our thanks also go to our typist, Dolores M. Davidson.

STEWART L. TUBBS
SYLVIA MOSS

Contents

SITUATION

Anxiety/Changes in Self-Esteem/Isolation

POPULAR AND UNPOPULAR PEOPLE

Involvement and Arousal/Some Dimensions of Interpersonal Relations

STRUCTURED TWO-PERSON COMMUNICATION: THE INTERVIEW

Standardized and Unstandardized Interviews/ Questions and Answers/Interview Structure/ Responsibilities of the Interviewer and the Respondent

GROUP DYNAMICS

Conformity/Social Influence/The Quality of Group Problem Solving/The Role of Group Member/Cohesiveness

GROUP STRUCTURE

Group Size/Communication Networks/ Leadership

CORRELATES OF EFFECTIVE GROUPS

Idea Development and Problem Solving/ Resolution of Conflict/Patterns of Decision Making/Testing the Group's Effectiveness

THE GROUP EXPERIENCE

THEORIES OF GROUP DEVELOPMENT

The Two-Phase Theory/The Three-Phase Theory

PERSONAL EXPERIENCE

A Case Experience: Philip's Log/Case Analysis

THEORIES OF PERSONAL DEVELOPMENT

WHY SENSITIVITY TRAINING? SOME REASONS, OUTCOMES, AND EVALUATIONS

Positive Opinions/Negative Opinions/ Guidelines for Choosing a Group

SENSITIVITY TRAINING AND INTERPERSONAL COMMUNICATION: SOME PARALLEL GOALS

Introduction

part one

Chapter 1 The Process of Interpersonal Communication

OBJECTIVES

After reading this chapter the student should be able to:

1. Define the term "communication."

2. List and describe three characteristics of interpersonal communication.

3. Define effective communication in terms of five possible purposes or outcomes of interpersonal communication.

4. State five speaker responsibilities that enhance interpersonal communication.

5. State five listener responsibilities that enhance interpersonal communication.

1

Mr. A and Mr. B meet and exchange greetings:

A: "Hi!" (Hello, good morning.)
B: "Hi!" (Hello, good morning.)
A: "Warm enough forya?" (How are you?)
B: "Sure is. Looks like rain, though." (Fine. How are you?)
A: "Well, take cara yourself." (Okay.)
B: "I'll be seeing you."
A: "So long."
B: "So long."

Note that no information has been exchanged, at least on a verbal level, in this dialogue. "Indeed," it has been observed, "if there is any information, it is wisely withheld. It might take Mr. A fifteen minutes to say how he is, and Mr. B, who is only the most casual acquaintance, has no intention of devoting that much time to listening to him."[1] Now suppose that we push Mr. A and Mr. B forward in time. They are no longer casual acquaintances; they have become good friends. One day they meet by chance and decide to have dinner together. They spend a good part of the evening discussing Mr. A's problems with his son and Mr. B's new job.

The two encounters we have just described seem to have nothing in common; yet we can refer to each one as a form of interpersonal communication. It is difficult to see any respects in which these transactions are similar without some agreement about how we use the term "interpersonal communication."

WHAT IS INTERPERSONAL COMMUNICATION?

What do you think of when the word "communication" is used? Students' answers to this question typically range from the use of electric circuits to prayer. "There must have been a breakdown in communication" is one of the tritest and most overused expressions heard today. Communication is a subject so frequently discussed that the term itself has become *too* meaningful—that is, it has too many different meanings for people. Agreeing on a working definition is the first step toward improving our understanding of this complex phenomenon.

Communication has been broadly defined as "the sharing of experience," and to some extent all living organisms can be said to share experience. What makes human communication unique is man's superior ability to create and to use symbols, for it is this ability that enables him to "share experiences indirectly and vicariously."[2] Let us keep this reference to man, the symbol-making animal, in mind as we consider an alternate definition:

> Communication, as I conceive it, is a word that describes the process of creating a meaning. Two words in this sentence are critical. They are "create" and "meaning." Messages may be generated from the outside— by a speaker, a television screen, a scolding parent—but meanings are generated from within. This position parallels that of Berlo when he writes, "Communication does not consist of the transmission of meaning. Meanings are not transmitted, or transferable. Only messages are transmittable and meanings are not in the message, they are in the message-users." Communication is man's attempt to cope with his experience, his current mood, his emerging needs. For every person is a unique act of creation, involving dissimilar materials. But it is, within broad limits, assumed to be predictable or there could be no theory of communication.[3]

For the time being, then, let us say that **communication** is *the process of creating a meaning.* This is at least a partial definition of communication, one we shall want to expand in discussing communication outcomes.

The term "interpersonal communication" may still be confusing to you. Does interpersonal communication occur anytime two or more people interact? Does it occur when people exchange letters or talk on the phone? Does it include communication between author and reader, playwright and actor, and telecaster and viewer? As we use the term in this book, it does not include these kinds of contacts. **Interpersonal communication** refers only to *face-to-face, two-way communication.* This distinction limits our discussion by omitting written communication and communication through such media as radio and television. Furthermore it implies that the number of people participating in the communication event is relatively small.

How much of our time involves interpersonal communication? One study examined how 173 people from various occupations spent their time.[4] Every person kept a log of his communication activities for each fifteen-minute period throughout the day. These activities were speaking, conversing, listening, reading, and viewing television. (In this study "speaking" referred to speaker-audience communication and "conversing" to less formal, two-way exchanges. Writing was not considered a communication behavior.) The respondents estimated that almost three-quarters (72.8 percent) of their waking hours involved communication activities. Members of certain occupations—salesmen, teachers, and administrators—averaged even more. Excluding the time the subjects spent reading and viewing television, the study still found an average of 52.4 percent of their waking hours devoted to three types of communication activities: speaking, listening, and conversing. These are the activities we classify as interpersonal communication.

Interpersonal communication events include more informal, everyday exchanges than they do any other type of communication. They include most of the communication activities we engage in from the time we get up until we go to bed. Such activities can be thought of as **transactions**. Harris offers a simple but very useful definition of a transaction as a situation wherein "I do something to you and you do something back."[5] We enter into and move out of such encounters several times each day with little or no prior arrangement, and many of the rules regulating behavior in these encounters are not even known to us, at least on a conscious level. There are exceptions. In an interview, for example, the roles of interviewer and respondent are fairly well defined. As group members we may have to follow an agenda. We may even find ourselves addressing an audience and still be engaging in interpersonal communication. An activity is interpersonal communication if it meets three criteria: (1) all parties must be in close proximity, (2) all parties send and receive messages, and (3) these messages include both verbal and nonverbal stimuli.

That all parties must be in close proximity follows from our definition of interpersonal communication. We have to be within a somewhat limited physical distance of one another to communicate face to face. This point seems obvious. Less obvious but no less important is the fact that there seems to be an informal distance classification to which we adhere, usually without being aware of it. Chapter 7, on the nonverbal message, describes how the physical distance between people has a distinct effect on how they communicate. Different distances seem appropriate for different messages. If you doubt this statement, try discussing an intimate subject with someone who is standing 5 feet away from you.

We expand our definition still further when we observe that all parties send and receive messages. You are sitting in a booth having coffee with someone you hardly know but think you might like to go out with. Each of you is both a sender and a receiver of messages; the interaction depends on the two of you. As you start to talk, one of you usually asks about the other's hometown, interests, activities, friends, and so on. As you hit on mutually interesting topics, you tend to steer your conversation in those directions and to drop other subjects that seem to lead nowhere. If you can't find topics that are mutually satisfying or if you find you are really at opposite poles on a number of issues, you may want to terminate the exchange altogether, as these people did:

LARRY: So you're an art major, huh?

GAIL: Yes, I really feel this is the only major that gives me the freedom to *create*.

LARRY: I really don't know too much about artists or art.
GAIL: Well, I'm also interested in music. In fact I play the piano.
LARRY: Do you like Roger Williams? I think he's cool.
GAIL: Oh, I can't stand Roger Williams.
LARRY: Oh, sorry.
(*Silence.*)

We can see now how the outcome of interaction constantly changes as a result of the responses of both parties. What each says—indeed whether he continues to say anything—depends to a great extent on what the other person says and does. That is, each relies on feedback from the other communicator, or as one author has defined it, "the return to you of behavior you have generated."[6]

Compare any recent face-to-face encounter you have had with your present activity—sitting and reading a book. Are there times when you would like us to back up and explain something over again? Or do you wish you could change the subject? Can a member of the audience change the script of a play by interacting with the playwright? Obviously not. But how an actor interprets the script may be influenced by feedback from the audience. It is true that television viewers may write letters to a network concerning a given program and that enough letters or responses to a rating survey will affect the future of the program. But this interaction is not so immediate as the interaction that results from a conversation, and the viewers are not face to face with the television personality. Thus, although playwright and telecaster both originate messages, their communication would not be considered interpersonal.

We have shown that all parties involved in interpersonal communication send and receive messages. Our third point is that these messages include both verbal and nonverbal stimuli. We tend to think of interpersonal communication solely as speech communication. Yet we respond to a person's facial expressions, eye movements, hand gestures, dress, and posture as well as to other nonverbal stimuli he transmits. Sometimes nonverbal stimuli supplement verbal stimuli; sometimes they contradict them; sometimes they replace them entirely.

If you want to see how dependent we are on nonverbal cues, strike up a conversation with someone (whom you know well, preferably). Then give him absolutely no response, verbal or nonverbal. Just look at him and listen. After a while he starts saying things like "You know what I mean?", "What do you think?", and "Do you follow me?" If you don't look at him, his reaction is likely to be even more rapid and intense. If you try this technique on someone you don't know (a stranger seated next to you on a plane, for example), his response is likely to be silence after a relatively short time. When we are face to face, our behaviors really do have an immediate effect on others.

One of the best media available for studying interpersonal communication is the videotape recorder, though even videotape loses some of the nuances of eye contact, vocal inflection, postural cues, and the like. The audiotape recorder is another valuable aid and one that is perhaps more accessible to you. As you continue this course, try to make recordings of your own communication behaviors.

WHAT IS EFFECTIVE INTERPERSONAL COMMUNICATION?

Students sometimes say that interpersonal communication is effective when a person gets his point across. This is but one measure of effectiveness. More generally, **interpersonal communication is effective** *when the stimulus as it was initiated and intended by the sender corresponds closely with the stimulus as it is perceived and responded to by the receiver.* We can also represent effectiveness by an equation. If we let G stand for the person who generates the response and P stand for the perceiver of the response, then communication is whole and complete when the response G intends and the response P provides are identical:[7]

$$\frac{P \text{ meaning}}{G \text{ meaning}} = 1$$

We rarely reach 1—that is, perfect sharing of meaning; we approximate it. And the greater the correspondence between our intention and the response we receive, the more effective we have been in communicating. At times, of course, we hit the zero mark: there is absolutely no correspondence between the response we want to produce and the one we receive. The drowning man who signals wildly for help to one of his friends on a sailboat only to have his friend wave back is totally ineffective, to say the least.

We can't judge our effectiveness if our intentions are not clear; we must know what we are trying to do. What makes that first definition of effectiveness inadequate ("when a person gets his point across") is that in communicating we may try to bring about one or more of several possible outcomes. We shall consider five of them here: understanding, pleasure, attitude influence, improved relationships, and action. Let us examine them one by one.

Understanding

Understanding refers primarily to *accurate reception of the content of the intended stimulus.* In this sense a communicator is said to be effective if his receiver has an accurate understanding of the message he

10   has tried to convey. (Of course, he sometimes conveys messages unintentionally that are also understood quite clearly.)

     Primary breakdowns in communication are *failures to achieve content accuracy.* For example, the service manager of an oil company had a call one winter morning from a woman who complained that her oil burner was not working. "How high is your thermostat set?" he asked. "Just a moment," the woman replied. After several minutes she returned to the phone. "At 4 feet 3½ inches," she said, "same as it's always been." This confusion is typical of a failure to achieve understanding. Like most primary breakdowns it should be relatively easy to remedy through clarifying feedback and restatement.

     As we add more people to a communication context, it becomes more difficult to determine how accurately messages are being received. This is one of the reasons that group discussions sometimes turn into free-for-alls. Comments begin to have little relation to each other, and even a group with an agenda to follow may not advance toward the resolution of any of its problems. Situations such as these call for more clarifying, summarizing, and directing of group comments. (See Chapter 9.)

     With respect to public communication, much has been written about how to improve understanding when speaking to inform—with "understanding" often being referred to as "information gain." The basic thing for the public speaker to remember is that the feedback he receives is often quite limited; he should therefore make a concerted effort to be as objective and precise as possible in explaining his subject. The use of supporting materials—examples, analogies, and the like—help clarify an explanation of almost any subject. (See Chapter 11 for a discussion of the use of supporting materials.)

Pleasure

Not all communication has as its goal the transmission of a specific message. In fact the goal behind the recently emerging Transactional Analysis school of thought is simply to communicate with others in a way which ensures that each person gains a sense of "I'M OK—YOU'RE OK."[8] What is sometimes referred to as **phatic communication** is intended simply to maintain human contact. Many of our brief exchanges with others—"Hi," "How are you today?", "How's it going?"—have this purpose. Bull sessions, Coke dates, cocktail parties, coffee breaks, and rap sessions are more structured occasions on which we come together to enjoy the company and conversation of others. (Some think that the word "rap," incidentally, comes from the word "rapport," which refers to a sympathetic relationship between people.) The purpose of public, or speaker-audience, communication can also be pleasure; the after-dinner speech and the speech intended to entertain fall in this category.

The degree to which you find communication pleasurable is closely related to your feelings about those with whom you are interacting. If you repeatedly find that your communication with a particular person is not enjoyable, you may discover some of the reasons in Chapter 5. By and large, communication that has enjoyment as its primary purpose should be natural and spontaneous. To plan a good time or to try to maneuver people into having a good time is usually foolhardy —unless, of course, you are preparing a speech to entertain.

Attitude Influence

Suppose that five politicians meet to determine the best way to reduce cost overruns on military contracts and that they reach a stalemate because of their extreme differences of opinion. Such situations are often erroneously referred to as "communication breakdowns." If the disputing parties understood each other better, it is assumed, their differences would be eliminated and an agreement would be reached. But understanding and agreement are by no means synonymous outcomes. When you understand someone's message, you may find that you disagree with him even more strongly than you did before.

Drawing by Charles M. Schulz. © 1970 United Feature Syndicate, Inc.

In many situations we are interested in influencing a person's attitude as well as in having him understand what we are saying. As we shall see in Chapters 3 and 4, the process of changing and reformulating attitudes goes on throughout our lives. In two-person situations attitude influence is often referred to as "social influence"; the dynamics of social influence is discussed in Chapter 5. Attitude influence is no less important in the small group. For example, consensus among group members is an objective of many problem-solving discussions (see Chapter 9), and the development of new attitudes toward oneself and others is an outcome desired by many therapeutic groups (see Chapter 10). In public communication contexts the process of attitude influence is usually referred to as "persuasion," a topic examined at length in Chapter 11.

In determining how successful your attempts to communicate have been, remember that you may fail to change a person's attitude but still get him to understand your point of view. In other words, a failure to change someone's thinking is not necessarily a failure to communicate with him.

Improved Relationships

It is commonly believed that if a person can select the right words, prepare his message ahead of time, and state it precisely, perfect communication will be ensured. But total effectiveness requires a positive and trusting psychological climate. When a human relationship is clouded by mistrust, numerous opportunities arise for distorting or discrediting even the most skillfully constructed messages. Voters may well be suspicious of their mayor's promise that if reelected he will fulfill all the campaign promises he failed to keep during his first term in office. A young woman will probably discount her date's assurances that he is very interested in her after he cancels an appointment for the third or fourth time. A professor may begin to doubt the excuses of a student whom he sees holding court at the student union an hour after he was too sick to take the midterm.

We mentioned primary breakdowns in communication—those that occur when the content of the message is not understood accurately. By contrast, **secondary breakdowns** are *disturbances in human relationships which result from misunderstandings.* They stem from the frustration, anger, or confusion (sometimes all three) caused by the initial failure to understand. Because secondary breakdowns tend to escalate, they are difficult to resolve. By acknowledging that the initial misunderstandings are a common occurrence in daily communication, we may be able to tolerate them better and avoid or at least minimize the damaging effects of secondary breakdowns.

There is another kind of understanding, of course, that can have a profound effect on human relationships: understanding another person's motivations. At times each of us communicates not to convey information but to be "understood" in this second sense. Throughout this text we shall discuss various facets of human relationships: motivation (Chapter 3), interpersonal choice (Chapter 5), group cohesiveness (Chapter 9), interpersonal relations in unstructured situations (Chapter 10), source credibility in public communication (Chapter 11), and interpersonal trust (Chapter 12). We hope to show that all these concepts are bound together by a common theme: the better the relationship between people, the more likely it is that other outcomes of effective communication will also occur.

Action

Some would argue that all communication is useless unless it brings about a desired action. Yet all the outcomes discussed thus far—understanding, pleasure, attitude influence, improved relationships—are important at different times and places. There are instances, however, when action is an essential determinant of the success of a communicative act. An automobile salesman who wants you to think more favorably of his car than his competitor's also wants you to act by buying the car; his primary objective is not attitude change. A math tutor is far from satisfied if the student he is coaching says he understands how to do a set of problems but fails to demonstrate that understanding on his next exam. And we might question the effectiveness of a finance committee that reaches consensus on how to balance a budget yet fails to act on its decision.

Eliciting action on the part of another person is probably the communication outcome most difficult to produce. In the first place it seems easier to get someone to understand your message than it is to get him to agree with it. Furthermore, it seems easier to get him to agree—that he should exercise regularly, for example—than to get him to act on it. (We realize that some behaviors are induced through coercion, social pressure, or role prescriptions and do not necessarily require prior attitude change. Voluntary actions, however, usually follow rather than precede attitude changes.) If you are trying to prompt action on the part of the receiver, you increase your chances of getting the desired response if you can (1) facilitate his understanding of your request, (2) secure his agreement that the request is legitimate, and (3) maintain a comfortable relationship with him. This is not to say that the desired action will automatically follow, but it is more likely to follow if these three intermediate objectives have first been accomplished.

COMMUNICATION RESPONSIBILITIES

Once you know what effective interpersonal communication is, the next step is to improve your own communication behavior. This change can occur if you are willing to accept the responsibilities described in the next few pages. Since we are speaking about two-way communication, each of you will have responsibilities as both a speaker and a listener.

The Speaker's Responsibilities

First, be audible. Speak loudly enough so that your listener can hear you without undue strain.

Second, be clear. If you find yourself saying, "I know what I mean, but I just don't know how to say it," it's possible that you have not thought through your message. Think before you speak.

Third, be aware that your listener may not have understood you.

In other words, acknowledge the many possibilities for misunderstanding as a normal part of daily communication.

Fourth, be willing to ask questions of your listener to see if he understands you. Offer him an opportunity to ask for clarification. The professor who finishes a technical lecture with the remark, "Now, are there any stupid questions?" obviously doesn't get responses of any kind. Contrast his behavior with that of another professor who periodically asks, "Do you know what I mean?" or "Are you still with me?"

Finally, be willing to restate and clarify your message. Sometimes when questioned we repeat what we have just said, using the identical words and a louder, angrier tone of voice. Or we become even more hostile: "What do you mean, you don't get it? I just finished explaining it." This is hardly a response that fosters two-way communication. It's the type of reaction that ridicules the listener and makes it less likely that he will even acknowledge any future misunderstandings.

Your various responsibilities as a speaker are interdependent. If you are aware that the other person may have misunderstood you, you are more willing to restate your message in different terms. You are also more likely to ask him questions from time to time to see if he does understand.

The Listener's Responsibilities

First, let the speaker know if he is inaudible. Don't just sit there straining to hear; ask him to speak more loudly and if necessary to repeat what you have missed.

Second, let him know that you are attentive. Look at him. Nod or shake your head. Your response need not be verbal, but you should react in some way to show him that you are listening.

Third, if the speaker's message is unclear, let him know that you have not understood him. Be tactful about it, and be willing to accept some of the responsibility for not understanding, but let him know when you need a point clarified.

Fourth, be aware that you may not have understood the speaker. Don't be impatient if he loses you occasionally. Misunderstandings and their subsequent clarification are a normal part of the communication process. Try to keep from getting angry about them.

Finally, be willing to paraphrase what you think the speaker means. This is the best check on how the message as received compares with the message as intended. If you can restate the speaker's message to his satisfaction, then you are both more likely to understand the other's position.

As the listener gives feedback to the speaker, he provides some stimuli, and the speaker becomes the receiver. If you have been the listener and now begin to speak, you must take up the procedures of a good speaker. When roles shift so do responsibilities.

Before you take on these responsibilities more deliberately, we have a word of caution for you. Don't overdo it. One writer calls this annoying your friends clinically.[9] For example, during a family quarrel the shortest route to the door is to announce calmly to your overwrought parents that their argument is the result of a secondary breakdown in communication.

Summary

Human communication is unique because man's superior ability to create and use symbols enables him to share his experiences indirectly. In studying interpersonal communication we limit ourselves to a portion of that experience: face-to-face, two-way communication. All interpersonal communication events fulfill three conditions. First, all parties are in close proximity. Second, all parties send and receive messages, and the outcome of interaction constantly changes as a result of their responses. And third, these messages include both verbal and nonverbal stimuli.

The second half of the chapter was concerned with what constitutes effective communication. We established that interpersonal communication is effective to the degree that the stimulus as it is intended by the sender corresponds with the stimulus as it is perceived and responded to by the receiver. We learned that effectiveness is closely linked to intention and that in communicating we usually want to bring about one or more of several possible outcomes. Five of the major communication outcomes—understanding, pleasure, attitude influence, improved relationships, and action—were considered, and our discussion concluded with an analysis of our dual communication responsibilities as speaker and listener.

Review Questions

1. Provide your own personal definition of communication. How is it similar to or different from the definitions given in the text?
2. State three characteristics of interpersonal communication. How does interpersonal communication differ from other types of communication?
3. List five outcomes of interpersonal communication. Give an example of each.
4. What is effective communication? Think of arguments for and against the types of communication effectiveness that have been

16 described in this chapter. Are there some that the text has not included? Are there some it has discussed that you think should not be included? What do you think is the most important outcome of interpersonal communication?

5. How do the communication responsibilities of a speaker and a listener differ? How well do you think you assume either set of responsibilities? Are you a better speaker or listener? How do you think you might use this information to improve yourself?

Exercises

1. Start a personal log in which you record your daily reaction to perhaps ten members of your class. Only some will impress you (favorably or unfavorably) at first. Note details of their behavior. Describe your own feelings as candidly as possible.
2. Observe several communication events and keep a record of the outcomes that resulted. Which outcomes occurred more frequently than others? Under what conditions did these outcomes appear to occur most frequently? How can you explain these results?
3. What speaker or listener responsibilities were ignored or violated when disruptions in communication occurred in the situations just described?
4. Write a one-page case study in which you have experienced or observed some sort of communication breakdown. Then write an analysis of the causes of the problem and suggest a way to resolve it.

Suggested Readings

Barnlund, Dean C. *Interpersonal Communication: Survey and Studies.* Boston: Houghton Mifflin, 1968. This book is perhaps the single most comprehensive book available on the subject of interpersonal communication. A valuable in-depth sourcebook, it contains summaries of many points of view along with thirty-seven articles covering a wide range of topics.

Berne, Eric. *Games People Play.* New York: Grove Press, 1964. This delightful best seller offers a framework for analyzing human interaction. Part I presents the Parent, Adult, Child mode of psychiatry, a neo-Freudian formula which is easy to follow and use. In Part II, Berne explains certain recognizable behaviors in terms of games, including such notable ones as, "Now I've Got You, You Son of a Bitch," "Ain't It Awful," and "Rapo."

Watzlawick, Paul, Beavin, Janet, and Jackson, Don. *Pragmatics of Human Communication.* New York: Norton, 1967. This book offers an excellent explanation of several basic principles of communication, relating them to such areas as psychiatry and existentialism. The principles are then applied in an analysis of the interaction in the play/movie "Who's Afraid of Virginia Woolf?" in Chapter Five.

Notes

[1] Eric Berne, *Games People Play* (New York: Grove, 1964), p. 39.

[2] Robert S. Goyer, "Communication, Communicative Process, Meaning: Toward a Unified Theory," *Journal of Communication,* 20 (1970), 4–5.

[3] Dean C. Barnlund, "Toward a Meaning-Centered Philosophy of Communication," *Journal of Communication,* 11 (1962), 199.

[4] Larry A. Samovar, Robert D. Brooks, and Richard E. Porter, "A Survey of Adult Communication Activities," *Journal of Communication,* 19 (1969), 301–307.

[5] Thomas A. Harris, I'M OK—YOU'RE OK (New York: Harper & Row, 1967), p. 12.

[6] Joseph Luft, *Of Human Interaction* (Palo Alto, Calif.: National Press, 1969), p. 116.

[7] Goyer, p. 10.

[8] Harris, p. 50.

[9] Luft, p. 41.

Chapter 2

A
Model
of
Interpersonal
Communication

OBJECTIVES

After reading this chapter the student should be able to:

1. List at least two characteristics of models.

2. State two criteria that may be used to evaluate models.

3. Describe what is meant by the term "input" as it is used in the communication model.

4. Distinguish between physiological filters and psychological filters.

5. List four types of communicative stimuli and give an example of each type.

6. Identify three primary channels of interpersonal (that is, face-to-face) communication.

7. Distinguish between technical and semantic interference and give an example of each.

8. Explain what is meant by the term "signal-to-noise ratio."

9. Describe two concepts about the nature of interpersonal communication emphasized by spiral (or helical) models.

10. Describe three effects of time on interpersonal communication.

11. Draw and label a model of interpersonal communication using the following terms: communicator 1, communicator 2, input, filters, communicative stimuli, channels, interference, and time.

2

In both the physical and the social sciences, it is now popular to talk about "models." We are all familiar with the term "model" as it refers to a line-for-line replica of a thing—a building, an airplane, or even a living cell. But when scientists use the term, they refer to something broader and more abstract. Some equate "model" with "theory"—a kind of theory in miniature. In fact, Simon and Newell have argued that a model, or analogy, is one of three main kinds of theories, the other two being verbal and mathematical theories.[1]

Others feel that it is more precise to consider a model as a scientific metaphor, that is, an extended comparison between the subject we want to study and some object or process. For example, we might have a model of the heart as a pump; in this case the comparison is drawn from mechanics. Kaplan has tried to refine the concept of the scientific metaphor even further by suggesting that it is more accurate to view "as models only those theories which explicitly direct attention to certain resemblances between the theoretical entities and the real subject-matter."[2]

Lately the communication process itself has served as a model for explaining other phenomena. Thus the transmission of nerve impulses has been described in terms of a communication model. And in discussing human behavior one writer refers to communication as "the only scientific model which enables us to explain physical, intrapersonal, interpersonal, and cultural aspects of events within one system."[3]

Unlike the metaphors of literature, those of science need not consist of words. They may be equations. Or they may be made out of paper, wire, wax, steel, or any other material. The important thing to remember is that models are *made*—by men. They do not exist in nature though their terms may be drawn from nature. In short, models are abstractions from nature. Thus many models can describe the same object or process or series of events. Each offers us another way to organize and classify data, another way to see relationships between parts. Each identifies and makes explicit the elements—or to use a scientific term, the "variables"—to be studied. Kaplan explains this advantage of a model succinctly: "As inquiry proceeds, theories must be brought into the open sooner or later; the model simply makes it sooner."[4]

"If so many models exist, then how do we know which one is correct?", you might ask. This is an important question, for as we shall see many models have been proposed to describe the communication process just as many have been proposed to describe the operation of the heart or for that matter the human psyche. Theorists agree that there is no single true model just as there is no single correct metaphor. They propose that instead of thinking of models as true or false, we evaluate them in terms of two criteria. First, how effectively does the model permit us to organize data and make successful predictions about such data? And second, how much research does the model generate? Keep in mind that the model can prove valuable even if the research simply uncovers that the model is a misleading one.

One advantage of using a model is that it makes explicit the assumptions and interests of the model builder. It tells you what elements he intends to examine; indirectly it also tells you what he is not examining. For example, the model of interpersonal communication in Figure 1, which we shall explore in some detail, is concerned not so much with what happens within each communicator as with more directly observable and measurable experiences—what happens *between* communicators and how their interaction evolves and changes over time. Instead of presenting a cross section of one moment in a communication event, the model tries to give you a sense of the movement of communication in time. This is called a **process model of** communication.

Some of the terms in which our model is explained—the metaphors, if you will—are taken from the study of the computer (for example, "input" or "information"), and others are from telecommunication (for example, "channel" and "interference"). This does not mean that interpersonal communication is synonymous with the operation of either a computer or a telephone. A model cannot be taken literally or applied rigidly to all phenomena. It is a framework from which we are able to generalize. A model simplifies reality. Therefore, to explain a given communication event, we may have to put back the particulars of that event. We may even have to revise our model to accommodate new experiences. With these warnings in mind, let us turn to Figure 1.

This is a model of the most basic interpersonal communication event; it involves only two people. We shall call them communicator 1 and communicator 2. Both are sources of communication, and at different times each originates and receives communicative stimuli. Thus the communication process as represented in this model can be initiated from either the right or the left side. Communicator 1 may originate the first message and communicator 2 may be the first to perceive the transmitted stimuli, but this order is dictated by chance. For example, when you got up this morning, did you speak first to someone, or were you spoken to first? You probably don't even remember because in most exchanges who speaks first is a matter of chance. It is arbitrary to call yourself either a speaker or a listener: you are both. Even while you are speaking, you are simultaneously observing the

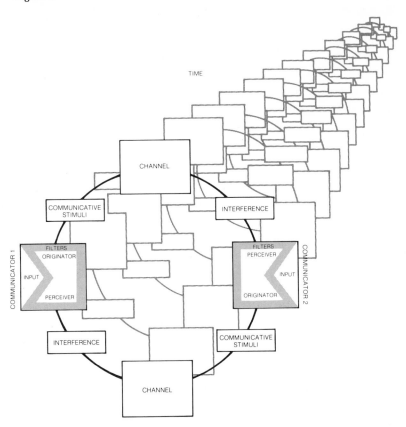

The Tubbs Communication Model

other person's behavior and reacting to it. This is also true of the other person as he interacts with you.

Only under a few circumstances does one of the two people characteristically initiate communication, and these situations usually involve differences in status, with the first speaker often higher in status. We shall discuss the effects of status on communication in Chapter 8; for the sake of simplicity, however, we shall consider the people in our model without reference to their status.

COMMUNICATOR 1

Let us take a closer look at communicator 1 as he tries to send a message to communicator 2. What kinds of human characteristics does

24   he have that would be important in the communication process? Obviously his mental capacities are of central importance. Inside his brain are millions of nerve cells that function together to store and utilize his knowledge, attitudes, and emotions. As students of communication we want to know something about the experiences that shape knowledge, attitudes, and emotions. We want to know what makes communicator 1 distinct from any other communicator—in effect, what makes him the person he is.

Input

Like those of any other human being, communicator 1's senses are continually bombarded by a wealth of stimuli from both inside and outside his body. All that he knows and experiences—whether of the physical or the social world—comes to him initially through his senses. Borrowing from computer terminology we call these raw data **input**, *all the stimuli—both past and present—that give us our information about the world.*

From the accounts of explorers, castaways, and prisoners of war, we can learn what it is like to experience a long period of isolation, but even such people ordinarily have some sensory stimulation. The effect of radically decreased input—in solitary confinement, for example—is more difficult to imagine. You can get some notion of how dependent we are on a steady flow of stimuli by supposing that your senses were shut off one by one. Imagine what it would be like to be without them for a day or just an hour or even fifteen minutes.

To make the situation concrete, suppose a psychologist hires you for more than twice what you could usually earn to spend several days (probably three or four) lying on a bed in a cubicle that measures 8 by 4 by 6 feet. To limit your tactile sensations, you wear cotton gloves and cylinders of cardboard on your arms from below your elbows to beyond the tips of your fingers. Translucent goggles allow you to see diffused light but no patterned stimuli. Your perception of sound is also cut to a minimum. You can speak with the experimenter by using an intercom, but such exchanges are not frequent. The only breaks in this routine are eating or going to the toilet. How long do you think you would last, and how would you feel during and after the experiment?

We know the answers to these questions because in 1953 a group of researchers at McGill University, in Montreal, performed this experiment. They wanted to study the effects of **sensory deprivation**, or *extremely limited sensory intake,* on normal human beings. From the description in the preceding paragraph, you can see that the test conditions were monotonous but not frightening. There were simply very few stimuli. Yet most of the subjects felt their experience had been unpleasant, and few lasted longer than two or three days. Some felt disoriented and were easily upset. Some daydreamed much of the time. Others had blank periods. One remarkable finding was that many people experienced hallucinations; these ranged from geometric patterns to actual scenes. Not all the hallucinations were visual. Some participants heard speech or music. One reported that his head felt detached from his body. It seems as though when a person's input is limited, he starts creating it for himself.

Several sensory deprivation studies were done at McGill during the 1950s, and research is still going on in Canada and the United States. Although much remains to be learned about the effects of limited sensory input, psychologists have shown that we depend on stimuli not only for our initial knowledge about the world but also for our daily functioning. One psychologist sums up the findings of sensory deprivation research this way: ". . . human beings are individually, socially, and physiologically dependent not only upon stimulation, but upon a continually varied and changing sensory stimulation in order to maintain normal, intelligent, coordinated, adaptive behavior and mental functioning."[5]

The reason you find it so difficult to imagine yourself in a situation that provides little or no input is that most of the time you do receive "varied and changing sensory stimulation." In fact, you usually have more input than you can possibly be aware of. For most of us there are almost too many stimuli. In addition to the normal input of human life, city dwellers are besieged by the noises and distractions of an urban environment. And wherever we live the mass media provide us with a deluge of information. Under ordinary circumstances then, so many stimuli assail us at a conscious level that we can experience only a small portion of the total. You can illustrate this for yourself. Right now you are primarily aware of reading this page in this book. Try moving your toes. Are you now aware of your shoes, socks, or bare feet? You have just brought this sensory input to the conscious level. The sensations are always there, but you probably were not experiencing them at a conscious level.

What you are aware of at any time is determined by what you as a perceiver *select* out of the total input. Because your capacity to register sensory stimuli is limited, you cannot take in everything. You choose certain aspects of your environment. The American philosopher and psychologist William James has explained the process of selection in terms of interest, or attention: "Millions of items of the outward order are present to my senses which never properly enter into my experience. Why? Because they have no *interest* for me. *My experience is what I agree to attend to.* Only those items which I *notice* shape my mind— without selective interest, experience is an utter chaos."[6]

You can see the selection process at work if you relate an incident to someone, ask him to relate it to another person who has not heard it, and then have the second person relate it to a third. Each person will give a slightly different version of the incident, for each selects differently out of the total stimuli. As we discuss selection, bear in mind that it need not be a totally conscious process.

Filters

No two people—not even identical twins—have the same input, even when their environment seems constant. In addition, no two people perceive things in quite the same way. Selection explains why communicators in general are different and why they often disagree even when given what seems to be the same information. In our model, selection is represented by the filters through which all input or sensation must pass. Simply put, **a filter** is *a limit on our capacity to sense or perceive stimuli*. Filters are of two kinds: physiological and psychological. We shall call them "perceptual filters" and "sets" respectively.

Perceptual Filters. How much do you trust your senses? Most of us trust our senses so much that we are offended at the suggestion that we might have observed something inaccurately. "But I saw it with my own eyes," we counter. Yet we are often unaware of the many stimuli that are filtered out of our experience. We cannot see infrared and ultraviolet light rays. We cannot hear the sound of a dog whistle because it has too high a frequency for human ears. These **perceptual filters** are *biological limitations that are built into man*, and they cannot be reversed. Moreover they vary from one person to another so that we differ in the degree to which our senses are accurate.

Perhaps the most troublesome perceptual filter to the human communicator is the limit on his ability to hear. Sometimes we think we hear a person say one thing when actually he said another. We then act on the basis of what we think he said. Many communication difficulties are rooted in this kind of misunderstanding.

Sets. Other forms of selection can be just as strong as perceptual filters. For example, ask someone to complete the following sentence:

> *P-o-l-k* is pronounced *poke*, and *f-o-l-k* is pronounced *foke*, and the white of an egg is pronounced . . . ?

Although the white of an egg is called "albumen," you will find that most people answer "yolk." Miller explains this reaction as a verbal habit.[7] Because of what precedes the last part of the sentence, we expect a word that will rhyme with "polk" and "folk." **Set** is the word psychologists use to describe this *expectancy or predisposition to respond*. As we shall see throughout this text, we have sets not only about words and objects but also about other human beings. Here is how set functions when we look at a piece of sculpture:

When we step in front of a bust we understand what we are expected to look for. We do not, as a rule, take it to be a representation of a cut-off head; we take in the situation and know that this belongs to the institution or convention called "busts" with which we have been familiar even before we grew up. For the same reason, we do not miss the absence of color in the marble any more than we miss its absence in black-and-white photographs. . . .[8]

We have sets about all kinds of experience. For example, some people—especially in telephone conversations—are so accustomed to being asked how they are that after saying "Hi" or "Hello," they answer "Fine" to what the other party has just said, even if it is something like "I tried to call you earlier in the day." In daily communication we have all sorts of sets. Some are useful and give meaningful patterns to our lives; others interfere with our ability to perceive accurately and respond appropriately.

The Influence of Filters on Communication. How can we improve our interpersonal communication by knowing about perceptual filters and sets? If you know that human beings are capable of making perceptual errors, you may be willing to say, "I thought it was such and such, but I might be wrong." A great deal of interpersonal conflict stems from the fact that many people do not realize the fallibility of their senses. Then too, even if they know they are wrong, sometimes they are unwilling to admit it. There is now convincing evidence that in some situations we are more persuasive and effective if we do not try to force our point of view on the other person. In fact, if we press him, we may reinforce his opposition to our point though he appears to be agreeing with it.

As you speak with someone, you formulate ideas that become the content of the communication event. How accurately your message is received depends on the other person's perceptual filters and sets. Remember that his psychological and physiological characteristics will influence which stimuli he perceives and how he perceives them.

COMMUNICATIVE STIMULI

Looking again at the model in Figure 1, we can think of the message that communicator 1 transmits as being conveyed in the form of communicative stimuli. Most formal models of communication speak simply of messages; they do not single out communicative stimuli per se. If they did, they would probably divide them into two basic categories. First, they would determine whether words were used—whether the stimuli were verbal or nonverbal. Second, they would establish whether the communicator wanted to transmit the stimuli—whether they were intentional or unintentional. Thus four types of stimuli are transmitted: (1) intentional verbal, (2) unintentional verbal, (3) intentional nonverbal, and (4) unintentional nonverbal. As we examine these types remember that most messages contain two or more types of stimuli and that they often overlap.

Verbal Stimuli

A **verbal stimulus** is *any type of spoken communication that uses one or more words.* Most interpersonal communication falls within the category of **intentional verbal stimuli**; these are *the conscious attempts we make to communicate with others through speech.*

Intentional verbal stimuli may be classified according to the elements in the message that influence how it is received by the other person. Suppose you want to persuade a friend to stop taking drugs. You have several options for how to do this. You can tell him that he is going to be arrested or that you will stop seeing him if he doesn't quit. You can present him with some medical statistics and let him draw his own conclusions. You can cite the opinion of a psychiatrist. You can sum up both sides of the issue by stating its pros and cons or just state your own point of view. In short, you need to choose among **message variables**, or *alternate ways of presenting a single message.* (See Chapter 11 for a discussion of message variables relating to public communication.)

Much of the research on interpersonal communication concerns verbal message variables. Among the questions that have been studied are whether scare tactics or emotional appeals are persuasive, whether you should state both sides of an issue or give a simple statement of your own viewpoint, and whether you should allow the other person to draw his own conclusions from your argument or draw them yourself. The relative effectiveness of the variables is usually measured by which persuades people most readily to change their attitudes.

Unintentional verbal stimuli are *the things we say without meaning to.* Freud argued that all the apparently unintentional stimuli we transmit—both verbal and nonverbal—are unconsciously motivated. We cannot discuss the merits of this argument here, but we can cite an amusing example of a slip of the tongue described by one of Freud's colleagues: "While writing a prescription for a woman who was especially weighed down by the financial burden of the treatment, I was interested to hear her say suddenly: 'Please do not give me *big bills,* because I cannot swallow them.' Of course, she meant to say *pills.*"[9]

Everyone makes slips occasionally. For example, one of the authors heard a young man say that on a scale from 1 to 5, he rated the college football team 7. He probably intended to say "on a scale from 1 to 10." A speech professor once explained to his students that "With a singular subject you must use a plural verb." He did not realize what he had said until his students started to laugh. Sometimes it is only when we get feedback from others (in this instance, laughter) that we become aware we have even transmitted such stimuli. Then we can correct ourselves and proceed from there. In general, unintentional stimuli—both verbal and nonverbal—tend to increase in number if the person is a poor communicator.

Nonverbal Stimuli

Nonverbal stimuli cannot be described as easily as verbal stimuli, probably because the category is so broad. They include all the non-verbal aspects of our behavior: facial expression, posture, tone of voice, hand movements, manner of dress, and so on. In short, *they are all the stimuli we transmit without words or over and above the words we use.*

Let us first consider **intentional nonverbal stimuli**, *the nonverbal stimuli we mean to transmit.* Sometimes we rely exclusively on non-verbal stimuli; sometimes we use them to reinforce verbal stimuli. For example, you can greet someone by smiling and nodding your head, or you can say "Hello" and also smile or wave. At times we deliberately use nonverbal stimuli to cancel out a polite verbal response and indicate our true feelings: the verbal message may be positive, but the tone of voice and facial expression indicate that we mean something negative. Maintaining eye contact with a person who is speaking to you is another nonverbal stimulus. It conveys interest and attention, offers feedback to the speaker, and in some cases tells him whether you understand or agree with what he is saying.

Interpreting nonverbal stimuli can be difficult, and it may require some insight to determine whether or not they are intentional. Many expressions that seem unintentional are in fact deliberate. Think of a weary clerk in the complaint department of a large store. She has been told that the customers must be treated politely—even when they are offensive. There must be many times when she would like to express her annoyance. She can do this by speaking politely but purposely conveying her mood through her tone of voice. Similarly a friend who assures you that "Nothing is wrong" lets you know that something is very wrong by casually dropping his lip and lowering his voice. Most of us use such tactics from time to time, which makes them easier to spot in others.

Thayer has stressed the notion that much of what we are as a person "communicates" itself every time we behave.[10] A great deal of this behavior is unintentional. Some writers on the subject go so far as to assert that what we communicate is what we are. **Unintentional nonverbal stimuli** are *all those nonverbal aspects of our behavior trans-*

mitted without our control. For example, one of the authors once told a student speaker to relax. "I am relaxed," the student replied in a tight voice, speaking over the rattling of a paper he was holding. A problem frequently raised in management classes is that store managers unintentionally communicate anger or impatience to their customers. This is a situation different from that of the angry clerk in the complaint department: she does not depend on the good will of the customer, but the store manager does, and he wants to control his nonverbal cues.

Controlling nonverbal stimuli is a very difficult task. Facial expressions, posture, tone of voice, hand gestures—what some writers have called "body language"—often give us away. Ralph Waldo Emerson phrased it well when he remarked to a speaker, "What you are speaks so loudly that I cannot hear what you say." And of course the better a person knows you, the more likely he is to pick up your nonverbal expressions, even if you don't want him to. Lest we paint too dark a picture, however, we should add that as your communication skills improve, you may find that the number of unintentional stimuli you transmit will decrease significantly.

CHANNELS

A communicator rarely thinks about the **channels** of communication shown in Figure 1. Usually he becomes aware of them only when one or more are cut off or when some sort of interference is present. For example, if there is a large vase of flowers between two people trying to talk across a dinner table, both communicators lose a lot because they are unable to see each other's faces. They may even find it too unsettling to carry on a conversation without the presence of facial cues. In interpersonal communication you rely not only on hearing what the other person is saying but on seeing his face when he speaks as well as when you do.

If you are talking on the telephone, the channels that transmit the communicative stimuli are the telephone wires. The channels of face-to-face communication are the sensory organs. Although all five senses may receive the stimuli, you rely almost exclusively on three: hearing, sight, and touch. For example, you listen to someone state an argument, or you exchange knowing glances with a friend, or you put your arm on someone's shoulder.

Often several channels are used simultaneously. In general, the more channels you use, the more likely you are to communicate successfully because you increase the number of transmitted stimuli. Remember though that the more channels you use, the greater the possibility that you will transmit unintentional stimuli. In addition, there may be situations in which we want to limit the channels of communication. If you are applying for several jobs, you may choose to send in résumés rather than attend personal interviews so that you may delay committing yourself to any one position.

INTERFERENCE

Once a communicator has initiated a message, he almost always assumes that it has been received. He is puzzled or annoyed if he is misinterpreted or gets no response. He may even have taken special pains to make his message clear. Isn't that enough? he asks. In effect, he wants to know what went wrong between the transmission and reception of his message.

The communication scholar would give him the answer, **interference**, or **noise**—that is, *anything that distorts the information transmitted to the receiver or distracts him from receiving it*. In communication theory the terms "interference" and "noise" are synonymous. "Interference" is probably a more appropriate word, but because "noise" was the term first used in studies of telecommunication, you should be familiar with it too. Claude Shannon and Warren Weaver, the authors of one of the earliest communication models, spoke of the noise that could interfere with the transmission of a signal. And in discussing the problem of noise in relation to television, Cherry indicates its broader meaning by saying that " 'noise' refers to any disturbance or interference, apart from the wanted signals or messages selected and being sent."[11]

If you think of noise as "any disturbance or interference," you will soon realize that noise need not be sound. It can be visual, for example. Winston Churchill was once quite successful in creating a lot of noise without uttering a word. The members of Parliament were being addressed by a speaker of an opposing party. Looking very intent, Churchill bent down and groped along the floor, pretending to search for a missing collar button. He succeeded in distracting almost all the members of Parliament from listening to the speech. Whether Churchill accomplished what he intended is another question. Festinger and Maccoby have found that under some circumstances people who are distracted when listening to a communication tend to change their attitudes more in the direction of the communication.[12]

Technical and Semantic Interference

We can distinguish between two kinds of interference: technical interference and semantic interference. **Technical interference** refers to *the factors that cause the receiver to perceive distortion in the intended information or stimuli.* And the speaker himself may create the distortion: if he has a speech impediment or even if he simply mumbles, he may have difficulty making his words clear to another person. Someone at a party may not be able to hear the response of the person he is talking to because the stereo is blaring or because other people standing nearby are speaking so loudly. In this case the interference is simply the transmission of the sounds of other people in conversation. So as you can see, noise is relative, not absolute.

The second type of interference is **semantic interference**, which occurs when *the receiver does not attribute the same meaning to the signal that the sender does.* For example, two people get into a heated argument over the causes of crime. One argues that they are mainly "economic" and the other that they are largely "social." Only after considerable discussion do they realize that they are referring to much the same thing; they are simply using different words to describe their ideas.

Disagreements about meaning are so common that one writer makes the distinction between meaning to the speaker and meaning to the listener.[13] The closer the fit between the two meanings, of course, the more complete the communication. We shall have a great deal more to say about meaning in Chapter 6 when we discuss language. Remember though that it is possible for people to attribute different meanings to nonverbal messages.

Signal-to-Noise Ratio

We can also think of noise, or interference, in terms of how it affects information. Cherry writes, "Noise is the destroyer of information and sets the ultimate upper limit to the information capacity of a channel. . . ."[14] **Signal-to-noise ratio** is the term often used to denote *the relationship between the essential information in a message and the extraneous or distracting factors.* You may know people whose interpersonal communication is characterized by a little signal and much noise. Occasionally they are charming; more often they are boring and annoying.

Shakespeare was a master at portraying the exasperating quality of "noisy" replies. This is the way that Polonius, the lord chamberlain, tells the king and queen that Hamlet is mad:

> My liege, and madam, to expostulate
> What majesty should be, what duty is,
> Why day is day, night night, and time is time,
> Were nothing but to waste night, day and time.
> Therefore, since brevity is the soul of wit,
> And tediousness the limbs and outward flourishes,

> I will be brief: your noble son is mad:
> Mad call I it; for, to define true madness,
> What is't but to be nothing else but mad?
> But let that go.

To which the queen briskly answers:

> More matter, with less art.[15]

Let's consider a more familiar kind of dialogue:

FRED: How do you get to Detroit from Flint?
SAM: Well, gosh, I've taken several ways. Back in the 1950s I used to go along Dixie Highway, but that isn't as good any more. I remember that road because that's where I learned to drive. I still enjoy driving on a Sunday afternoon. Do you?
FRED: Yes, but how do I get to Detroit?
SAM: Detroit—oh, yes, Detroit. Now there's a real city. Some people wouldn't agree with me, but I've always liked Detroit. Say the best way to get to Detroit might be to take Interstate 75.

To Fred, Sam's last sentence is signal; all the rest is noise. Fred asks a simple question and gets far more than he wants. For his purposes much of the information Sam provides is useless. At first glance, we might say that Sam is a bore or that he can't concentrate because his mind wanders. Yet the reasons Sam supplies all the detail about himself may be complex. He may feel that this is the way to be friendly. He may be trying to communicate something more about himself so that Fred will take greater interest in him. He may be stalling for time as he tries to remember the name "Interstate 75" so that he won't lose face. Certainly he is unaware of the poor impression he is making on Fred.

Eliminating Interference

Some interference will always be present in human communication. Yet even if we cannot expect to eliminate it completely, identifying its major sources can help us communicate more effectively. As we have seen, interference can exist in the context of the communication, in the channel, in the communicator himself, or in the receiver of the message. The sources we can do most to minimize, of course, are those that lie within ourselves.

During emergencies it is essential to convey messages promptly and clearly with as little superfluous information as possible. In reporting an accident, for example, you know that you must not go into needless detail; your intention is to get help as quickly as possible. Under more relaxed conditions you are apt to be less aware of

34 creating interference, however. Take the person who habitually monopolizes conversation. He gives others little opportunity to respond meaningfully. As a result they become bored or hostile. One way he may notice this habit in himself is to recall whether he does most of the talking when he is with others. If he does, he is probably talking too much and saying too little. He can always ask the others if they would like to hear more. He should also watch their nonverbal cues. If they seem restless and inattentive, it is probably because they would like to be talking also.

COMMUNICATOR 2

At this point our model departs from several current models that create the illusion that communication has a definite starting point with the sender and a termination point with the receiver. When communicator 2 in Figure 1 has received a message, we have come only halfway through the continuous and ongoing process that is communication. For each receiver of a message is himself a sender of messages, and his uniqueness as a human being ensures that his attempts to communicate will be very different from those of the other person in the model. For example, his cultural input may be quite unlike that of communicator 1. His filters, both physiological and psychological, will be different. The stimuli he transmits will be different. Even his selection of channels and his sources of difficulty, or interference, may differ.

The present model includes these differences as inherent parts of the communication process. Although the lower half of the circle lists the same elements as the upper half—input, filters, communicative stimuli, channel, interference—and these elements are defined in the same way, they are always different in content from those in the upper half. The transmission and reception of a single message is only one part of our model. More than any other type of communication (mass or organizational communication, for example), interpersonal communication is characterized by its interdependent participants and the explicit and immediate feedback between them. If we lose sight of one of the participants, we are no longer studying what we set out to study.

TIME

Once communicator 2 responds to communicator 1, their interaction can be represented by a circle. But as their exchange progresses in time, the relationship between them is more accurately described by several circles. In fact, all but the briefest exchanges entail several communication cycles. Thus time itself becomes the final element in our model.

We have tried to convey the presence of time in Figure 1 by representing communication in the form of a spiral, like an uncoiled spring. Some writers prefer to symbolize time as a helix; the only difference between these forms is that the spiral is usually regarded as two-dimensional whereas the helix is thought of as three-dimensional. We shall treat them as identical.

Spiral (or helical) models emphasize the effect of the past on present or future behavior. Dance sums up this emphasis in the following way:

> At any and all times, the helix gives geometrical testimony to the concept that communication while moving forward is at the same moment coming back upon itself and being affected by its past behavior. . . . The communication process, like the helix, is constantly moving forward and yet is always to some degree dependent upon the past, which informs the present and the future.[16]

The spiral also illustrates that participants in the communication process can never return to the point at which they started. Their relationship must undergo change as a result of each interaction. Let us look briefly at some of the ways in which time changes communication.

First, time affects the *intensity* of interpersonal relationships. Marathon encounter groups tacitly acknowledge this principle. The participants are brought together for an extended period—usually six to twenty-four hours. As they learn to express themselves more openly, the interaction reaches a high level of intensity. If the group were to meet only one hour a week for six to twenty-four weeks, such intensity would be difficult to achieve. In terms of the model, it is as though we were pulling the ends of the spring farther and farther apart. The important thing to remember is that a human relationship is not constant; its intensity is affected by the amount of time that passes between encounters.

The effect of time is often dramatized in relationships between people who are far apart in age. Consider communication between mother and child, for example. Here the *mode*, or quality, of communication changes over time. At first the communication is essentially nonverbal. The infant signals his needs for food and comfort by wailing, but he cannot use language. The mother responds by satisfying his needs; she may speak to him as she does this, but she does not expect him to respond. Slowly the child learns to communicate in other ways. He begins to smile when he is happy or amused. Even his crying changes. Later he learns to point at something he wants. At about age one he learns to walk and can lead his mother toward something he can't reach himself. By this time he often can say two or three words, and he shows clear evidence that he understands many more. His mother has already begun to discipline him, and whether he listens or not—probably not—he understands the word "no." By the end of the second year, the child's vocabulary has expanded to such a degree that he can sometimes make up simple two- or three-word sentences such as "Paul cake" or "Me cup." As he masters language, his mother can communicate with him in new ways. Nonverbal communication still takes place, but the shift in emphasis from nonverbal to verbal makes possible a change in the kind of relationship that evolves between mother and child.

In addition to changing intensity and mode, time can also change the *style* of communication. When two people first meet, they usually try to be as explicit as possible in their communication. Even if the two share several interests, one does not assume that the other knows what he is thinking or trying to say. This kind of insight develops only after long acquaintance. Sometimes two people get to know each other so well that each can anticipate much of what the other is trying to communicate. We frequently see this relationship in married couples or very close friends; to use the term of the Russian psychologist Vygotsky, their speech becomes "abbreviated."[17]

This kind of communication has two limitations. First, speech can become too abbreviated; one person can take for granted that he knows what the other is thinking but be wrong. Second, people who use abbreviated speech can unwittingly alienate a third party by making him feel left out; he may be at a loss to understand much of what the other two are talking about.

Thus the effect of time on communication is not always constructive. It would be ideal if time always moved interpersonal transactions toward greater and greater effectiveness. But we know, for example, that communication between parent and child becomes more difficult as the child reaches adolescence. Time does not always erase differences. Indeed it can have a negative effect on communication. If two friends quarrel bitterly, the passage of time may help transform their anger into total alienation because it incorporates repeated misunderstandings that reinforce the original disagreement.

Throughout this text we shall try to point out the effects of time on communication. Implicit in this emphasis is our belief that time is one of the most relevant variables in the study of human communication. If it does nothing else, the spiral model should remind us that communication is not static and that it thus requires different methods of analysis from a fixed entity. Dance sums up the problem so well that we simply quote his statement here:

> The means of examining something in a quiescent and immobile state are quite different from the means of examining something that is in constant flux, motion, and process. If communication is viewed as a process, we are forced to adapt our examination and our examining instruments to the challenge of something in motion, something that is changing while we are in the very act of examining it.[18]

The model identifies some of the major elements that exist in all interpersonal communication. We have discussed such communication only in its simplest form. As we add more communicators, change the kind or amount of interference, or vary the stimuli transmitted, our subject increases in complexity. We shall see this especially when we turn to the study of small groups. As you read on you may want to look at other models, some of which are mentioned in the books at the end of this chapter. You may even want to try your hand at developing a model of your own. In either case remember that each communication event you will study has something unique about it, and no model can be used as a blueprint of the communication process.

Summary

In this chapter we defined models as scientific metaphors and discussed some of their advantages and limitations. We presented a model to help us conceptualize the relationships among the elements of interpersonal communication. Both communicators in our model, like all human beings, originate and perceive communicative stimuli. Both are dependent on the steady flow of physical, social, and cultural input, and both select from the total input through their perceptual filters and sets.

We then discussed the components of a message in terms of the types of stimuli transmitted: verbal and nonverbal, intentional and unintentional. We learned that though all five senses are potential channels for receiving stimuli, face-to-face communication relies primarily on hearing, sight, and touch and that interference, or noise, may distort signals.

We saw that all the elements in the first communicator's half of our communication cycle—input, filters, communicative stimuli, channels, and interference—are different for the second communicator because of his uniqueness as a human being. Finally, we examined the effect of time, a crucial variable in all studies of communication. In our model, time was represented by numerous circles in the form of a spiral.

Review Questions

1. What are two characteristics of models? What criteria may be used to evaluate the worth of models?
2. What is input and how does it influence a person's communication?
3. How do physiological and psychological filters differ?
4. Name the four types of communicative stimuli. Give a specific example of each that you have experienced.

5. What are the three primary channels of interpersonal communication?
6. Explain the difference between technical and semantic interference and give an example of each.
7. What is signal-to-noise ratio?
8. What do spiral (or helical) models suggest about the nature of interpersonal communication?
9. Discuss intensity, mode, and style of face-to-face communication as functions of time.

Exercises

1. a. Draw and label a model of interpersonal communication. If possible, include components that can be appropriately labeled as communicator 1, communicator 2, input, filters, communicative stimuli, channels, interference, and time. To what extent does the model reflect the three characteristics of interpersonal communication (see Objective 2, Chapter 1)?
   b. Examine the model carefully and formulate five statements that describe how two or more components of the model may interrelate and influence communication effectiveness as defined in Chapter 1 (see Objective 3).
   c. To what extent would your model meet the criteria for evaluating models?
2. Select a group of about ten students and ask them to discuss one of the case problems listed in the Appendix. Observe the group and, if possible, tape-record the discussion. Analyze the group's communication in terms of intentional, unintentional, verbal, and nonverbal stimuli.
3. Write a short paper in which you analyze the strengths and weaknesses of the communication model in this chapter. Compare and contrast it with some other models that may be found in the books in the Suggested Readings.

Suggested Readings

Budd, Richard, and Ruben, Brent (eds.). *Approaches to Human Communication.* Rochelle Park, N.J.: Hayden, 1973. This excellent sourcebook brings together a vast array of articles dealing with communication theory. Communication theory is applied to such diverse subject areas as art, economics and marketing, general systems theory, history, international behavior, nonverbal behavior, organizational behavior, and therapeutic transaction.

Dance, Frank E. X. (ed.). *Human Communication Theory: Original Essays.* New York: Holt, Rinehart and Winston, 1967. This excellent collection of essays contains interesting articles that cover communica-

tion theory from the perspective of different fields of study, including
anthropology, neurophysiology, psychiatry, psychology, and sociology.

Notes

[1] Herbert A. Simon and Alan Newell, "Models: Their Uses and Limitations," in Edwin Paul Hollander and Raymond G. Hunt (eds), *Current Perspectives in Social Psychology* (New York: Oxford University Press, 1963), pp. 79–91.

[2] Abraham Kaplan, *The Conduct of Inquiry: Methodology for Behavioral Science* (San Francisco: Chandler, 1964), p. 265.

[3] Jurgen Ruesch, in Jurgen Ruesch and Gregory Bateson, *Communication: The Social Matrix of Psychiatry* (New York: Norton, 1968), p. 5.

[4] Kaplan, p. 269.

[5] Charles A. Brownfield, *Isolation: Clinical and Experimental Approaches* (New York: Random House, 1965), pp. 74–75.

[6] William James, *Principles of Psychology*, Vol. I (New York: Dover, 1950), p. 402.

[7] George A. Miller, *Language and Communication* (New York: McGraw-Hill, 1963), p. 227.

[8] E. H. Gombrich, *Art and Illusion*, 2nd ed. (New York: Pantheon, 1961), p. 60.

[9] A. A. Brill, quoted in Sigmund Freud, *The Psychopathology of Everyday Life*, in *The Basic Writings of Sigmund Freud*, ed. and tr. by A. A. Brill (New York: Modern Library, 1938), p. 82.

[10] Lee O. Thayer, "On Theory-Building in Communication: Some Conceptual Problems," *Journal of Communication*, 13 (1963), 230.

[11] Colin Cherry, *On Human Communication*, 2nd ed. (Cambridge, Mass.: M.I.T. Press, 1966), p. 42.

[12] Leon Festinger and Nathan Maccoby, "On Resistance to Persuasive Communications," *Journal of Abnormal and Social Psychology*, 68 (1964), 359–366.

[13] Cherry, pp. 116–117.

[14] Cherry, p. 176.

[15] *Hamlet*, act 2, sc. 2.

[16] Frank E. X. Dance, "Toward a Theory of Human Communication," in Frank E. X. Dance (ed.), *Human Communication Theory: Original Essays* (New York: Holt, Rinehart and Winston, 1967), p. 295.

[17] Lev Semenovich Vygotsky, *Thought and Language*, ed. and tr. by Eugenia Hanfmann and Gertrude Vakar (Cambridge, Mass.: M.I.T. Press, 1962), p. 141.

[18] Dance, pp. 293–294.

The Psychology
of Interpersonal
Communication

part
two

Chapter 3 Social Behavior and Motivation

OBJECTIVES

After reading this chapter the student should be able to:

1. Distinguish between respondent learning, instrumental learning, and social learning.

2. Distinguish between the concepts of generalization and discrimination as they apply to learning.

3. Describe the phenomenon of social facilitation and give at least two examples of how it affects behavior.

4. Explain how the concepts of reinforcement (both positive and negative) and feedback operate in interpersonal communication.

5. Define the terms "comparison level" and "comparison level for alternatives" and give an example of each.

6. Describe how need for affiliation, need for achievement, and Machiavellianism influence communication style.

3

A human being can be a human being only because other people have taught him, directly and indirectly, explicitly and implicitly, how to be human and what the important characteristics of the world, human and nonhuman, are that he is going to have to live with.[1]

Writers in many disciplines have repeatedly emphasized the importance of social interaction as an influence on the developing individual. Studies of infants raised in orphanages and monkeys raised in isolation show us that interaction is a necessity of life. In fact, some theorists have argued that mind and self actually emerge as a result of social experience and that communication is responsible for that emergence.

Essentially this chapter is concerned with the first element of our model, the communicator himself, and the learning processes by which his communication behaviors develop out of his interactions with other human beings. Our interest in learning is twofold: we want to know how communication behaviors, like other social behaviors, are learned, and we want to suggest how some of these behaviors can be modified through new experiences.

SOME PRINCIPLES OF LEARNING THEORY

In one of the most famous experiments in **respondent learning**, or *classical conditioning,* a hungry dog is shown a light just before he receives food. The food is a natural positive stimulus that always produces a salivating response. The light is a neutral stimulus. After the two stimuli, food and light, have been paired a number of times, the dog salivates whenever he sees the light even if he receives no food. His response is then said to be "conditioned." This response has limited usefulness to the dog because it is not adaptive: it will not produce a change in his environment—that is, it will not bring him food. But in studying social behavior we are interested primarily in learning that can produce environmental change.

Instrumental Learning

A good part of the learning that does produce environmental change is **instrumental learning**. We can best explain its principles by describ-

46   ing another animal experiment, this one derived from the work of B. F. Skinner.

In front of you is a box that contains a hungry pigeon. Aimlessly he pecks around the box, scouting for food. In time he pecks at a window in the box that happens to be illuminated, and he is immediately given a pellet of food. The food pellet is his **reinforcement**, or his *reward for giving the desired response*. After a number of such reinforcements, the pigeon learns that he can get food for himself simply by pecking at the window when it is lighted. This behavior is *instrumental* in getting the reward. Incidentally the reward, or reinforcer, need not be a positive stimulus. It can be the removal of some noxious or aversive stimulus: a pigeon may learn to peck at the window in order to avoid an electric shock.

Since the pigeon in the Skinner box sounds somewhat remote from human concerns, suppose we turn to a study of human behavior. One team of researchers wanted to determine whether the vocalizations of infants could be influenced by the responses of the adults who cared for them.[2] The researchers observed the infants for two days, the "baseline period," and tallied the normal frequencies of their vocalizations (or discrete, voiced sounds). During the next two days, the "conditioning period," experimenters held their heads about 15 inches away from the infants for three minutes nine times each day. Each time an infant vocalized, an experimenter made three immediate responses: he gave the infant a broad smile, he made three sounds ("Tsk, tsk, tsk"), and he lightly touched the infant's abdomen. The last two days constituted the "extinction period." **Extinction** is *the elimination of a response—* in this case, vocalizing—*by withholding reinforcement*. Now the experimenter remained silent and expressionless whenever the infant vocalized.

The results are shown in Figure 2. During the conditioning period vocalizations significantly increased, but they returned to about the base-line level when the adult responses of social encouragement were withdrawn. In our discussion of feedback, we shall see that vocalizing is only one aspect of communication that can be modified by social reinforcers.

At first glance the experiments we have just described seem to have little application to the complexities of adult social life; yet the concepts of instrumental learning have been used to explain an enormous range of human behaviors. Perhaps it will help if we consider the nature of reinforcers. Food is a reinforcer for the pigeon in the Skinner box. Smiles, "tsk" sounds, and abdominal tickles are reinforcers for the infant. Reinforcers for an adult might be praise, agreement, higher grades, social acceptance, job promotions, and simply human companionship. The basic principle is always the same. Each human being emits hundreds of responses. Some are reinforced whereas others are

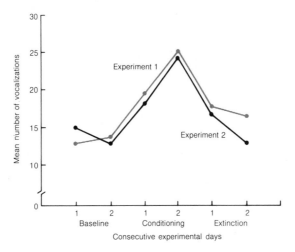

Mean Number of Vocalizations on Consecutive Experimental Days

SOURCE: Harriet Rheingold, Jacob Gewirtz, and Helen Ross, "Social Conditioning of Vocalizations in Infants," *Journal of Comparative and Physiological Psychology*, 52 (1959), 69. Copyright 1959 by the American Psychological Association and reproduced by permission.

discouraged. The reinforcement of a given behavior increases the probability that that behavior will occur again. One interesting theory is that just such a process may account for at least one form of stage fright, or speech anxiety. According to Heider, children who are continually suppressed in their efforts to express themselves tend to develop an aversion to other communication situations.[3]

Once we acquire a new response, we often **generalize** it—we *apply it to situations that are similar but not identical* to those in which we learned it. Since no two stimuli are identical, generalization has an important function. It has been proposed, for example, that without the ability to generalize it would be impossible to learn language.

How do we learn which behaviors are appropriate for which situations? A successful debater who has been reinforced for his rigorous use of logic, his verbal aggression, and his criticism of his opponent's weaknesses may have a hard time adapting to the cooperative spirit of a problem-solving discussion. If he applies his debating behavior to this setting, he is in for trouble. Debating and problem solving both require communication skills, but the differences in situation require differences in behavior. The principle involved here is **discrimination**, or *learning that a behavior has different consequences in different situations.* To some degree all social learning depends on our ability to discriminate and react selectively.

Skinner and his followers believe that the principles of instrumental learning can account for almost all social behavior. Yet a major criticism has been their inability to explain how new behaviors are acquired. According to proponents of instrumental learning, a behavior must be emitted before it can be reinforced. But how can it be emitted if it is new?

Social learning, a much broader-based theory of behavior acquisition proposed by Bandura and Walters, accounts for the acquisition of many novel responses through **modeling,** or *imitation.*[4] In other words, it is argued that we need not perform behaviors and be reinforced for them in order to learn. We can acquire many new responses simply by observing them in others.

A model need not be directly observed. Bandura and Walters found that after children were shown a film of an adult kicking and pummeling a doll, they imitated the aggressive behavior in their play. There were several versions of the film. Imitation of aggressive behavior was greatest when the film showed the adult model being rewarded for his actions and least when the model was punished for them.[5] Most introductory speech and communication courses make use of both live and symbolic models to teach communication skills. Students watch fellow students give speeches that are then critiqued; they see videotapes of actual speeches that are later evaluated in class; and they read and analyze the merits of various printed speeches.

Much of what is known about modeling is closely linked to the study of socialization. Although his parents are usually the first and most significant models for any young child, he rarely grows up to be a carbon copy of any single human being. As he develops, numerous models are available to him: his brothers and sisters, other relatives, friends, neighbors, and teachers. He also reads stories and sees films that dramatize the behavior of symbolic models. Out of all the behavior that he observes, he imitates only selected responses. In certain respects, he may pattern himself after a favorite uncle. If he notices that his kid brother gets his own way by throwing temper tantrums, he may also give temper tantrums a try. If the tantrums get him what he wants, they will probably persist.

In this connection it is important to note that a child does not always model himself after the person who receives the greatest rewards. He may imitate a person who has the power to grant the rewards. Bandura, Ross, and Ross found that after observing a group of adults, children imitated the adult who controlled rewards—even if that adult did not make use of the rewards (toys) himself—in preference to an adult who received and made use of them.[6] Perceived power seems to be a crucial determinant of modeling.

Although they do not dismiss the biological differences between males and females, social learning theorists have argued persuasively that many of the psychological differences between the sexes are learned during the socialization process. In their view there are certain **sex-typed behaviors**—that is, *behaviors that typically elicit rewards for one sex that differ from those granted to the other.* These behaviors are learned both by direct reinforcement and by modeling.

Consider aggressive behavior. Even at age three, boys exhibit more aggressive and negativistic behavior than girls. This difference seems to exist in children from many other cultures, and it is often said that males are instinctively more aggressive than females. Social learning theorists remind us, however, that aggression is likely to bring different consequences for a boy and a girl even at the tender age of three. Children are quick to learn that the girl who never hits other children is a "little lady" but that the boy who never hits is a "sissy." Differential reinforcement of aggressive behavior becomes even more pronounced as children grow older. Seven-year-old Billy may be encouraged to "hit back" by his father, but Billy's sister is likely to hear that girls "don't fight." Apparently little girls are still expected to be made of "sugar and spice and everything nice."

This is not to say that girls do not know how to express aggression or that they are incapable of acting aggressively. We have to distinguish between the *acquisition* of a new response and its *performance.* Girls observe a great many aggressive models just as boys do. They perform less aggressive behaviors because they receive more negative consequences (criticism, rejection, and so on) than boys receive for the same behaviors. On the other hand, dependency behaviors seem to work in reverse, with girls performing more dependent behaviors than boys because the former receive more positive consequences. Achievement is another behavior that seems to be sex-typed, at least to some degree, as we shall see when we discuss motivation.

Another social learning concept is **vicarious reinforcement**, the proposition that *when we observe others being reinforced for a given behavior we are more likely to perform that behavior.* Vicarious reinforcement has been used as a technique for reducing speech anxiety in college students.[7] Students who observe others communicating successfully are more likely to try these communication behaviors themselves. Apparently we expect to receive the same reinforcement as others do. Miller reports that the delivery of a speaker who has observed an audience reaction to a preceding speaker will become disrupted and nonfluent if he receives an audience response different from that of the first speaker. In fact, ". . . the sequence of responses to the two speakers had greater impact upon delivery than did approval or disapproval of the speaker himself."[8]

Thus social learning theorists explain social behavior in the language of learning theory, but in doing so they broaden the definition of learning considerably. For them socially accepted and/or adaptive behavior is acquired not only through reinforcement, generalization, and discrimination but through modeling and vicarious reinforcement. For example, all learning theorists agree that aggressive behavior that is directly reinforced increases. Social learning theorists add that observing aggressive social models who receive rewards or do not receive punishment increases the probability that the observer will behave aggressively.

Much of our scientific knowledge about how social behaviors are learned is still elementary. We have seen, however, that the social learning process has a great many implications for the study of interpersonal communication. Before exploring these further let us take note of a social phenomenon that affects how well behaviors will be performed.

Social Facilitation

Have you ever been in an audience composed of only a few people scattered throughout all the seats? How do the responses of the audience differ from those of an audience whose members are seated close to one another? Or have you ever noticed how a few people in an audience beginning to laugh or applaud start almost everyone doing it? This shows how others influence our behavior. A special case of this type of influence is known as **social facilitation**—*the enhancing effect of the presence of others on a person's performance.*

The earliest study of this phenomenon was conducted by Triplett in 1897.[9] He found that people who were required to turn a fishing reel 150 times did better when they competed in the presence of others than in isolation. The research of Triplett and others led Allport to introduce the term "social facilitation" in 1924.[10] Later research has shown that social facilitation occurs only under certain conditions. For example, the student who is required to give a talk before a communication class and who has decided not to prepare often does rather poorly. He is also more likely to experience speech anxiety. Conversely the well-prepared student feels greater self-confidence, and his performance is usually enhanced by his high arousal level, which is stimulated by the presence of an audience. In other words, the presence of others generally inhibits your ability to learn or perform new responses (solving a new mathematics problem at the board, for example), but it enhances your ability to perform well-learned responses.

FEEDBACK AS A REINFORCER

In writing about feedback systems in computers and other machines, Norbert Wiener, the founder of cybernetics, observes that when "the information which proceeds backward from the performance is able to change the general method and pattern of performance, we have a process which may well be called learning."[11] When we examine feedback solely in interpersonal terms, we can be more specific and say that feedback reinforces some behaviors and extinguishes others. For example, one story has it that a psychology instructor who had been teaching the principles of instrumental learning was actually conditioned by his own class. The students decided to give him reinforcement by taking lots of notes, looking attentive, and asking questions whenever he moved to his right. Whenever he moved to his left, they tried to extinguish this behavior by not taking notes, being inattentive, and not asking questions. He was just about teaching from the right front corner of the room when he realized what was happening.

Influencing Through Feedback

Interpersonal feedback can influence the outcome of interaction in some rather subtle ways. For example, an interviewer's biases or even his characteristics can affect the responses of the person being interviewed. Thus Cantril found that Democrat interviewers received more pro-Democrat responses than Republican interviewers, who in turn obtained more pro-Republican responses than Democrat interviewers.[12] It has also been shown that blue-collar interviewers receive more favorable responses on labor questions than white-collar interviewers.[13] There is a strong possibility that feedback from the interviewer accounts for these findings.

There is considerable evidence to justify the generalization that just about any verbal behavior can be reinforced through the use of "Good" or "Mmm-hmm." One team of researchers even found that during an interview a simple head nod was enough of a reinforcer to encourage the respondent to talk more. The results of their experiment lend support to the view that nonverbal as well as verbal feedback can have a sustained effect on the receiver's subsequent communication behavior. Their experiment, like many others on the effects of feedback, employed a design similar to that of the study of infant vocalization described earlier: a base-line period followed by a period of conditioning, or reinforcement, and then an extinction period.

In an attempt to determine the precise operations of head nodding and vocal reinforcers in less structured interpersonal communication, Dittmann and Llewellyn seated pairs of subjects 5 feet apart and facing each other at a slight angle (a seating arrangement normally adopted by strangers).[14] They were asked to converse with each other for two separate time periods of two minutes each on any subject that interested them. During the first period one person was to do most of the speaking and the other the listening; during the second they were to reverse the speaking and listening roles. Several consistent patterns of behavior emerged:

1. Head nod or vocal response is usually followed by some comment. This cue seems to be used as an indication to the first speaker that the other person now wants to speak.
2. Head nods and vocal responses frequently occur together and in that order, and they are far more likely to occur when the first speaker drops his voice, indicating the completion of an idea.
3. A speaker tends to look at his listener as he approaches the end of a statement and to look away as he begins one. The person listening gives better eye contact than the person speaking, so that when the speaker does look at his listener as he ends a statement, it may serve as a cue that he is now ready to listen.
4. "You know" is used by a speaker to tell the listener that he wants some feedback on how he is being received.

Dittmann and Llewellyn's study emphasizes a concept we spoke of in Chapter 1 and developed in Chapter 2: the interdependence of the participants in the communication process. It is significant for two reasons. First, it describes a relatively normal conversation rather than a rigged encounter. Second, it reminds us of the wealth of cues exchanged at specific points in a conversation in which one person relinquishes the role of speaker and the other person, who was listening, assumes it. Research has shown that as communicators we expect such responses from others and find them reinforcing. If we do not receive them, we tend to evaluate the other person negatively.[15] The implications for the student are obvious. Providing feedback is an essential aspect of both the speaker's and the listener's responsibilities, as we tried to suggest in Chapter 1.

Students often say that they do not like to talk if they are just agreeing with or adding to what someone else has already said. They feel that their comments will be repetitious and have no value. Yet there is considerable evidence that showing agreement or clarifying what someone else has said is functional behavior that elicits greater participation from other communicators. Scheidel and Crowell found that in small groups a full 35 percent of the discussion was devoted to feedback, most of it consisting of statements that either supported or clarified what had already been said. The experimenters suggest that one possible explanation for the substantial amount of feedback is "the reinforcing effect of the agreement comments which occur in the feedback process."[16] They also show that the tendency to give feedback is characteristic of highly task-oriented people, not just those who seek social approval. In fact, task-oriented group members seem to use feedback primarily as a tool for accomplishing the group goal more effectively. The same reinforcing phenomenon takes place in speaker-audience contexts.

The Information Value of Feedback

In addition to its task functions, feedback is also an important source of information about the self. A person's **self-concept**, *one's relatively stable impressions of oneself*, develops in part out of the feedback he receives from those around him. In fact, some psychiatrists take the position that a person evaluates himself primarily on the basis of how he thinks he is evaluated by others.

It is known that feedback has a direct effect on level of self-esteem, one of the chief measures of self-concept. When people are asked to predict their own performance on a test—whether of their social, intellectual, or physical competence—and are later given feedback on how well they scored, they revise their predictions for the next experimental task in the direction of that feedback. This is true regardless of whether the feedback is accurate or not.

From a survey of more than fifty studies of speech communication feedback, Gardiner concluded that "Sources who receive positive audience response will develop more favorable attitudes toward themselves and toward the audience than sources who receive negative audience response."[17] He also found strong evidence that negative feedback can inhibit a speaker's delivery and that this effect is reflected in fluency, rate of speech, voice loudness, nervousness, stage fright, eye contact, and body movement.

It should be emphasized, however, that negative reactions can also be valuable in improving communication skills. In a speech class designed to correct voice and diction problems, the instructor paired off the students. Each time one member of a team exhibited a "poor" communication habit, the other immediately called it to his attention. Most students found it a frustrating but rewarding experience.[18] Jenkins suggests a related value of feedback when he writes about prediction in interpersonal communication:

> Accuracy in predicting responses to communicative efforts tends to improve if an awareness of the results of one's attempts accompanies experience. For example, one learns what kind of behavior will be rewarded or accepted and what kind of behavior will result in punishment or rejection. . . . only through a set of experiences in a variety of groups can one learn that he must adjust his behavior and his predictions to the particular body with which he is associating. (Some, never learning this, have unvarying habits of communication.) As a person gains this insight, he becomes able to communicate appropriately and readily.[19]

REWARDS AND MOTIVATIONS

There are no absolute rewards in human interaction. Several studies have shown that people with similar attitudes or other perceived

54 similarities are more capable of reinforcing each other than people who are dissimilar. One communication scholar sums up the point, *"Reward has to be defined in terms of the receiver."*[20]

Analyzing human interaction in terms of rewards and costs, Thibaut and Kelley offer an excellent theoretical framework from which to view these differences. For each of us the outcome, or consequences, of any interpersonal encounter will simply be the rewards we receive from interacting with a given person minus the costs we incur. **Rewards** are defined as *"the pleasures, satisfactions, and gratifications"* we enjoy, including the fulfillment of any of our needs. **Costs** are *"any factors that operate to inhibit or deter the performance of a sequence of behavior."*[21] Costs include not only negative feelings but the fatigue and stress resulting from interaction.

Thibaut and Kelley assume that in all our interactions we actively seek positive outcomes from others and that we are constantly comparing the outcomes that different people provide for us. In fact, each of us has a standard for evaluating the rewards and costs of a relationship according to what he feels he "deserves." This standard is his **comparison level** (CL) , or *minimum level for positive outcomes,* and it is in great part determined by the quality of his previous outcomes. A high-powered person who is self-confident and outgoing usually has a relatively high CL.

One's CL is his criterion for judging a relationship at a given moment. He also has a **comparison level for alternatives** (CL_{alt}), which is his *criterion for deciding whether to continue or terminate any relationship.* Obviously involvement in any human relationship automatically reduces to some extent the ability to form others. CL_{alt} is the lowest level of outcomes we find acceptable in a relationship as measured against all other opportunities. The greater the rewards a person can produce for himself, the higher his CL_{alt}. We are constantly comparing each of our relationships with possible alternatives, and when the outcomes we receive drop below CL_{alt}, we terminate the relationship. Some time ago a television commercial made the point quite bluntly. The scene opens with a rather plain couple parked on a beach in a flashy new car. Then along comes a terrific-looking girl in a bikini. She asks the fellow if the car is his, and he invites her to sit in it. As the commercial ends we see the plain girl standing alone on the beach, shouting at the other two as they drive off. In this example the young man's alternatives suddenly improved with the acquisition of a new car—and his choice of dates changed rather abruptly.

We have seen how social learning influences and shapes our subsequent behavior patterns. To a large extent, this shaping determines our needs and expectations—our comparison levels, if you will. Early in their work Thibaut and Kelley emphasize the relationship between rewards and need satisfaction. To some degree it is the strength of one's various needs that determines what is rewarding for him. Therefore if we know more about motivation, we can make some predictions about differences in communication behaviors. In the following pages we shall look at three dimensions along which some of these differences can be measured.

The Need for Affiliation

One variable that has a great influence on communication behavior is **need for affiliation** (N Aff), or *the need to be with others*. Most of the rewards for a person rated high in need for affiliation come directly from human companionship. Therefore he tends to be friendly and avoids disagreements. His communication behaviors contrast sharply with those of a low affiliater. For example, the high affiliater seats himself closer to the other person; he smiles more often; he nods his head more often to indicate agreement or gain approval; he uses more arm and hand gestures.[22] In general the high affiliater gives a great deal of supportive nonverbal feedback. And if he is relatively self-confident, he also tends to be more verbally supportive and affectionate to others.

Whether the need to affiliate is innate or learned is an issue still unresolved. We do know that a correlation exists between affiliative need and birth order so that only children and first-borns rank highest in their need to be with others.[23] And as we shall see in Chapter 5, anxiety-producing situations intensify this need.

The Need for Achievement

A second motive that bears on communication style is **need for achievement** (N ach)—that is, *the need to demonstrate competence and to gain recognition for accomplishments*. Like the rewards of the person with strong affiliative needs, those of the high achiever are, at least to some degree, social. He wants to excel, to attain some high standard, whether it is in business, sports, or academic life, but he is also concerned with how others will respond to his accomplishments. His communication is characterized by relatively frequent attempts to build up his own confidence and establish his dominance over others while at the same time attracting attention to himself. We also expect the high achiever to talk more than others, especially in situations where there is an objective to be reached (that is, task-oriented situations).

McClelland, who has done some of the most outstanding research on achievement motivation, pokes fun at the high achiever when he writes:

> Some psychologists think that because I've done so much on N ach I must like the kind of people who have a strong need for achievement. I don't. I find them bores. They are not artistically sensitive. They're entre-

preneurs, kind of driven—always trying to improve themselves and find a shorter route to the office or a faster way of reading their mail. . . . Yes, it's an efficiency kind of thing, but it also includes taking personal responsibility to solve problems and achieve moderate goals at calculated risks—in situations that provide real feedback. You can see why most innovative businessmen score high on N ach.[24]

A recent study of speech anxiety in college males linked need for achievement to level of self-confidence.[25] It was found that high achievers were more self-confident as well as less likely to experience speech anxiety. Low achievers tended to have less self-confidence and to have more anxiety about speaking before others.

Most of our generalizations about achievement motive are based on data obtained from male subjects. The data on women are strangely different. For example, women who have a strong need for achievement, particularly very intelligent women, also tend to rate very high on measures of anxiety. This discrepancy has usually been interpreted as evidence that women do not have the competitive needs that men do—that they have, in fact, a will to fail. Not content with this explanation, Horner pursued the question by examining what consequences women expect as a result of high achievement.[26] She found that whereas men expect positive outcomes as a result of their accomplishments, women often link achievement with negative outcomes, such as social rejection and loss of femininity.

Two interesting comparisons have been made between high affiliaters and high achievers. A study of small groups found that high achievers give more suggestions about procedures, offer more opinions, draw attention to themselves more often, and integrate past communication more than high affiliaters.[27] Earlier evidence of the more task-oriented approach of high achievers comes from a study by French.[28] Subjects had to choose between a work partner who was a competent stranger and one who was a less competent friend. High achievers made their choices on the basis of competence; high affiliaters chose on the basis of friendship.

Machiavellianism

Suppose that we look at communication behavior not in terms of whether the need to achieve goals is high or low but in terms of how a person interacts with others as he attempts to reach his goals. The study of this dimension of personality began with the construction of a questionnaire in which people were asked to express the extent to which they agreed or disagreed with a series of statements about human nature. Here are some sample items:

Barnum was very wrong when he said there's a sucker born every minute.

It is safest to assume that all people have a vicious streak and it will come out when they are given a chance.

There is no excuse for lying to someone else.

Most men forget more easily the death of their father than the loss of their property.

Anyone who completely trusts anyone else is asking for trouble.[29]

The questionnaire was the first of a series of scales designed to measure **Machiavellianism**, *manipulative behavior in interpersonal relationships.* In the laboratory so-called high Machs and low Machs have been brought together in a number of ingenious games and situations involving bargaining, changing attitudes, and social influence. A basic difference between the two types seems to be that the high Mach, while not unconcerned about the success of his own behavior, shows greater emotional detachment. For example, the high Mach does not assume that his partner in a game will be loyal; nor does he feel betrayed when the partner is not. And if the stakes are high enough, he has little difficulty advocating a position that is contrary to what he believes.[30] The high Mach manipulates more, wins more, persuades others more, and is himself less frequently persuaded. His first concern is the task at hand. Christie and Geis call the high-Mach pattern of behavior the "cool syndrome."[31]

The low Mach, on the other hand, is characterized as the "soft touch." The low Mach is first of all more susceptible to social influence. He frequently complies with the requests of others, changes his opinions, and becomes emotionally involved (a possible reason he loses to the high Mach as much as he does). His orientation is generally social; the high Mach is task-oriented.

Machiavellianism is a personality dimension particularly relevant to our study of communication because high Machs perform most differently from low Machs when there is face-to-face encounter and the situation is loosely structured. Machiavelli's critics labeled him an "opportunist"; his admirers, a "realist." Whatever our personal feelings about a manipulative approach to human relations, it is clear that the high Mach is very effective in face-to-face encounters—especially those that require bargaining, improvising, or persuasion. Thus he is especially successful in producing two of the five communication outcomes discussed in Chapter 1: attitude influence and action.

The high Mach's talent for improvisation is apparent in his superior ability to think on his feet when other people are present. We have already discussed the phenomenon of social facilitation: unlike most people, the high Mach is adept at learning or performing new responses in the presence of others. And in speech communication courses (though not in public speaking courses), it is the high Mach who tends to get the higher grade—presumably because these courses are more loosely structured and allow for a great many face-to-face exchanges between students.[32]

58   Differences between high and low Machs seem to be the result of a complex social learning process, though Christie and Geis believe that parental modeling is not a major influence. They suggest that "some manipulative behaviors are learned at an early age by being rewarded unintentionally by parents and by early exposure to nonfamilial socializing agents such as peers and mass media."[33]

Who are the high Machs in our society? The research findings seem to reverse our expectations.[34] It has been shown, for example, that college students have higher Mach scores than businessmen or Washington lobbyists and that younger people generally have higher scores than older ones. Furthermore the Machiavellian orientation seems to be on the upswing. We leave you wondering whether you yourself are a high Mach or a low Mach—and how you got to be that way.

Summary

Each of us comes to a communication event with certain established patterns, certain characteristic ways of responding. In this chapter we have tried to show that these are largely shaped by learning experiences and that some behaviors can be modified by new learning experiences.

Our study of how communication behaviors are acquired began with a review of several principles of instrumental learning: reinforcement, extinction, generalization, and discrimination. We then turned to social learning, a broader-based theory of behavior acquisition, which holds that socially accepted or adaptive behaviors can also be acquired through modeling. We saw that modeling and reinforcement are both important during the socialization process. We spoke next of the reinforcing effects of both verbal and nonverbal feedback and suggested that feedback can also influence self-concept.

In the final section we explored the relationship between reward and motivation and considered some ways in which three variables— need for affiliation, need for achievement, and Machiavellianism— affect communication style.

Review Questions

1. How do respondent learning, instrumental learning, and social learning differ?
2. Discuss the difference between generalization and discrimination in learning. What application do these concepts have to learning to communicate more effectively?
3. What is social facilitation? Give two examples of how social facilitation affects behavior.
4. How do the concepts of reinforcement and feedback operate in inter-

personal communication? Why is interpersonal feedback considered a reinforcer? What effect does feedback have on subsequent behavior?

5. What are comparison level and comparison level for alternatives? Provide an example of each in a hypothetical situation where young lovers are about to break up.

6. In what ways might need for affiliation, need for achievement, and Machiavellianism influence communication style?

Exercises

1. Refer to the model constructed for Exercise 1, Chapter 2. Describe and provide examples of how the principles of respondent learning, instrumental learning, and social learning apply to (a) the four types of communicative stimuli (see Objective 5, Chapter 2), and (b) five of the possible outcomes of interpersonal communication (see Objective 3, Chapter 1).

2. Examine a number of commercials presented over various media by analyzing how the concept of reinforcement is used in conjunction with the four types of communicative stimuli.

3. While in an informal conversation with someone, select a particular word or phrase he uses and reinforce him (for example, smile, nod, or say "good") each time he uses it. Determine the extent to which the frequency of its use increases.

4. Go to the personal log that you began for Exercise 1 in Chapter 1. Which of your comments illustrate the effects of social reinforcement or extinction on communication behaviors? What stimuli were used as reinforcers? Who used them? What were the results?

5. Make a list of three people whose friendship you value. Evaluate the effectiveness of their interpersonal communication with you and the part it plays in your relationship. What is it that sustains your attraction to each of them? Does this attraction have anything to do with social reinforcement, and if so, how?

Suggested Readings

Bandura, Albert, and Walters, Richard. *Social Learning and Personality Development.* New York: Holt, Rinehart and Winston, 1963. This fascinating little book contains an excellent summary of research in social learning. The effects of reward and punishment of behavior are discussed in terms of such topics as childhood violence as it relates to television viewing; spoiling children by rewarding temper tantrums; and overcoming one's fear of snakes.

Mann, Harriet, and others. "Four Types of Personality and Four Ways of Perceiving Time." *Psychology Today* (December 1972), 6:76–84. Despite a ponderous title, this is an easily read article in which Mann defines four personality types and their ways of seeing reality.

60   Ruch, Floyd L. "Personality—Public or Private." *Psychology Today* (October 1967), 1:46–47, 58–60. This is a thoughtful examination of the invasion-of-privacy issue as it relates to personality testing of job applicants. Based on his own studies and research in previous experiments, Ruch states that testing for sociability is essential for filling executive positions. A good discussion-starter, particularly when exploring the definition of privacy.

Notes

[1] Joseph Church, *Language and the Discovery of Reality* (New York: Random House, 1961), p. 137.

[2] Harriet Rheingold, Jacob Gewirtz, and Helen Ross, "Social Conditioning of Vocalizations in Infants," *Journal of Comparative and Physiological Psychology,* 52 (1959), 68–73.

[3] Mary Heider, "An Investigation of the Relationship Between Speech Anxiety in Adults and Their Indication of Parental Suppression of Communication in Childhood" (M.A. thesis, University of Kansas, 1968).

[4] Albert Bandura and Richard Walters, *Social Learning and Personality Development* (New York: Holt, Rinehart and Winston, 1963), p. 50.

[5] Albert Bandura, "Vicarious Processes: A Case of No-Trial Learning," in L. Berkowitz (ed.), *Advances in Experimental Social Psychology*, Vol. II (New York: Academic, 1965), pp. 1–55.

[6] Albert Bandura, Dorothea Ross, and Sheila A. Ross, "A Comparative Test of the Status Envy, Social Power, and Secondary Reinforcement Theories of Identificatory Learning," *Journal of Abnormal and Social Psychology,* 67 (1963), 527–534.

[7] Kim Giffin and Kendall Bradley, "Group Counseling for Speech Anxiety: An Approach and a Rationale," *Journal of Communication,* 19 (1969), 22–29.

[8] Gerald R. Miller, "Variations in the Verbal Behavior of a Second Speaker as a Function of Varying Audience Responses," *Speech Monographs,* 31 (1964), 114.

[9] N. Triplett, "The Dynamogenic Factors in Pacemaking and Competition," *American Journal of Psychology,* 9 (1897), 507–533.

[10] Floyd Allport, *Social Psychology* (Boston: Houghton Mifflin, 1924), p. 283.

[11] Norbert Wiener, *The Human Use of Human Beings: Cybernetics and Society* (New York: Avon, 1967), p. 84.

[12] Hadley Cantril, *Gauging Public Opinion* (Princeton, N.J.: Princeton University Press, 1944).

[13] Daniel Katz, "Do Interviewers Bias Results?", *Public Opinion Quarterly,* 6 (1942), 248–268.

[14] Alan Dittmann and Lynn G. Llewellyn, "Relationship Between Vocalizations and Head Nods as Listener Responses," *Journal of Personality and Social Psychology,* 9 (1968), 79–84.

15 Phoebe Ellsworth and J. Carlsmith, "Effects of Eye Contact and Verbal Content on Affective Responses to a Dyadic Interaction," *Journal of Personality and Social Psychology,* 10 (1968), 18.

16 Thomas Scheidel and Laura Crowell, "Feedback in Small Group Communication," *Quarterly Journal of Speech,* 52 (1966), 277.

17 James C. Gardiner, "A Synthesis of Experimental Studies of Speech Communication Feedback," *Journal of Communication,* 21 (1971), 31.

18 Stewart L. Tubbs and Gail A. Tubbs, "Speaking and Listening," *Today's Education,* 61 (1972), 23.

19 David Jenkins, "Prediction in Interpersonal Communication," *Journal of Communication,* 11 (1961), 134.

20 David K. Berlo, *The Process of Communication* (New York: Holt, Rinehart and Winston, 1960), p. 89.

21 John W. Thibaut and Harold H. Kelley, *The Social Psychology of Groups* (New York: Wiley, 1959), p. 12. Italics added.

22 Howard Rosenfeld, "Instrumental Affiliative Functions of Facial and Gestural Expressions," *Journal of Personality and Social Psychology,* 4 (1966), 65–72.

23 Stanley Schachter, *The Psychology of Affiliation* (Stanford, Calif.: Stanford University Press, 1959), p. 37.

24 David McClelland, "To Know Why Men Do What They Do," *Psychology Today,* 4 (1971), 36.

25 Kim Giffin and Shirley M. Gilham, "Relationships Between Speech Anxiety and Motivation," *Speech Monographs,* 38 (1971), 70–73.

26 Matina Horner, "Fail: Bright Women," *Psychology Today,* 3 (November 1969), 36–38, 62.

27 Joel Aronoff and Lawrence Messé, "Motivational Determinants of Small-Group Structure," *Journal of Personality and Social Psychology,* 17 (1971), 319–324.

28 Elizabeth G. French, "Motivation as a Variable in Work-Partner Selection," *Journal of Abnormal and Social Psychology,* 53 (1956), 96–99.

29 Richard Christie and Florence L. Geis, *Studies in Machiavellianism* (New York: Academic, 1970), pp. 17–18.

30 Michael Burgoon, Gerald R. Miller, and Stewart L. Tubbs, "Machiavellianism, Justification, and Attitude Change Following Counterattitudinal Advocacy," *Journal of Personality and Social Psychology,* 22 (1972), 366–371.

31 Christie and Geis, pp. 285–313.

32 Michael Burgoon, "The Relationship Between Willingness to Manipulate Others and Success in Two Different Types of Basic Speech Communication Courses," *The Speech Teacher,* 20 (1971), 178–183.

33 Christie and Geis, p. 338.

34 Robin Widgery and Stewart L. Tubbs, "Machiavellianism and Religiosity as Determinants of Cognitive Dissonance Following Counterattitudinal Advocacy" (paper delivered at the annual convention of the International Communication Association, Atlanta, 1972).

Chapter 4
Interpersonal Perception

OBJECTIVES

After reading this chapter the student should be able to:

1. Define the term "psychological set" and give at least two examples.

2. Describe two ways in which person perception differs from object perception and what implications these differences have for interpersonal communication.

3. Explain what is meant by the primacy effect and how it relates to interpersonal communication.

4. Identify at least three influences on stereotype perceptions.

5. State three generalizations from research studies about individual ability to judge people.

6. Identify four characteristics associated with the ability to make accurate perceptions of others.

7. List two ways that perception and interpersonal communication effectiveness can be improved.

One winter day in New York, a smartly dressed woman walked into Tiffany and asked to see some diamond rings. The salesman obliged and she went through the tray, removing her own diamond to try on one ring after another. But she could find nothing to her satisfaction and so thanked the salesman and left. A block away, at Harry Winston (a major competitor of Tiffany's), she did the same thing but again left without making a purchase. It was more than an hour later that the Tiffany salesman discovered that a ring with a large diamond was missing from one of the trays; in its place was a ring with a much smaller diamond. And then he remembered the smartly dressed woman. It wasn't very long before the salesman at Harry Winston made a similar discovery—but his loss turned out to be more unfortunate. The ring was the missing diamond from Tiffany and had to be returned to that store.

The woman who carried through these unusual daylight robberies must have been very confident of the impression she would create. No doubt wearing a diamond ring helped. Yet the impression she created was based not only on her clothing or her jewelry; handsomely dressed women are a common sight in places such as Tiffany. How did she do it?

This incident really happened. It interests us here because it dramatizes how deceptive impressions of others can be—even when other people share our impressions. As communicators we depend on our perceptions of other human beings in almost every aspect of our daily life. The way we perceive others determines the kind of communication that takes place between us; in some cases it even determines whether communication takes place at all. In this chapter we shall examine in some detail what happens when we make a judgment about another person. Let us begin with a look at the process of perception itself.

PERCEIVING PEOPLE AND OBJECTS: A COMPARISON

Our total awareness of the world comes to us through our senses. Thus our perceptions—whether of tables and chairs or coffee cups or other human beings—have a common basis. Yet curiously two people will often disagree in their judgments about a third. The reasons for this difference of opinion become clearer when we consider the ways in which interpersonal perception and perception in general are similar.

First, as we know from Chapter 2, we cannot take in everything; that is, we perceive only part of the available stimuli. The inherent structures of our sense organs—our perceptual filters—limit our capacity to perceive. These limitations exist whether we are experiencing an object or a person. Although we all have these limitations, they vary considerably from one individual to another. Some of us have keener vision than others, some better hearing, and so on. We all see the world a bit differently, and no one sees it completely.

Second, our past experiences influence what we select and the way we perceive it. For example, quickly read the words in Figure 3.

Figure 3

Do you notice anything unusual? Readers often overlook the extra word "the" in the triangle because of their past reading experiences. We are so accustomed to seeing words in groups that we often do not perceive single words. Similarly we often judge a person by the group in which we meet him; we generalize about him on the basis of earlier experiences that seem comparable.

We know that expectations, or psychological sets, have a profound effect on our perceptions of objects. Given an ambiguous stimulus, a hungry man is more likely to perceive food objects, for example, than is a person who has just eaten. Psychological set also affects our perception of people. A defensive person is more apt to perceive strangers as hostile than a self-confident person is. Before you read any further, take a look at the picture of the young woman in Figure 4. Do you see a young woman? Do you also see an old woman? The phrase "the picture of the young woman in Figure 4" led you to perceive the illustration in one way first, but after a while you should be able to see both a young woman and an old one. Try showing this illustration to a friend. Tell him that it is a picture of an old woman, and see whether your statement affects his perception.

Figure 4 is a deliberately ambiguous illustration. Psychologists have made good use of such ambiguous stimuli in testing personality. One such test, the Thematic Apperception Test (TAT), consists of a set of

Figure 4

A Test of Psychological Set

Source: C. M. Mooney and G. A. Ferguson, "A New Closure Test," *Canadian Journal of Psychology,* 5 (1951), 129–133.

twenty pictures. As each picture is shown, the person being tested is asked to make up a story about it. The degree to which his story reveals his past experiences and expectations can be striking. For example, a simple illustration of an elderly woman opening the door to a room was shown to a young man who had formerly been a bombardier in the air force. He responded as follows:

> She has prepared this room for someone's arrival and is opening the door for a last general look over the room. She is probably expecting her son home. She tries to place everything as it was when he left. She seems like a very tyrannical character. She led her son's life for him and is going to take over again as soon as he gets back. This is merely the beginning of her rule, and the son is definitely cowed by this overbearing attitude of hers and will slip back into her well-ordered way of life. He will go through life plodding down the tracks she has laid for him. All this represents her complete domination of his life until she dies.[1]

At the time the young man was tested, he was undergoing psychological treatment. Facts that were later brought to light confirmed that his story clearly reflected his personal problems and that his relationship with his mother strongly resembled the one he had described. The stimulus that elicited his story, however, could evoke a virtually infinite number of interpretations. Each of us has a story for that picture.

Early philosophers, among them John Locke, compared the human mind to a *tabula rasa*, a blank tablet, on which impressions were made. Today we know that perception is not a passive state in which stimuli are received and automatically registered. On the contrary, perception is an active process in which the perceiver selects, organizes, and interprets what he experiences.

Like object perception, person perception may be thought of in terms of three elements: the perceiver, the object of perception, and the context within which the object (in this instance, another human being) is viewed. The perceiver, who shall be referred to as *P*, is of course influenced by his own attributes as well as by those of *O*, the person who is being perceived. The cues that *P* gets from *O* are often called **proximal stimuli**; these are *the attributes of a person as seen through the eyes of the perceiver*. The context, or setting, within which the process of interpersonal perception occurs is both physical and psychological, as we shall see.

Psychologists do not agree about how far we can go in saying that the perception of people resembles the perception of objects. Tagiuri points out an important respect in which the two acts of observation differ:

> Person perception is special . . . in that the similarity between perceiver and perceived is greater than in any other instance. Banal as this may seem, it has far-reaching consequences. The most obvious one of these is that the perceiver is probably maximally inclined and able to use his own experience in perceiving or judging or inferring another's state or intentions. Perceived and perceiver, in general, react similarly to events. This may be viewed as empathy or projection or whatnot. . . .[2]

In other words, to some degree, however slight, we assume that the other person shares some of our characteristics, that he resembles us in some ways. We are—or so we think—familiar with some of his experience. Such assumptions may help us perceive more accurately. For example, if I know that you have just returned from a funeral, on the basis of my own experience I will probably interpret your silence as depression rather than indifference. On the other hand, we often misinterpret what we perceive precisely because we assume other people are like us. If I assume that your taste in music is like mine, when I offer to play some rock music, I may interpret your remark "Oh, great!" as genuinely enthusiastic though it is clear to most people from your facial expression that your reply was sarcastic.

Another way in which perceiving people differs from perceiving objects is that our perceptions and misperceptions influence and keep on influencing our interactions with others—because they keep responding to these perceptions. Sometimes people correct our misperceptions. But occasionally we get further and further afield, and one misinterpretation leads to still another. The following exchange, which took place in an office of a psychiatric research institute, is a good example:

VISITOR: Good afternoon. I have an appointment with Dr. H. My name is Watzlawick [VAHT-sla-vick].

RECEPTIONIST: I did not say it was.

VISITOR: (taken aback and somewhat annoyed) But I am telling you it is.

RECEPTIONIST: (bewildered) Why then did you say it wasn't?

VISITOR: But I said it was![3]

By this time the poor receptionist thought the visitor a new psychotic patient of Dr. H's; the visitor, who was applying for an assistantship at the institute, felt himself the victim of an incomprehensible and insulting joke. The whole incident hinges on the misperception of a word. When the visitor said "My name is Watzlawick," the receptionist thought he had said, "My name is not Slavic."

Person perception then is a special form of perception, and it will require some specific attention and study. Although in passing we shall point out other similarities between object perception and person perception, our primary concern in this chapter will be with how we form our impressions of others and with the accuracy of those impressions.

FORMING IMPRESSIONS OF OTHERS

Most people form impressions of others quite easily; yet they would find it difficult to explain how they do so. In fact, many feel that they make their judgments intuitively. Tagiuri describes the process of personality assessment well when he writes, "Regardless of the degree of skill which an adult may have in appraising others, he engages in the process most of the time without paying much attention to how he does it."[4]

We are accustomed to using the word "impression" about our judgments. We speak of being "under the impression" or of someone as making a "lasting impression," a "false impression," or a "good impression." Even our legal system reflects the degree to which we rely on snap judgments. Before a trial begins prospective jurors are screened by the defense and the prosecution. In addition to raising specific objections to certain candidates for the jury, both the defense and the prosecuting attorney have several peremptory challenges; that is, they are each allowed to reject a certain number of would-be jurors without

70   stating their reasons. An attorney often makes his decision rapidly though it is a complex one and is probably based on several considerations. He will probably take into account his perception of the potential juror, his perception of his client, and the impression he feels that his client will make upon that juror. And of course the attorney for one side might be more than willing to accept a juror whom opposing counsel found objectionable.

Attorneys usually seem to be rather skilled perceivers, accustomed to formulating judgments about others very quickly. But think of the members of the jury. They will be meeting and evaluating many people for the first time—and presumably doing this entirely on their own. If the case is a controversial or sensational one, the jurors may be kept apart from other people until the time they make their decision. They will be instructed not to discuss any aspects of the trial outside the courtroom, even with friends or family. In a short time each juror will probably have formed an impression of most if not all of those involved in the case being tried—including the witnesses, the defense attorney, the prosecuting attorney, and even the judge.

Because a juror's final judgment about the person on trial can have dramatic consequences, it is important to consider how he forms his initial impressions and whether those impressions will have any effect on his later perceptions. Our own evaluations of people also have important if less dramatic consequences, so we might all benefit from looking more closely at how an impression of another person is formed.

A Private Theory of Personality

As we have seen, our own attributes as perceivers influence not only what we see but how we interpret what we see. Many people are quite confident of their perceptions about others, and some even like to think of themselves as amateur psychologists. Actually each of us seems to hold what has been described as a "**private theory of personality**":

> One factor that determines the content we tend to select (in order to fill in a sketchy impression) is our general notion of "what goes with what" in people. This notion in fact constitutes a private theory of personality that each of us has and that determines, to a considerable extent, how we judge others. This private theory is almost never stated or examined and is therefore referred to by psychologists as an "implicit theory of personality."[5]

You can see private personality theory at work in many shorthand attempts to size up people. For example, you might be asked, Is a glass with water to its midpoint half-full or half-empty? This question is a layman's way of finding out whether your view of life is optimistic (half-full glass) or pessimistic (half-empty glass). He is using your answer as a basis from which to generalize about your personality and to predict something about your future behavior. In fact, one of the major uses of personality evaluation is to explain and predict behavior on the basis of very limited information.

The First Impression

Ideally, as we learn more about a person, we come to perceive him in the light of this new information so that our impressions are revised and refined. But is this true? Does a first impression enhance or interfere with later knowledge, or does it have no effect at all? Psychologists have long puzzled over these questions and have undertaken many studies of impression formation. Those conducted by Luchins on the **primacy effect** are among the most significant.

In one of Luchins' experiments, the subjects were divided into two groups: the E-I group and the I-E group. Members of the E-I group were first asked to read this description of a young man named Jim:

Jim left the house to get some stationery. He walked out into the sun-filled street with two of his friends, basking in the sun as he walked. Jim entered the stationery store which was full of people. Jim talked with an acquaintance while he waited for the clerk to catch his eye. On his way out, he stopped to chat with a school friend who was just coming into the store. Leaving the store, he walked toward school. On his way out he met the girl to whom he had been introduced the night before. They talked for a short while, and then Jim left for school.

They then read a second paragraph:

After school Jim left the classroom alone. Leaving the school, he started on his long walk home. The street was brilliantly filled with sunshine. Jim walked down the street on the shady side. Coming down the street toward him, he saw the pretty girl whom he had met on the previous evening. Jim crossed the street and entered a candy store. The store was crowded with students, and he noticed a few familiar faces. Jim waited quietly until the counterman caught his eye and then gave his order. Taking a drink he sat down at a side table. When he had finished the drink he went home.[6]

Members of the second group, I-E, read the same material about Jim, but the paragraphs were given to them in reverse order. After reading the descriptions each member of both groups was asked to write a personality sketch of Jim and to predict how Jim would behave under various circumstances not described in the paragraphs.

Luchins had arranged the material so that the first paragraph given to group E-I described a predominantly extroverted person whereas the second described someone who could be characterized as introverted. He wanted to find out whether the order in which the paragraphs were read would influence the conception of personality. The results of his experiment confirmed that this was indeed so: most E-I members described Jim as an extrovert; most I-E members described him as an introvert. Yet both groups read the same paragraphs; it was only their order that varied.

You might have guessed that if paragraph order were at all influential, it would be the second paragraph, the one most *recently* read, that would be decisive. But once we know that a primacy effect exists, it is tempting to look back and speculate about how this might work. If you reverse the order of the paragraphs above so that they appear as they were read by the I-E group, you will be able to see how such divergent interpretations of the same descriptions could be given.

The fact that first impressions can have such dramatic effects on judgment is disturbing. We all know how often first impressions can be mistaken ones, and we also know how often decisions depend on first impressions. Imagine, for example, that you are being interviewed for membership in the fraternity you prefer or for your first job in your chosen profession.

But the situation is not as alarming as it might seem at first glance. Luchins found that if people were warned not to make snap judgments before they read the descriptions or if they were given simple arithmetic problems to do before reading the second paragraph, the primacy effect was reversed or eliminated completely. Several other studies of primacy and recency confirm Luchins' finding that the primacy effect is not inevitable.

There are many times, however, when a primacy effect exists, and we must examine more closely its influence on interpersonal communication. If you look once more at the model in Figure 1, you will recall that each perceiver should be receiving input and feedback. Yet the primacy effect blocks both input and feedback. To illustrate, if *P* is confident that he has judged *O* accurately, he is of course much less interested in receiving feedback about his impression of *O*; in other words, *P* is not receptive to feedback. Most of you have been in *O*'s place more than once. In a sense, it is as if you were invisible. No matter what you do or say, the other person does not seem to respond; he has made up his mind, and you cannot affect his judgment about you. The frustration of being in such a position is summed up in the statement, "It's like talking to a wall."

Demonstrating this situation in terms of Luchins' experiment, let us say that a participant in group E-I—call him Ted—has completed his impression of Jim after reading the first paragraph. Rightly or wrongly Ted feels confident that Jim is an extrovert. Confidence of this sort is interesting. In his analysis of Luchins' experiments, Brown points out that almost all the subjects were quite willing to answer questions about Jim's behavior that were totally unrelated to the information they had read about him; for example, "Is he: (a) shy; (b) more shy than forward; (c) more forward than shy; (d) forward; (e) none of these?" Only a few subjects asked how they were supposed to know such things.[7]

Most of Luchins' subjects freely answered questions about Jim because they felt they knew him. Given information about some of his behavior, they inferred several other things about him and confidently predicted how he would behave in other social situations.

Now imagine Luchins' test in reverse—suppose you are given the following list of words describing Jim and asked to write a personality sketch of him:

energetic	ironical
assured	inquisitive
talkative	persuasive
cold	

Several years before Luchins' experiment, Asch used this list to learn more about how impressions of others are formed. He read each of the seven adjectives to a group of students and asked them to write a full impression of the person described. There were two important findings from the Asch experiment.

First, the students were able to organize the scanty information they received and to create a consistent, unified impression, though there is a great deal of variation in their personality sketches, and they all go beyond the terms of the original description. Here are two samples:

He seems to be the kind of person who would make a great impression upon others at a first meeting. However as time went by, his acquaintances would easily come to see through the mask. Underneath would be revealed his arrogance and selfishness.

Possibly he does not have any deep feeling. He would tend to be an opportunist. Likely to succeed in things he intends to do. He has perhaps married a wife who would help him in his purpose. He tends to be skeptical.[8]

Second, Asch found that certain trait names are more influential than others in forming the personality sketches. When one of the adjectives on the list was substituted for its opposite, the personality descriptions were radically different. Can you guess which of the seven traits was the crucial one? In the Asch experiment it was the word "cold." Half the students heard the list read with the trait name "warm" substituted for "cold." When in another experiment Asch substituted the pair "polite-blunt" for "warm-cold," he found that these traits had a relatively small effect on the way personality impressions were formed. To most of his subjects, whether a person is warm or cold was more important than whether he is blunt or polite. Thus we can say that in the minds of most people, some traits are more central or more heavily weighted than others.

74   Trait Associations

Since 1946 several studies have been made of how people believe traits are linked together. Students in an economics course at the Massachusetts Institute of Technology were unwitting participants in one such experiment by Kelley. They were told that their instructor was out of town and that the department was interested in evaluating a new lecturer. All the students were given a brief biographical note about the lecturer on the pretext that they would later be asked to fill out forms about him. What they did not know was that the biographical notes differed. Half the students received the biographical note with this sentence:

> People who know him consider him to be a rather warm person, industrious, critical, practical and determined.

The other half received the same note but with a single word changed so that it read:

> People who know him consider him to be a rather cold person, industrious, critical, practical and determined.[9]

After the lecturer had finished speaking and left the classroom, the students were asked to describe him and to rate him on fifteen different characteristics. Kelley found that those who had read the "warm" biographical note usually described the lecturer as social, popular, and informal. Those given the "cold" description felt he was neither sociable nor popular; they thought of him as formal and self-centered.

Indirectly, experiments such as those of Asch and Kelley tell us that certain traits influence our judgments more than others. For a long time most psychologists believed that impressions of others were often interpreted on the basis of what they called the "halo effect," the tendency to extend a favorable impression of one trait to other traits—in other words, a tendency for the perceiver to exaggerate the uniformity of personality. You might think of your friend as honest and polite, for example, just because you consider him intelligent. And if your first impression of a person is unfavorable, you might attribute many other undesirable traits to him. This explanation sounds reasonable, but we know now that the concept is too simple to account completely for the way we interpret our perceptions. Certain traits are clearly more decisive in or central to our judgments than others. Psychologists are still learning about **trait associations**, and it will be some time before they can isolate all the traits critical to the process of person perception.

Personal Generalizations and Stereotypes

One's private theory of personality is in large part based on generalizations, many of which are derived from personal experience. If Jane favors boys of fraternity XYZ, for example, then she may be attracted to Phil simply because he is a member. Similarly, if she thinks math students are creeps, then she may refuse a first date with one regardless of whether he fits her personal definition of math students. If your luggage is stolen while you are traveling in Italy, you may come to feel that Italians are dishonest. If you have seen several Swedish films, perhaps you have come to believe that all Swedish women are beautiful.

In saner moments we realize that generalizations based on limited personal experience can be inaccurate and misleading. Jane may find that the next member of fraternity XYZ she dates is a creep. You may get to know members of a wonderful Italian family who practically take you into their home. The first Swedish girl you actually meet may be unattractive.

But how we perceive others also depends on our shared experience. Thus many of the generalizations we make are culturally determined. We call them **stereotypes** when they are *biased or false generalizations*. Relying on stereotypes rather than on direct perceptions can result in embarrassing social situations. The story is told, for example, of an elderly club member who was attending a distinguished public dinner in London:

> [He] was disconcerted to find himself seated next to a silent Chinese. Wanting to be courteous, however, he leaned toward him and asked, tentatively, "Likee soupee?" The Chinese looked at him briefly, nodded, but said nothing, and conversation lapsed. However, it appeared that the Chinese was a foreign guest of some note, for as coffee was served he was called upon to say a few words. He rose, bowed, and made a fifteen minute speech in impeccable English about the sociological significance of the European Common Market. Amid polite applause, he then sat down, turned to his abashed English neighbor, and, after the briefest of pauses, asked softly: "Likee speechee?"[10]

There can be no doubt that race membership affects our perceptions of others. Malpass and Kravitz found, for example, that people of one race (both black and white were studied) were better able to recognize pictures of members of their own race than pictures of members of another.[11] A more light-hearted illustration of this phenomenon is depicted in a popular cartoon. The setting is a Chinese restaurant in the United States. All the waiters are Chinese; all the customers are Americans. In the foreground a waiter holding a tray with a covered dish on it is conferring with several other waiters. "I can't remember which customer ordered this," he says. "They all look alike."

Stereotypes extend not only to social and ethnic groups. They can refer, for example, to physical attributes. Nor are all stereotypes negative. Think of the American stereotype of young women with blonde hair. Advertising for hair dye makes use of it in such slogans as "Is it true Blondes have more fun?" and "If I've only one life . . . Let me live it as a Blonde." Right now the length of hair rather than its color has become the issue. A few decades ago a "longhair" referred to someone (particularly a man) who was devoted to the arts, especially to classical music. Today a young person with long hair is referred to as a "hippy" —and sometimes as a "radical."

Physical attributes have considerable influence on our first impressions of others. One study showed that pictures of people can be separated into groups of attractive or unattractive on the basis of facial features. And it is significant that in our culture attractive people are judged to have better character than unattractive people.[12]

Citing earlier studies, Secord points out that in addition to stressing physical attributes, each culture emphasizes certain facial cues. Several decades ago in our own culture, he notes, the amount of lipstick a woman wore was "more important than the shape of her ears." And people are usually perceived as more intelligent, reliable, and industrious when they are wearing glasses.[13] No doubt you have seen people who are aware of the power of this stereotype and exploit it to create an impression. Politicians and moderators of talk shows seem inclined to do this.

Conversely, status differences can affect our perception of physical attributes. In one study a speaker named Mr. England was introduced to each of five different college classes by a different title:[14]

Class 1   A student from Cambridge
Class 2   A demonstrator in psychology from Cambridge
Class 3   A lecturer in psychology from Cambridge
Class 4   Dr. England, senior lecturer from Cambridge
Class 5   Professor England from Cambridge

When students were asked to estimate Mr. England's height, it was found that the mean estimate given by each class increased from class 1 to class 5; that is, the class 2 estimate was greater than the class 1, the class 3 greater than the class 2, and so forth. In other words, the higher Mr. England's status, the taller the students thought he was.

In each of the examples of stereotyping discussed, a person is considered to have attributes generally ascribed to the group of which he is a member. He is not perceived as a unique human being; he is seen as a member of a certain category of human beings. Although some generalizations about categories are valuable to us in daily experience, generalizations about human beings tend to distort our perceptions and to interfere with our ability to make accurate judgments.

Unlike the primacy effect, however, personal generalizations or stereotypes cannot be eliminated simply by alerting the perceiver to their dangers. Crockett and Meidinger have found for example that people who are authoritarian and closed-minded seem to do more stereotyping than those who are not.[15] But one cannot simply tell a person to be less authoritarian.

CHARACTERISTICS OF ACCURATE PERCEIVERS

Whether certain types of people are in fact generally more accurate in their perceptions of others is an important issue in the study of communication skills. For if some people are more accurate judges than others, it would be instructive to find out what their characteristics are. Certainly we all know people who feel their perceptions to be accurate. The first question then that we shall raise is whether there is a relationship between self-confidence and accuracy of perception. Does self-confidence about our ability to judge others make a difference in how we see them?

There are some social situations in which self-confidence can make a difference. Consider the person who expects to be rejected by other people. Perceiving others as hostile or unfriendly, he often acts defensive or overly superior, and his behavior may very well help produce the rejection he fears. On the other hand, a person who expects to be accepted by others, who perceives them as friendly, is often outgoing and congenial, and his behavior will account in good measure for his popularity. These people help confirm their own expectations. In such situations a favorable self-concept may lead to success and an unfavorable self-concept to failure. This phenomenon is called the "self-fulfilling prophecy." In terms of our communication model, we might say that a person who begs the question receives no feedback. Although he finds his beliefs about the other communicator confirmed, we cannot say that his judgments are based on accurate perceptions.

Crockett and Meidinger tried to find out what made the difference between people who have confidence in their perceptions of others and those who lack this confidence. Were the more confident people also more accurate in their evaluations of others? No. The researchers found that there was not necessarily a correlation between accuracy of perception and confidence in that perception.

If self-confidence is no measure of accuracy, what is? Surely, you might say, some people are more skilled or astute in evaluating others. Perhaps you even considered yourself a "good judge of character." For a long time psychologists have tried to determine whether some people are indeed better judges than others. Although the problem seems clear-cut, research findings are contradictory. Only one study supports the view that there is a general ability to judge people.[16] Other studies do not confirm this finding. On the contrary, they suggest that (1) some people are easier to judge than others (perhaps because they are more open or straightforward), (2) some traits are easier to judge than others, and (3) people are better at judging those who resemble themselves.

From what we know at present, it seems likely that judging ability may be quite specific to the situation. Psychologists have also found this to be true for other traits. Although it is assumed, for example, that a person who tells the truth in one situation will not lie in others, an early study of children by Hugh Hartshorne and Mark Arthur May (1928–1930) shows that this is a questionable assumption; an individual's interpretation of moral conduct will vary from situation to situation. Other traits vary with circumstances. The late Igor Stravinsky, one of the foremost composers of the twentieth century, was known for his self-assurance and commanding intellect. Stravinsky was unafraid; he openly referred to music critics as "pests" and once announced that his music was "not to be discussed or criticized." Yet this formidable man "was so nervous when performing in public that he thrice forgot his own piano concerto."[17]

Our ability to judge other people seems to vary just as much as other traits. One thing that affects our judgment is whether we are alone or in the presence of other people when we are perceiving someone. In one study female college students were asked to view a person bargaining in two different situations.[18] The bargainer was very cooperative in the first situation and very competitive in the second. All the subjects were able to distinguish between the two types of bargaining behaviors quite easily. When a subject was one of a group of four observers, however, and the answers of the other three were rigged to disagree with hers, in every case she was influenced by group opinion. Later the subjects filled out questionnaires designed to measure their perception of the bargainer; their answers showed that group influence had been so strong that when their perceptions did not correspond with those of the group, the subjects denied what they had seen with their own eyes. In fact, they believed the opposite of what they had seen.

Majority or group opinion is just one instance in which context—the third element of perception—exerts its subtle influence on person perception. Yet despite the fact that accurate person perception varies from one situation to another, psychologists generally agree that certain characteristics seem to be associated with sound perceptions of others.

First, the ability to draw inferences about people from their behavior seems related to accurate perception. Second, intelligence is a prime factor. Third, people who score low on tests of authoritarianism tend to be better judges of others. They are less rigid in their expectations, judging more from what they know about the person and assuming less that he is like themselves. And fourth, those with a high degree of objectivity about themselves tend to have insight into the behavior of others. Openness and awareness of one's own shortcomings seem to play a part in this process.

How does this information relate to improving our effectiveness as communicators? We certainly cannot improve our intelligence directly —and the ability to draw sound inferences about people from their behavior probably depends in part on intelligence. Nor can we simply tell ourselves to be less rigid or authoritarian. Social psychologists have shown that attitudes are rarely changed so easily. The one thing we can do is become conscious of and less defensive about our own limitations. As we shall see, this fourth characteristic is one of the most important for our purposes.

IMPROVING PERCEPTION AND COMMUNICATION

Failures or breakdowns in communication frequently occur because (1) people have inaccurate perceptions of each other and (2) they are unaware that their perceptions are inaccurate. The Kelley experiment described in a previous section provides us with some information on this subject. Among students given the description of the lecturer as "warm," 56 percent participated in the classroom discussion; among those informed that he was "cold," only 32 percent engaged in any classroom discussion. This trend is borne out in everyday experience. If you are told, for example, that a girl you know only casually is snobbish or stand-offish, you are not likely to ask her out on a date. If you feel that your instructor is stubborn and somewhat hostile, you probably won't consider questioning him about why he gave you such a low grade on the last exam. Kelley's experiment confirms that our perceptions of others can determine not only the kind of communication that takes place but whether or not we attempt to communicate at all.

It would seem then an easy matter to facilitate more effective interpersonal communication by simply improving the accuracy of our perceptions. Yet the three elements of perception—the perceiver, the object of perception, and the context within which the perception occurs—are so interwoven that one cannot be analyzed apart from the others. The most important thing the perceiver can do is take into account the need to make perceptual adjustments as any of these three components varies.

The second source of misunderstanding—lack of awareness that one's perceptions may be inaccurate—is closely linked to the first. Improved perception and improved communication can occur only after we realize that our perceptions are personal, subjective, and therefore subject to error. One of the authors remembers a conversation in which two people disagreed about their perceptions of a third. When one was asked whether she was sure of what she was saying, she replied, "Would I say it if it wasn't true?" Her statement shows an obvious lack of awareness that human perceptions are subject to error. As long as she was unwilling to admit that possibility, there was little chance that an effective exchange of viewpoints could take place. It is difficult to think clearly in a dispute, but the next time you are involved in one, try to ask yourself, "Could my perception have been somewhat wrong?" Have the other person ask himself the same question. If you both answer it affirmatively, an effective sharing of ideas is much more likely than if either or both of you answer negatively (we shall discuss this at greater length in Chapter 10).

It would be utopian to say that more accurate person perception always makes for more effective communication. Nevertheless communication in both long-term and short-term relationships is often enhanced when the participants perceive each other accurately. For example, if a husband knows his wife, he can react to her more effectively in many situations. Notice the difference between these two conversations:

Conversation 1

WIFE: Would you help me with the shopping today?
HUSBAND: No, I want to watch a ball game on television.
WIFE: You never want to do anything with me any more.
HUSBAND: Oh, that's not true.
WIFE: *(starting to cry)* I sometimes wonder if you love me any more.

Conversation 2

WIFE: Would you help me with the shopping today?
HUSBAND: Well, I did want to watch a ball game on television. Could you wait until after the game? It's not that I don't want to go. I just don't want to miss the game.
WIFE: Well, I think it will be too late to go after the game.

The husband in conversation 1 reacts only to the most obvious content of his wife's message. The husband in conversation 2 knows from past experience that sometimes if his wife asks him to accompany her she also wants to know whether he values simply being with her. He is sensitive to the more subtle relationship aspects of his wife's requests and tries to respond to her total message.

We need not be speaking of marital communication; the same principles apply to relationships that precede marriage and to many less intense interpersonal encounters. For example, the interview relies heavily on accurate interpersonal perception despite the fact that it usually involves a relatively short-term relationship. Here is a situation in which two or more people meet to exchange information—ordinarily about a subject that has been decided on beforehand. The interview is often an important vehicle for formulating interpersonal impressions. In a selection or job interview, it is each person's intention to size up the other's attributes. Interpersonal perception is one of the prime objectives. In an evaluative interview an employee's work is appraised by a supervisor, and guidelines for improved job performance are discussed. Several studies have shown that two of the most important objectives of evaluative interviews are that the employee perceive the supervisor as helpful and constructive rather than critical, and that the supervisor and employee perceive effective job performance in a similar way.

We have tried to suggest that interpersonal sensitivity is a requirement in both long- and short-term encounters. Later in this book we shall discuss a technique for increasing one's level of awareness (Chapter 10) as well as some differences between perception of the self and perception of others (Chapter 12). In the chapter that follows, we shall see that although early impressions depend to a great extent on a person's physical appearance, as contact with a person continues, the content of his messages (both verbal and nonverbal) plays a major role in modifying our perception of him.

Summary

In the present chapter it has been our intention to demonstrate that interpersonal perception is an active process in which the perceiver selects, organizes, and interprets what he experiences. After suggesting some parallels and distinctions between person and object perception, we focused on how our impressions of other human beings are formed. We spoke of private personality theory, primacy and recency effects, trait centrality and trait associations, and personal generalizations and stereotypes. We saw that our impressions, while formed with relative ease, are not necessarily accurate. Some characteristics of accurate perceivers were mentioned, but judging ability itself was seen as specific to the situation. In concluding we discussed inaccurate perception as a source of communication breakdowns and illustrated how improved perception contributes to effective communication.

Review Questions

1. What is psychological set? Give an example.
2. How is person perception different from object perception?
3. What is the primacy effect? How does it relate to interpersonal communication?
4. Discuss three influences on stereotype perceptions.
5. What are three generalizations from research studies about individual ability to judge people?
6. Discuss four characteristics associated with accurate perception of others.

7. How can perception and interpersonal communication effectiveness be improved?

Exercises

1. Select one of the case problems listed in the Appendix. Ask five people to read the same case problem and write a short position paper supporting a solution to the problem. Examine the solutions offered in terms of differences and similarities in person perception. How do the following concepts relate to the similarities and differences:
   a. psychological set
   b. psychological filter (see Objective 4, Chapter 2)
   c. primacy effect
   d. stereotype perceptions
2. Write down some of the perceptions you have of your classmates. Then refer to your earlier comments in your personal log. Have you changed or confirmed some of your original impressions?
3. Think of a person who impressed you one way at first but differently later. What factors made the difference? Did *the person* actually change, or did *your perception* change? Which perception do you think is more accurate?
4. In a paragraph describe a person you know who you think is an effective interpersonal communicator. List all the attributes that seem to contribute to this effectiveness. Now think of a poor communicator. What characteristics seem to cause the ineffectiveness? What characteristics do you possess that affect how you perceive these two people?
5. Think about your day-to-day interaction with others. How is your communication affected by (a) your self-concept, (b) your perception of others, and (c) the context of the perception? How could you improve all of these?
6. Interview a person who does a lot of interviewing. Discuss communication and interpersonal perception with him. Have him elaborate on how he perceives interviewees and what cues he looks for in assessing them.

Suggested Readings

Fabun, Don. *Communications: The Transfer of Meaning.* Beverly Hills, Calif.: Glencoe Press, 1968. This colorfully illustrated and highly readable booklet serves as an excellent, entertaining primer on communication. It indicates several practical applications of communication theory and relates perception to communication.

Hastorf, Albert, Schneider, David, and Polefka, Judith. *Person Perception.* Reading, Mass.: Addison-Wesley, 1970. This brief paperback introduces the subject of interpersonal perception, discussing basic issues and numerous research findings in perception as well as impression formation, attribution theory, and interpersonal behavior resulting from person perceptions.

Rosenthal, Robert. "Self-Fulfilling Prophecy." *Psychology Today* (September 1968), 2:44–51. This author proves that an experimenter influences his subjects. Time after time, no matter what the conditions, whether the subjects were human or not, the group that was expected to do better on the tests *did* do better—even when the positive correlation existed only in the experimenter's mind!

Notes

[1] Magda B. Arnold, "A Demonstrational Analysis of the TAT in a Clinical Setting," *Journal of Abnormal and Social Psychology*, 44 (1949), 100.

[2] Renato Tagiuri, Introduction, in Renato Tagiuri and Luigi Petrullo (eds.), *Person Perception and Interpersonal Behavior* (Stanford, Calif.: Stanford University Press, 1958), p. xi.

[3] Paul Watzlawick, Janet Helmick Beavin, and Don D. Jackson, *Pragmatics of Human Communication* (New York: Norton, 1967), p. 94.

[4] Tagiuri, p. ix.

[5] David Krech, Richard S. Crutchfield, and Norman Livson, *Elements of Psychology*, 2nd ed. (New York: Knopf, 1969), p. 801.

[6] A. S. Luchins, "Primacy-Recency in Impression Formation," in C. I. Hovland and others (eds.), *The Order of Presentation in Persuasion*, Vol. I (New Haven, Conn.: Yale University Press, 1957), pp. 35–36.

[7] Roger Brown, *Social Psychology* (New York: Free Press, 1965), p. 618.

[8] S. E. Asch, "Forming Impressions of Personality," *Journal of Abnormal and Social Psychology*, 41 (1946), 261.

[9] Harold H. Kelley, "The Warm-Cold Variable in First Impressions of Persons," *Journal of Personality*, 18 (1950), 433.

[10] Dennis Bloodworth, *The Chinese Looking Glass* (New York: Farrar, Straus and Giroux, 1967), p. 6.

[11] Roy Malpass and Jerome Kravitz, "Recognition for Faces of Own and Other Race," *Journal of Personality and Social Psychology*, 13 (1969), 330–334.

[12] Robin Widgery and Bruce Webster, "The Effects of Physical Attractiveness upon Perceived Initial Credibility" (paper delivered at the annual convention of the National Society for the Study of Communication, Cleveland, 1969).

[13] P. F. Secord, "Facial Features and Inference Processes in Interpersonal Perception," in Tagiuri and Petrullo, pp. 308, 313.

[14] Paul Wilson, "Perceptual Distortion of Height as a Function of Ascribed Academic Status," *Journal of Social Psychology*, 74 (1968), 97–102.

[15] W. H. Crockett and Thomas Meidinger, "Authoritarianism and Interper-

84   sonal Perception," *Journal of Abnormal and Social Psychology,* 53 (1956), 378–380.

[16] Victor B. Cline and James M. Richards, "Accuracy of Interpersonal Perception—A General Trait?", *Journal of Abnormal and Social Psychology,* 60 (1960), 1–7.

[17] "Igor Stravinsky: An 'Inventor of Music' Whose Works Created a Revolution," *The New York Times,* April 7, 1971, p. 48.

[18] Stewart L. Tubbs, "Interpersonal Trust, Conformity, and Credibility" (paper delivered at the annual convention of the Speech Association of America, New York, December 1969).

Chapter 5

The Bases of Interpersonal Choice

OBJECTIVES

After reading this chapter the student should be able to:

1. State two similarities and two differences between the Scale of Social Distance and the Behavioral Differential.

2. List three advantages of the sociometric test.

3. Describe two ways in which proximity affects interpersonal relationships.

4. State the basic assumption of cognitive consistency theories.

5. Explain the relationship between interpersonal attraction (that is, liking), familiarity, and proximity.

6. State the relationship between interpersonal attraction and similarity.

7. Draw two diagrams, one depicting a balanced state and one depicting an unbalanced state.

8. Describe three alternative strategies that one might employ to balance an unbalanced state.

9. Discuss three variables that qualify generalizations about attitude similarity.

10. Contrast the theory of complementary needs with the research findings on the relationship between perceived similarity and interpersonal attraction.

11. Describe three situations that influence communicator choice and give an example of how each affects interpersonal attraction.

12. Identify at least two attributes of persons generally perceived by others as providing consistent positive reinforcement.

13. Identify at least four attributes of generally disliked persons.

5

In an offhand way we notice who is popular and who is not—who, so to speak, gets chosen. We also notice that we tend to interact with some people more frequently than we do with others. But beyond saying that we seek the company of A or that we turn the corner every time we see B coming, we find the patterns of likes and dislikes within a group of people difficult to account for. We express our preferences when we choose our friends, our school leaders, our roommates, our dates, and—most important—our marriage partners; yet it often seems that the choices we make are random. How, if at all, are the choices we make as communicators related? And what are the reasons that we are attracted to some people and put off by others?

These are the themes of this chapter, and they will lead us back quite directly to the study of communication: "To know the lines of attraction and avoidance within a social system," writes Barnlund, "is to be able to predict where messages will originate, to whom they will flow, and much about how they will be received."[1] We begin with a look at some systematic ways of measuring attraction.

MEASURES OF INTERPERSONAL CHOICE

Today numerous measures of interpersonal choice are available, and most of them stem from the early study of attitude. In 1925 Bogardus made one of the first systematic attempts to measure attitude when he devised the **Scale of Social Distance**, a questionnaire concerning how intimate a person will allow himself to be with members of various groups.[2] Bogardus was interested in our attitudes toward people of other cultures. Each subject was given a list of nationalities and asked to indicate whether he would accept people of a given group in the following relationships:

1. To close kinship by marriage
2. To my club as personal chums
3. To my street as neighbors
4. To employment in my occupation in my country
5. To citizenship in my country
6. As visitors only to my country
7. Would exclude from my country

88   As you can see, Bogardus tried to create a continuum of social intimacy, with item 1 indicating the highest degree of closeness permitted and item 7 the lowest.

The Bogardus scale was the basis for several later measures of attitude. One extension of Bogardus' work is Triandis' **Behavioral Differential**, which measures attitudes toward any single person or group of persons, not just those of different nationalities.[3] The subject is first given a description of a stimulus person or group of persons and then asked to predict how others will behave toward that person or group. The accompanying scale is a sample item from the test.

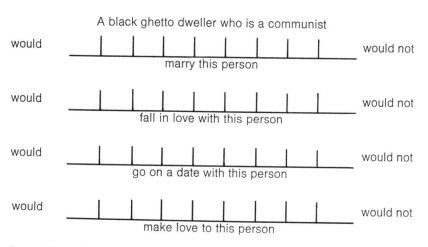

SOURCE: Harry C. Triandis, *Attitude and Attitude Change* (New York: Wiley, 1971), p. 53.

In a typical study a subject might make as many as 1,000 judgments of this kind: he might, for example, rate 50 stimulus persons using 20 rating scales for each.

Tests such as the Scale of Social Distance and the Behavioral Differential tell us a great deal about our attitudes toward various social groups, but they describe our attitudes in hypothetical situations. They tell us little about our feelings toward the people we know and interact with on a daily basis: family members, friends, classmates, committee members, neighbors. To measure the choices we have in fact made or are likely to make, Moreno developed the **sociometric test**.[4]

Like Bogardus and Triandis, Moreno asked his subjects questions, but the questions were about people they actually knew, not anonymous Russians, Italians, or Swedes or hypothetical black ghetto dwellers. The test is a simple one. Essentially it is a means of determining the pattern of preferences and rejections within a group of people. In private each member specifies those with whom he would like to engage in a given activity; in many versions of the test, he also indicates those with whom he would not care to participate. Obviously, as the situation changes, the test choices vary. Consider the criteria you would use to answer these questions:

1. With whom would you most like to discuss a problem?
2. Whom would you pick to represent the class as a good communicator?
3. With whom would you like to work on a project?

The sociometric test has several advantages. First, it is easy to administer: it has been used with children and even adapted to study the communication patterns within an entire community. Second, it is easy to score. And third, its results can be set out in tables, statistics, or diagrams. The diagram—or **sociogram**, as it has come to be called—is especially popular because of its visual power. It uses geometric figures to represent the group members and lines to represent their choices and rejections.

Figures 5 and 6 are sociograms drawn up from data obtained in a sensitivity training group. Figure 5 illustrates the answers to the question, "Whom would you like to have as a leader?" The question behind Figure 6 was, "With whom would you like to be better friends?" You

Figure 5

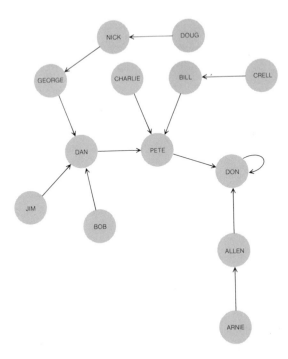

Whom Would You Like to Have as a Leader?

Figure 6

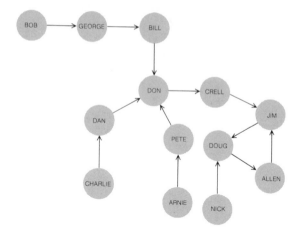

With Whom Would You Like to Be Better Friends?

can see from the two sociograms that when the choice criterion was changed, the results were distinctly altered. Power and popularity are often distinct qualities. Although Dan and Pete are most frequently chosen as leaders, Don is the person most frequently chosen as a potential friend. In Moreno's terms Dan and Pete are the **overchosen members** of the group in Figure 5; Don is the overchosen member in Figure 6. Sociograms also identify **isolates**, those who are not chosen by anyone. The isolates in Figure 5 are Doug, Jim, Bob, Arnie, Crell, and Charlie; in Figure 6 they are Bob, Charlie, Arnie, and Nick. **Cliques,** or *subgroups,* are also reflected in sociograms; see Jim, Doug, and Allen in Figure 6, for example. Thus a sociogram summarizes information about interpersonal preferences among members of a given group and also identifies a number of communication links within it.

Despite its dramatic summary of social relations, however, the sociogram, like other measures of interpersonal choice, is descriptive. To determine why we make the choices we do, we must look at some of the research on attraction and some of the theories proposed to explain the findings. Another issue we shall discuss—and you might begin to consider this question yourself—is what the specific situations, personal attributes, and behaviors are that cause people to be chosen or rejected.

PROXIMITY

The most obvious determinant of communicator choice is **proximity,** or *geographic closeness.* We can state the principle simply. Other things being equal, the more closely two people are located geographically, the more likely they are to be attracted to one another.

The effects of proximity are seen in a number of ways. If you are not within a reasonable distance of another person, your chances of meeting and becoming friends are quite slim. How many friends do you have who live more than 3,000 miles away from you? Probably very few unless you formerly lived in another country or people from another region spent some time in yours. In support of the notion that proximity fosters attraction, researchers have found that you are far more likely to marry a person who is geographically close to your home or school than someone living or studying far away.[5]

Once we get to know people, proximity also affects whether our relationships will continue. A great number of friendships and court-ships are damaged by the effects of physical separation. A Frenchwoman living in the United States commented to one of the authors on how easily she could get to know Americans. Then she added with some hesitation that if these new acquaintances moved or came from another part of the country, she never heard from them again. One thing she may not have considered is the vastness of this country when compared with France. The drive from northern to southern France can be made in a day—certainly an easier distance over which to maintain a friend-ship than the distance between Maine and Florida. Perhaps the old saw "Out of sight, out of mind" has some validity simply because of the effort it takes to sustain relationships across many miles. Relationships that do continue despite this obstacle are maintained by the intensity of the rewards derived from them. In other words, the rewards outweigh the additional costs.

These conclusions about proximity are obvious, but what about the effect of much smaller distances on attraction? Are you more inclined to become friends with people who live next door than with those two blocks away? What about students who live on the same floor in your dormitory as opposed to those who live two floors beneath you? In their classic study of the Westgate and Westgate West housing projects, Festinger, Schachter, and Back asked residents, "What three people in Westgate or Westgate West do you see most socially?"[6] The greatest percentage of residents chose their next-door neighbors; the next most frequent choice was the neighbors who lived two doors away; and, in general, percentages dropped as a function of distance so that those who lived at opposite ends of a single floor chose each other least. Yet a look at the relationship between sociometric choice and distance on a single floor of a Westgate West building is startling: apartments are about 22 feet apart, and the greatest distance between apartments, those at opposite ends of the floor, is only 88 feet.

Why should a few feet make any difference in how friendships are formed, and why in general should proximity tend to produce attraction? A possible answer is suggested by the **cognitive consistency theories**, *a group of related theories all based on the assumption that human beings have a strong psychological need for consistency.* They want their beliefs, attitudes, feelings, and values to fit together, and so they try to maintain consistency and to create it where it does not exist. Each theory has its own terminology: one calls this drive a need for "balance," one for "congruity," and another for "consonance." In discussing proximity we shall rely primarily on **balance theory** as it has been presented by Heider, who seems to have been the first to formulate the basic concept on which all cognitive consistency theories are founded.

Balance theory is closely tied to the study of perception. When we perceive separate entities as belonging together, Heider says, we see them as a *unit.* There are many kinds of units: members of a family, players on a football team, citizens of a community, even a person and his property or actions might be perceived as a unit. Our *sentiments* are our positive or negative feelings about any *unit,* and Heider observes that we want our unit and sentiment relations to be harmonious, to correspond. Thus we are more comfortable psychologically if we extend our positive or negative feelings about some entities within a unit to all the entities within that unit. The Randalls are a family of five. If I like the three children and I also like Mr. Randall, it is more comfortable for me to like Mrs. Randall than it is to dislike her.

What has balance theory to do with proximity? Proximity, Heider maintains, is one of the factors that lead to unit formation; entities that are close to one another tend to be perceived as units. He gives us this example:

＊＊　＊＊　＊＊　＊＊　＊＊

Because of their proximity, we see these asterisks in groups of two. If we extend this principle to social perception, we infer that people in close proximity also tend to be seen as members of a unit.

Another unit-forming factor is similarity, which Heider illustrates this way:

＊＊ ── ＊＊ ── ＊＊ ── ＊＊ ── ＊＊

Despite equal space between all these signs, the similar signs tend to be seen in groups of two.[7]

We shall discuss similarity at some length, but we touch on it here because there seems to be some relationship between similarity and proximity. People with a common geographic location often have other things in common. Two families living on the same block in the inner city tend to be closer in socioeconomic level than either family would be to a family living in a high-rise apartment in another section of the city. Proximity also facilitates interaction, and as people interact they tend to share information and ideas and to influence one another. We expect, for example, that the views of a Kansas farmer will be more similar to those of another Kansas farmer than they will be to those of a resident of New York or San Francisco.

Familiarity

We may be able to explain the relationship between proximity and communicator choice without reference to balance theory. Zajonc reports a definite correlation between liking and **familiarity**. When he showed photographs of human faces to his subjects, he found that the more often a subject saw a particular face—the number of exposures varied from one to twenty-five—the more he liked it.[8] This experiment and others conducted by Zajonc, including some on language, suggest that familiarity in and of itself may increase liking. And proximity, of course, increases the frequency of interaction and thus the degree of familiarity.

If proximity were the only influence on attraction, we could easily predict what people would become friends simply on the basis of their physical distances from one another. Obviously this is not the case. We know from sociograms that given physical proximity we still favor some people and reject others. Proximity is clearly a precondition of communicator choice, but let us look at some other bases for attraction.

SIMILARITY

"An agreeable person," Disraeli once wrote, "is a person who agrees with me." In other words, we like people who appear to be similar to us. A funny and remarkably candid statement. More than three-quarters of a century later, it seems to be borne out by both theory and research. In one form or another, all cognitive consistency theories predict that we tend to attract and be attracted to people who have **similarities** to us and conversely that we tend to dislike and be disliked by those who differ from us.

Let us return for a moment to balance theory. Heider tells us that just as a person and his actions or possessions may be seen as belonging in a unit, so may a person and his beliefs and attitudes. He also says that ". . . we tend to like people who have the same beliefs and attitudes we have, and when we like people, we want them to have the same attitudes we have."[9] We want our attitudes and beliefs to be

94 shared because we want the entities or elements in various situations and our feelings about them to fit together. Consider these situations:

> Paul hates Arthur because he is so similar to Arthur.
> He always imitates people he dislikes.
> He hates Richard because Richard is similar to his friend Arthur.[10]

In each case, Heider explains, we sense an imbalance: certain factors do not add up. Imbalanced states disturb us. They create pressure. They lead us, Heider argues, to seek a state of equilibrium through change.

There are many applications of balance theory, but it is Newcomb who extended it specifically to interpersonal communication. He suggests that the phenomena of social behavior might more accurately be studied as "communicative acts" than as "interactions." In effect, he is saying that communication is one means by which we try to maintain balance—or, as he puts it, **symmetry**. He defines the simplest possible communicative act as a situation in which one person, A, transmits information to another person, B, concerning some thing, X. When A and B have similar attitudes or attractions toward X, their relations are symmetrical; when they have dissimilar attitudes or attractions toward X, their relations are asymmetrical.

What makes balanced, or symmetrical, relationships so desirable? Newcomb suggests two ways in which they are rewarding. First, greater agreement makes it easier to predict the other person's behavior. Second, the more similar A's and B's attitudes are, the more confident each becomes of his beliefs because he sees them validated. If these advantages are commonly experienced, Newcomb adds, ". . . communicative acts resulting in increased symmetry are likely to be rewarded, and symmetry is likely to acquire secondary reward value."[11]

Balance Theory in Practice

Balance theory has a simple way of mapping out balanced and imbalanced (or symmetrical and asymmetrical) states. In Figures 7–10, plus signs represent positive feelings, minus signs negative feelings, and arrows the direction of the feelings. Any situation represented by an even number or an absence of minus signs is balanced; if it is represented by an odd number of minus signs, it is imbalanced. To make this more concrete, we shall describe a situation in which two people have dissimilar attitudes toward a single issue.

Nina (A) and John (B) recently began dating. They are attracted to each other and agree about a lot of things. When they start discussing the Women's Liberation Movement (X), however, it turns out that John disapproves: "Women already have equal rights," he comments. Nina, a staunch advocate of Women's Lib, expresses her disagreement. Figure 7 illustrates this state of imbalance.

Figure 7

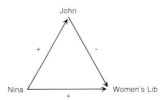

Consider the situation from Nina's point of view. Balance theory predicts that because she likes John she wants him to like the things she likes—in this case, Women's Lib. How much their difference in attitude bothers her will depend upon the strength of her feelings for both John and Women's Lib. To restore balance she may rationalize that John is not that appealing anyway. John's negative reaction to Women's Lib will then be counterbalanced by Nina's negative feelings toward him. Figure 8 depicts this balanced state.

Figure 8

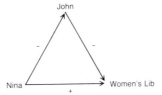

Nina has other alternatives. She may lower her opinion of Women's Lib and continue to go out with John. Nina and John will then like each other and both will disapprove of Women's Lib. As Figure 9 illustrates, this change will also achieve balance.

Figure 9

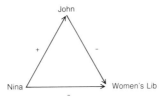

Or Nina can try to change John's attitude toward Women's Lib so that it is positive like her own. In this case, shown in Figure 10, all the elements will be positive: Nina and John will like each other and both will approve of Women's Lib.

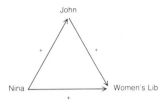

In any event our model depicts that Nina will not be comfortable with the situation described by Figure 7. As you can see from this simple illustration, our need to maintain psychological balance seems to be reflected in a great many day-to-day situations.

Drawing by Charles M. Schulz. © 1970 United Feature Syndicate, Inc.

Two Experiments in Attitude Similarity

In Chapter 2 we commented that one criterion of the effectiveness of a model is the amount of research it generates. By this standard all the cognitive consistency theories have contributed valuable models. Hundreds of experiments have been conducted to test the hypotheses of balance theory, for example. We shall look at two that explain more about the dynamics of interpersonal attraction.

The first is Brewer's study of how attitude change and interpersonal attraction work in a two-person situation.[12] Brewer's intention was to test some aspects of Newcomb's A-B-X model. A large group of students were given personality tests and then filled out questionnaires designed to rate their attitude toward capital punishment. Those who had strong opinions—either pro or con—were identified and selected as subjects for the experiment. Remember that Brewer then knew each subject's attitude toward capital punishment as well as something about his personality and the traits he preferred in others.

By means of verbal instructions, Brewer created conditions of high positive attraction (HPA) or low positive attraction (LPA) in his subjects. All participants were told that they would have a twenty-minute discussion with someone, but Brewer led the HPAs to believe that their partners would have personality traits highly compatible with their own and the LPAs to expect incompatible traits. Actually half the pairs in each of the two conditions had similar attitudes toward capital punishment and half had dissimilar attitudes. After the discussion each subject filled out a questionnaire on the issue again, indicating his own attitude and predicting his discussion partner's. Attraction to the discussion partner was also rated.

Brewer found perceived similarity in attitudes to be highly correlated with positive attraction. He also reports that following the discussions the HPA subjects tended to be more similar in their attitude toward capital punishment than LPA subjects. In short, as we communicate with someone whom we think is similar to us, we are likely to become more similar to each other in our attitudes toward a given issue. In addition, the more we perceive that person to be similar to us in attitude, the more we tend to be attracted to him.

Notice that here and often when we describe findings about similarity and attraction, we are speaking of *perceived* similarity. As Chapter 4 pointed out, our perceptions are not always accurate—they are often influenced by our expectations. For example, we expect people we like to agree with us on a wide range of topics, and we probably exaggerate the extent of this agreement. No doubt we also tend to overemphasize our differences with those we dislike.

Brewer's findings confirm some of the predictions of balance theory. But Brewer studied a single attitude: capital punishment. If the balance model holds, given adequate knowledge of people's attitudes, interests, values, backgrounds, and so on, we should be able to predict which people will become friends.

In examining the acquaintance process, Newcomb had a unique opportunity to pursue this line of reasoning. His subjects were male students, all strangers to each other, who transferred to the University of Michigan. In exchange for participating in the study through periodic testing, they were allowed to live rent free in a dormitory on campus for one semester. Before they came to the dormitory, Newcomb established on the basis of tests and questionnaires which students were similar in background, interests, values, and attitudes.

He found that on a long-term basis, students who remained friends had many similarities. In one group of seventeen men for example, three distinct cliques emerged. There was a group of five men who were all liberal in politics and religion, all intellectual, and all members of the arts college and who all rated high on aesthetic, social, and theoretical values. There was a three-man group plus one man classified as a semiisolate, or "hanger-on," in which three of the four were engineering students; all had practical interests and were rated high in economic and religious values. The third group consisted of three small-town Midwestern Protestants, two of them engineering students;

all three men were rated low in theoretical values. In this group of seventeen, four of the remaining five were considered extreme isolates, and the last appeared to be on the borderline between the first and second cliques.

Qualifications of Similarity Predictions

We have devoted most of our attention to attitude similarity, but as Newcomb's study makes clear, our backgrounds, experiences, values, and so on all influence our attraction to another person. Moreover there is a possibility that certain kinds of similarities do not foster attraction. Heider points out, for example, that though similar goals sometimes induce mutual liking, in competitive situations two people with identical goals often grow to dislike each other, primarily because of jealousy.[13] Two men vying for the same woman are unlikely to become friends. Two women who both want the same job probably will not like each other.

Therefore the fact that two people have some similar attitudes is not a sufficient basis on which to make predictions about whether they will like each other. We have to know something about other similarities. We also have to know something about three variables that affect attitude similarity: the proportion of issues on which two people agree, the salience of various attitudes, and whether reciprocity of liking is perceived.

Proportion of Issues. Our relationships with others are such that we rarely agree on all issues, even with our closest friends. Nevertheless we tend to agree with our friends on a greater **proportion of issues** than we do with those whom we dislike. Again this works two ways. We choose our friends because we agree on more issues, and we tend to agree on more issues because we are friends. Furthermore no single issue may make or break a friendship, but the proportion of issues on which we agree is a good indicator of whether it will continue. When computer dating has been successful, the reason is probably that though people matched on any single issue are not that likely to be attracted to one another, people matched on a substantial number of issues will in all probability be compatible.

Salience. A related consideration is attitude **salience**, or importance. To put it simply, some of our attitudes are more firmly established, more central to us, than others. Changing a salient attitude in order to make a situation more balanced is usually more difficult than changing a nonsalient attitude. Therefore agreement on salient attitudes is often crucial in determining our relationships with others. Two roommates may differ over which one should clean up the room, but they may still be friends despite their disagreement. If they disagree about whether to use drugs in the room, however, this issue potentially has far greater importance and is more likely to affect their relationship.

One young married couple we know disagreed on several apparently minor questions (where they would live, whether to buy a car, and so on) and were able to weather the storm. But differences about whether to start a family (the wife wanted a child; the husband did not) became so crucial that the marriage ended in divorce. Marriages between people who are dissimilar in religion, race, education, or socioeconomic status are more likely to end in divorce than marriages between people who are similar in these respects. One reason for this is probably that attitudes toward these factors often have great salience in intimate relationships between people; another is that any of these issues (education, for example) may be highly salient for one marriage partner and unimportant for the other.

Thus although the number of similar attitudes is important, we cannot make a simple tally of agreements and disagreements; not all attitudes have the same weight. We tend to like those who agree with us on a substantial proportion of highly salient issues.

Reciprocal Liking. Another variable that affects our attraction to others is whether **perceived reciprocity of liking** exists—whether we feel that the people we like also like us. Certainly we have all experienced situations in which our liking for a person is intensified by our feeling that he likes us too. When we like someone and our feeling is not reciprocated, we tend to lose interest in him. This common-sense prediction is supported by research findings.[14]

Knowing that another person likes us is rewarding because it increases our self-esteem. Sometimes the effect of that knowledge on our own judgments can be transparent. We are reminded of an incident that took place at a university faculty meeting during which a candidate for a job as an assistant professor in history was being evaluated. The candidate had previously expressed interest in sharing an office with one specific faculty member—let us call him Professor Jones. Each member of the history department was asked to rate the candidate on a scale from 1 to 10, with 10 being the highest positive evaluation. Most of the evaluations were between 5 and 8. When Professor Jones' turn came, he announced, "In my humble opinion I'd rate him a 10!"

It is reassuring to find that we are not always this vulnerable to flattery. In a review of research, Berscheid and Walster qualify the reciprocity-of-liking rule by observing that though esteem produces reciprocal liking and acts as a positive reinforcer, ". . . it is much more effective in producing liking when it is congruent with the subject's own evaluation of himself."[15] Flattery, it seems, does not get you everywhere.

Complementarity of Needs. Perhaps as you read about the influence of perceived similarity on interpersonal attraction, you thought about a couple you know who despite great differences in personality seem very compatible. "After all," you might ask, "aren't opposites supposed to attract?" Winch proposes a theory of **complementary needs** that seems to contradict some of the findings we have presented thus far.[16] Winch believes that in selecting marriage partners or even friends we are attracted to those most likely to satisfy our needs and that maximum gratification of needs occurs when two people have complementary rather than similar needs.

There are two types of complementarity. Two people may satisfy *different* needs for each other, as when A has a strong need to be protective and B has a strong need to be dependent; or they may satisfy the *same* need, as when A has a strong need to be dominant and B has a much less intense need to be dominant. Winch found that these predictions could be made regardless of a person's sex. Thus in the first example, A might be a woman and B a man, though our society usually casts women in the dependent role. Remember that Winch is speaking about complementary needs, not complementary attitudes, interests, or values. Two people might differ in the intensity of their needs for protection or dominance and still have many other similarities.

Most research has not substantiated Winch's theory; yet the principle of complementarity has an intuitive appeal. We can all think of instances in which it seems valid. If you cannot understand how someone as aggressive as A could marry a person as submissive as B, ask yourself how A would get along married to C, who is extremely aggressive too. Thibaut and Kelley offer the interesting speculation that some human relationships may be based primarily on similarity whereas others may be based primarily on complementarity. Perhaps, as they suggest, similarity and complementarity both contribute to the rewards of interaction.[17]

SITUATION

We qualified our statement about the effect of proximity on communicator choice with the phrase "other things being equal." We could qualify statements about similarity and communicator choice in the same way. But other things rarely are equal; there are other conditions that determine the rewards we receive from one another and therefore the choices we make. One of these is **situation**.

Experience and common sense tell us that we prefer to associate with some people in one situation and reject them in another. In other words, the situation itself may alter the standards by which we pick receivers in our communication attempts. We shall look at three kinds of situations that have this effect.

Anxiety

Anxiety-producing situations affect our need to interact or affiliate with others. Schachter was able to study this by telling college women that they were to be subjects in an experiment on the effects of electric shock.[18] One group was told that the shocks would be extremely painful; the other group was told that they would be mild and painless. A ten-minute "delay" was announced before the experiment, and the women were given the choice of waiting alone or with others. The choices they made were really what Schachter's experiment was all about. Schachter found that in the high-anxiety group (expecting painful shock), 63 percent of the women preferred to wait with others before the shock; in the low-anxiety group (expecting painless shock), only 33 percent of the women wanted company. The high-anxiety condition also produced a much more intense desire for affiliation than the low-anxiety. And though "Misery loves company," it isn't just any company: anxious subjects preferred to wait with others who were about to experience painful electric shock.

Schachter's experiment demonstrates that anxiety-producing situations can increase our need to affiliate and also change our criteria for choosing companions. Apparently the need to be comforted through sharing unpleasantness tends to supersede our other needs for associating with people. Boot camps and fraternity-pledging programs have long operated on this principle. People who share relatively unpleasant experiences often become more cohesive as a group—probably because together they find it easier to endure the hardships they are or will be experiencing.

Changes in Self-Esteem

A second situation that may influence communicator choice is a **change in the level of self-esteem.** Consider this example. Sam and Suzy have gone together for almost six months when suddenly she jilts him. Because he obviously is not good enough for Suzy, Sam's self-esteem is at an all-time low. Then along comes Valerie. Sam has never considered her as attractive or intelligent as Suzy, but she seems to be interested in him. Sam strikes up a romance on the rebound.

The rebound phenomenon, if we can call it that, illustrates what can happen to interpersonal choice as a result of a change in the level of one's self-esteem. An experiment by Walster explains something about how this works.[19]

Walster "hired" female college students to participate in a study of personality. Before the testing began each student "accidentally" met a male student, actually a confederate of the experimenter. By a strange coincidence he was also looking for the experimenter. As the couple waited the boy made it clear that he had a romantic interest in the girl. He talked to her for fifteen minutes, trying to arrange a date. After the experimenter appeared, the girl was given some personality tests and then given results that were rigged to alter her level of self-esteem. Some girls heard themselves described as mature, original, and sensitive. Others were told that they were weak, immature, antisocial, and lacking in leadership abilities.

After receiving the results of the personality tests, each subject was asked to give her honest evaluation of five people, including the student who had asked her for a date. As Walster predicted, girls who received negative personality assessments were more responsive to the boy's advances than girls who received positive test results. Her data suggest that when self-esteem has recently been lowered, our need for affiliation increases, and we become more accepting of affection from others. Under these conditions people we might have considered unappealing may now seem more desirable as companions.

Isolation

A third situation that influences our choice of receivers is isolation from the rewards of others. Although each of us has known occasional loneliness, brief isolation can sometimes be peaceful and pleasant. Prolonged isolation, however, is almost always unpleasant. Hence in prisons one of the severest forms of punishment is solitary confinement. Similarly prisoner-of-war camps often use isolation to break a prisoner's spirit. And think of the numerous cartoons in which a man shipwrecked on a desert island inhabited only by lovely native women eagerly greets a fellow countryman as "someone to talk to."

Each of these circumstances illustrates that social isolation tends to be less pleasant than interaction with others. Some researchers have found that as we are deprived of the rewards possible from human interaction, we become more receptive to those rewards. Thus a third influence on our communicator choices is the degree to which we have been isolated from contact with others. We would expect again that as we are deprived of social reinforcement, our strong need to interact with other human beings tends to override our standards for acceptable friends.

POPULAR AND UNPOPULAR PEOPLE

People with whom we associate on a continuing basis reward us in ways that make those associations worthwhile. Yet even when we are forced to communicate with people we have not chosen to interact with—on the job or in class, for example—we enjoy some people more than others because, to use Thibaut and Kelley's terms, they provide us with positive outcomes. No doubt sometimes this results from actual or perceived similarities or from other determinants of interpersonal attraction. Nevertheless the question remains: Are certain types of people more reinforcing than others?

In spite of some contradictory findings, the answer appears to be that there are some people who consistently provide positive outcomes for others. (These are the overchosen people in sociograms.) Think of someone you know who is exceptionally popular and try to pinpoint what it is that makes him that way.

One of his attributes may be *physical attractiveness*. Generally speaking, we are attracted to good-looking people. A study by Miller shows that we tend to associate high attractiveness with positive personality characteristics and low attractiveness with negative personality traits.[20] The effect of a person's physical appearance on our evaluation of him is usually greatest in the initial stages of our contact and diminishes as we become familiar with his other qualities.

Aside from liking physically attractive people because they are good to look at, we sometimes like them because we feel that by being seen with them, we will enhance our own image. The college man who consistently dates beautiful women is very likely to improve his own image among both his male friends and his prospective female acquaintances. The coed who dates handsome men is also increasing her self-esteem.

In addition to physical features, certain *behaviors* also appear to be more reinforcing than others. In more than one study, people who were seen as generous, enthusiastic, and affectionate were better liked than those described as stingy, apathetic, and cold. One summary of research tells us that popular people tend to be better-adjusted and more sociable, mature, and stable whereas less popular people tend to be more "aggressive-egocentric" or "withdrawn-shy."[21] It seems then that we can identify some behaviors that are generally more rewarding than others. Differences in situation will certainly exist, but given a set of behaviors, we may still be able to make some predictions about communicator choices.

Our interest in developing more effective patterns of interpersonal communication naturally leads us to the question: Are there some behaviors that are disliked by almost everyone? Or to use another frame of reference: Are there any relatively stable traits by which we can describe the isolate, the person who is rejected by others?

Delia approached this issue by asking each of his subjects to write a profile of a person he disliked.[22] Three types of descriptions appeared over and over again in his data, and all three were consistently disliked by a high percentage of the subjects.

In the first profile the person described is self-centered, arrogant, and conceited. This type of person is unrewarding to deal with because he thinks significantly more of himself than he does of anyone else. Interacting with him makes you aware of his lack of interest in your opinions and ideas and consequently diminishes your feeling of self-esteem.

The second profile is closely related to the first; it describes someone who is dogmatic, obnoxious, and pushy. Here is a person less concerned with the feelings and viewpoints of other people than with imposing his will on them. You usually respond to him in one of three ways. You fight fire with fire by imitating his offensive behavior: if he pushes you around, you push him around; if he insists that he is right, you are equally insistent in stating your opinion. Or you offer passive resistance: "Just because you have silenced a man does not mean you have convinced him" is the slogan of one contemporary poster. Your third alternative is to submit; but despite your response your attitude is again likely to be negative.

The third type of disliked person is someone who is two-faced, or insincere. Other studies confirm the high value we place on a person's intentions. Anderson found that in rating likable personality traits, his subjects valued sincerity above all others.[23] We also know that overheard conversations are more persuasive than direct ones—we are likely to believe completely in a speaker's sincerity if we think he does not know we are listening.[24] And apparently we are more susceptible to persuasion if we perceive his arguments as sincerely motivated.

Unfortunately few of us recognize our own portraits. We may be aware that we are acting insincerely, but we do not think of ourselves as obnoxious or domineering. We reserve those terms for others. One graduate student we know continually cuts into conversations with comments such as "Listen to me—I have the facts!" and "I hate to interrupt you with the facts. . . ." Yet he does not see himself as dogmatic. Nor does he see people roll their eyes when he starts to talk.

Delia seems to have hit upon three types of inherently unrewarding behavior. No doubt there are others. The specific behaviors are less important, however, than the concept that some people repeatedly provide negative outcomes and that they become the people least chosen by others.

Summary

Our study of communicator choice began with a review of three techniques for measuring attraction: the Scale of Social Distance, the Behavioral Differential, and the sociometric test. As we examined the bases for interpersonal attraction, some consistent patterns began to emerge.

We found that other things being equal, the closer two people are geographically, the more likely they are to be attracted to each other. We saw that we tend to attract and to be attracted to people who have attitudes similar to our own and that conversely we tend to dislike and be disliked by those who differ from us. To explain the relationship between proximity and liking, we turned to balance theory, and we elaborated on this model in our discussion of attitude similarity and liking. Other similarities—backgrounds, values, socioeconomic status, and so on—were also seen to be reinforcing and to increase attraction. We qualified our statements about the principles of attraction by noting some specific situations and behaviors that affect the rewards we receive from each other and therefore the choices we make.

Review Questions

1. How are the Scale of Social Distance and the Behavioral Differential similar? How are they different?
2. What are some advantages of the sociometric test?
3. How is proximity related to interpersonal attraction? How are familiarity and proximity related?
4. How is similarity related to interpersonal attraction? Discuss three variables that qualify generalizations about attitude similarity.
5. How does the theory of complementary needs compare with the research findings on the relationship between perceived similarity and interpersonal attraction?
6. Discuss three situations that influence communicator choice. Give an example of how each affects interpersonal attraction.
7. What are two attributes of people generally perceived as providing consistent positive reinforcement? What are four attributes of people who generally are disliked by others?

Exercises

1. Conduct a sociometric analysis in class or among a group of your friends. Choose several criteria, such as the ones on which Figures 5 and 6 are based, that seem relevant for different reasons. Go over the results of the sociogram by yourself, and try to determine the reasons that some people are overchosen and others are isolates.

2. Examine the following diagram of an apartment house. Using the concept of proximity as it relates to interpersonal attraction, discuss the probable relationships between the residents of each apartment (for example, which residents probably would engage most often in conversations).

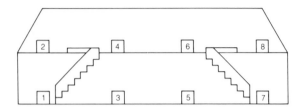

3. John is a motorcycle freak. Sally, John's girl friend, does not like motorcycles because she thinks they are dangerous.
   a. Using balance theory, draw a diagram depicting this relationship.
   b. List the alternatives available to Sally for balancing the situation and make a diagram for each alternative.

4. Describe a situation in which you entered into a relationship on the rebound. Analyze the positive and negative aspects of that relationship. If you were to encounter a similar situation, what, if anything, would you do differently?

5. Have some friends rate a number of topics on a scale such as the one shown here. Then create two paragraphs, one agreeing with the general attitude of the class on each issue—legalizing marijuana, for example—and one disagreeing. Put a byline on each of the two paragraphs, using fictitious names. Then have your friends indicate the extent of their attraction to the authors. See whether they prefer the person whom they perceive as holding an attitude similar to their own. This would validate the theory that perceived attitude similarity yields interpersonal attraction.

Strongly agree	Agree	Neither agree nor disagree	Disagree	Strongly disagree
5	4	3	2	1

6. Create a composite description of the kinds of people you are attracted to. What does this composite tell you about yourself?

7. Go back to the early entries in your personal log for this class, and identify some specific behaviors or events that caused you to like or dislike certain members. Interpret your findings in the light of the cost-reward framework discussed in Chapter 3.

Suggested Readings

Aronson, Elliot. "Who Likes Whom and Why." *Psychology Today* (August 1970), 4:48–51, 74. Experiments conducted by the author and three associates are the basis for theories on why people like (or do not like) one another. Some of the results are surprising. This is a well-written, easily understood article, good both as entertaining reading and for group discussion.

Berscheid, Ellen, and Walster, Elaine. *Interpersonal Attraction.* Reading, Mass.: Addison-Wesley, 1969. This short book offers a highly compact exposure to the subject of interpersonal attraction, including such topics as why certain people are attracted to each other; the effects of stress, loneliness, or insecurity on one's need to be liked; the effect of geographic proximity on our choice of friends and marriage partners; why we like those whom we think like us; and how we choose a partner in romance.

Chapman, A. H. *Put-Offs and Come-Ons: Psychological Maneuvers and Stratagems.* New York: Berkley, 1968. This psychiatrist has put together an insightful and entertaining inventory of interaction "maneuvers and stratagems" that people use on other people. He discusses come-on forces, which explain behaviors which attract people to one another, and put-off forces, which do the opposite. His inventory includes "Whine and Decline," "Temper Tantrum," "Love Will Come Later," and "Garbage Like Me."

Notes

[1] Dean C. Barnlund, *Interpersonal Communication: Survey and Studies* (Boston: Houghton Mifflin, 1968), p. 71.

[2] Emory S. Bogardus, "Measuring Social Distances," *Journal of Applied Sociology,* 9 (1925), 301.

[3] Harry C. Triandis, *Attitude and Attitude Change* (New York: Wiley, 1971), pp. 51–53.

[4] Jacob L. Moreno, *Who Shall Survive?* (New York: Beacon, 1953).

[5] Alvin Gouldner and Harry Gouldner, *Modern Sociology: An Introduction to the Study of Human Interaction* (New York: Harcourt, Brace and World, 1963), pp. 328–355.

[6] Leon Festinger, Stanley Schachter, and Kurt Back, *Social Pressures in Informal Groups* (New York: Harper & Brothers, 1950), p. 37.

[7] Fritz Heider, *The Psychology of Interpersonal Relations* (New York: Wiley, 1958), p. 177.

[8] Robert B. Zajonc, "Attitudinal Effects of Mere Exposure," *Journal of Personality and Social Psychology,* 9 (June 1968), 1–29.

108

9 Heider, p. 195.

10 Adapted from Heider, p. 180.

11 Theodore M. Newcomb, "An Approach to the Study of Communicative Acts," *Psychological Review,* 60 (1953), 395.

12 Robert E. Brewer, "Attitude Change, Interpersonal Attraction, and Communication in a Dyadic Situation," *Journal of Social Psychology,* 75 (1968), 127–134.

13 Heider, p. 197.

14 Brian F. Blake and Abraham Tesser, "Interpersonal Attraction as a Function of the Other's Reward Value to the Person," *Journal of Social Psychology,* 82 (1970), 67–74.

15 Ellen Berscheid and Elaine Walster, *Interpersonal Attraction* (Reading, Mass.: Addison-Wesley, 1969), p. 60.

16 Robert F. Winch, *Mate Selection: A Study of Complementary Needs* (New York: Harper & Brothers, 1958).

17 John W. Thibaut and Harold H. Kelley, *The Social Psychology of Groups* (New York: Wiley, 1959), p. 47.

18 Stanley Schachter, *The Psychology of Affiliation* (Stanford, Calif.: Stanford University Press, 1959), pp. 17–19.

19 Elaine Walster, "The Effect of Self-Esteem on Romantic Liking," *Journal of Experimental Social Psychology,* 1 (1965), 184–197.

20 A. Miller, "Role of Physical Attractiveness in Impression Formation," *Psychonomic Science,* 19 (1970), 241–243.

21 Barnlund, p. 79.

22 Jesse Delia, personal communication, December 29, 1971.

23 Norman H. Anderson, "Likableness Ratings of 555 Personality-Trait Words," *Journal of Personality and Social Psychology,* 9 (1968), 354–362.

24 Elaine Walster and Leon Festinger, "The Effectiveness of 'Overheard' Persuasive Communications," *Journal of Abnormal and Social Psychology,* 65 (1962), 395–402.

Basic Elements of Interpersonal Communication

part three

Chapter 6 The Verbal Message

OBJECTIVES

After reading this chapter the student should be able to:

1. Describe what is meant by the statement "The word is not the thing."

2. Distinguish between denotation and connotation.

3. Describe the Semantic Differential and give an example of a differential.

4. Distinguish between private and shared meanings.

5. Distinguish between egocentric speech and socialized speech.

6. Distinguish between a restrictive code and an elaborated code.

7. State the Whorfian hypothesis.

8. Describe two ways in which language and thought are related.

9. Discuss four imprecise uses of language and give examples of how each affects interpersonal communication.

10. Identify two sources of confusion about words or phrases, give an example of each, and describe how each can be minimized.

6

In *Through the Looking Glass,* one of Alice's most bewildering conversations was with Humpty Dumpty:

> ". . . and that shows that there are three hundred and sixty-four days when you might get unbirthday presents—"
>
> "Certainly," said Alice.
>
> "And only one for birthday presents, you know. There's glory for you!"
>
> "I don't know what you mean by 'glory,' " Alice said.
>
> Humpty Dumpty smiled contemptuously. "Of course you don't—till I tell you. I meant 'there's a nice knock-down argument for you!' "
>
> "But 'glory' doesn't mean 'a nice knock-down argument,'" Alice objected.
>
> "When *I* use a word," Humpty Dumpty said, in rather a scornful tone, "it means just what I choose it to mean—neither more nor less."
>
> "The question is," said Alice, "whether you *can* make words mean so many different things."
>
> "The question is," said Humpty Dumpty, "which is to be master—that's all."[1]

If we were to take sides in this argument, most of us would ally ourselves with Alice. Words, we would argue, have certain agreed-on meanings. This statement seems self-evident and quite reasonable. How then do we cope with the unsettling remark that a word "means just what I choose it to mean"? How do we establish the meaning of "glory"—or any other word? Let us approach the question of meaning through a closer look at the nature of language itself.

WORDS AND MEANINGS

To linguists the basic elements of language are sounds or, more precisely, distinctive features, which are components of sounds. To students of interpersonal communication, the basic elements of language are words, and words, as we know, are symbols. When we write the words "United States" in a notebook, we are obviously using some marks on a piece of paper to represent a particular land mass. People who speak other languages use other symbols to represent the same land mass—the French, for example, use "Etats-Unis" and the Spanish "Estados Unidos."

Symbols and Referents

A recent example of the arbitrary relationship between a word and the thing it symbolizes can be taken from the realm of science. The name of the space vehicle used to travel from the mother ship to the surface of the moon was originally "lunar excursion module"; later it was changed to "lunar module." In effect, we witnessed the words "lunar module" being created. Therefore, it is easy to recognize that the name was arbitrarily assigned to the vehicle so that it would be possible to communicate about it without pointing every time we referred to it.

In every branch of science, we have seen new words coined as a result of technological development—"antibiotic," "microwave," "photon," "DNA," and so on. There are 6,000 words just in the National Aeronautics and Space Administration's *Dictionary of Technical Terms for Aerospace Use*. And one writer comments that in the last twenty-five years ". . . advances in technology and communication media have produced a greater change in our language than in any similar period in history."[2]

Naming a space vehicle is a process somewhat similar to that of naming a newborn child. Initially no association exists between a name and the thing or person to be named. Similarly we could agree to call a vehicle that lands on the moon a "moon landing vehicle" or even a "xog." In this context it seems clear that a **word** is merely *a symbol of the object it represents.* The term "lunar module" only represents the vehicle. The vehicle itself is the **referent**, *the object for which the symbol stands.* Clearly the word is not the thing.

If words referred only to objects, no doubt our communication problems would be eased considerably. We could establish what referents we were speaking about with somewhat less difficulty. But words also refer to events, properties of things, actions, relationships, concepts, and so on. The referent of the term "Asian" seems clear. But suppose you are asked, "*Who* is an Asian, *what* is an Asian, and *what* does being an Asian mean to you?" These questions were addressed to a group of more than 200 authorities who were considered and who considered themselves Asians. There were many answers: Asia stands for a geographic concept, a political concept, an emotional concept, an ethnic theory, a fatalistic society, a kind of personality. In all, eighteen different interpretations of the word "Asian" emerged.[3] If we cannot find agreement on the word "Asian," what about terms that represent higher levels of abstraction? What are the referents of terms such as "ethics," "freedom," and "professionalism"?

The relationship between meaning and reference is well illustrated when we come upon words in a foreign language. If we see "ἄνθρωπος" ("*ánthrōpos*"), the Greek word for "man," for the first time, we have no way of determining what concept that word represents simply by looking at the word itself. Even with new words in our own language, we have to learn what concepts they represent. Notice how we carefully avoided saying, "what the words mean." Meanings are not inherent in words. Words in and of themselves are meaningful only after we have associated them with some referents. It is men who assign meanings to words.

Suppose you and a friend disagree about the meaning of "word." You turn to the dictionary to settle your differences only to find this formidable list:

1. A unit of language that functions as a principal carrier of meaning
2. Speech or talk
3. A short talk or conversation: "to have a word with someone"
4. An expression or utterance: "a word of praise"
5. A warrant, assurance, or promise
6. News, tidings, or information
7. A verbal signal such as a password
8. An authoritative utterance or a command: "His word was law"
9. The Scriptures
10. A proverb or motto
11. A recommendation: "to put in a word for someone"
12. To express
13. An expression of astonishment: "My word!"[4]

Meaning, it would seem, is not to be found in the dictionary. Instead the dictionary lists the uses or functions of language. "Dictionaries," one communication expert explains, "do not 'give meanings' or even definitions; they give more or less synonymous words or phrases."[5]

Denotation and Connotation

In discussing meaning some students of language make the traditional distinction between "denotation" and "connotation." We have said that words are meaningful only after we have associated them with some referents. When we speak of **denotation**, we refer to *the primary associations a word has for most members of a given linguistic community*. When we speak of **connotation**, we refer to *other, secondary associations a word has for one or more members of that community*. Sometimes the connotations of a word are the same for nearly everyone; sometimes they relate solely to one individual's personal experience. To most of us the word "fox" connotes guile or cunning. To a naturalist, a furrier, a chicken farmer, or a man who has just been bitten by a fox, the word "fox" may have completely different connotations.

Because words can elicit powerful emotional reactions, they are

THE BORN LOSER by Art Sansom. Reprinted by permission of Newpaper Enterprise Association.

often said to have negative or positive connotations for people. Take the word "housewife." Today "housewife" has strong negative connotations for so many women that the editors of several English-language dictionaries were recently interviewed concerning the possibility of introducing a substitute term. They commented that in the past "homemaker," "home manager," "household executive," "domestic engineer," and several other terms have been proposed and rejected. There seem to be no immediate plans for a change, however.[6]

As yet little research can be cited in the study of word connotations. One study investigated male and female responses to sex-related terms in an attempt to identify differences in response. Not surprisingly it was found that women tended to respond significantly less favorably than men to the following words:

Wife swapping
Husband swapping
Prostitute
Whore[7]

In another investigation male and female subjects were exposed to various words on a tachistoscope, and their galvanic skin responses (GSR) were measured as an index of their reactions. Although there were nonsignificant differences between responses to "good" words ("beauty," "love," "kiss," and "friend," for example) and "aversive" words ("cancer," "hate," "liar," and "death," for example), some words caused significant reactions in both men and women. These were called "personal" words and included the subject's first name, last name, father's first name, mother's first name, major in school, year in school, and school name. In general, subjects were more physiologically aroused by the personal words than by either the good or the aversive words.[8]

Some of the most influential research on the measurement of meaning has been conducted by Osgood and his associates, who developed an instrument called the **Semantic Differential**.[9] The Semantic Differential can *test a person's reaction to any concept or term*—sex, music, my mother, open enrollment, tree, ego, welfare, John Harris—so that in effect the number of semantic differentials is infinite. The test is a seven-interval scale whose limits are defined by sets of bipolar adjectives. In the accompanying scale, for example, we see a Semantic

War

Hot	____:____:____:____:____:____:____	Cold
Good	____:____:____:____:____:____:____	Bad
Relaxed	____:____:____:____:____:____:____	Tense
Cruel	____:____:____:____:____:____:____	Kind
Fast	____:____:____:____:____:____:____	Slow
Deceitful	____:____:____:____:____:____:____	Honest
Sharp	____:____:____:____:____:____:____	Dull
Active	____:____:____:____:____:____:____	Passive
Courageous	____:____:____:____:____:____:____	Cowardly
Powerful	____:____:____:____:____:____:____	Weak
Small	____:____:____:____:____:____:____	Large

Differential for the concept of war. The subject rates the concept by checking the interval between each pair of adjectives that best describes it. With this test the researcher can assess the subject's reaction to any number of concepts and then compare them with those of other people. He can also draw a line connecting each of the points made by the subject and thus create a profile of his concept of war.

Statistical analysis of the work of Osgood and his associates suggests that our judgments have three major dimensions: evaluation, potency, and activity. Thus we say that war is good or bad and cruel or kind (evaluation), that it is powerful or weak and small or large (potency), and that it is fast or slow and active or passive (activity).

The great appeal of the Semantic Differential is its flexibility. The procedure is so general that it can be precisely tailored to the needs and interests of the experimenter. And as one writer observed, though the technique was "intended to show how people *feel* about the concepts being rated . . . there is no reason in the world why it cannot be used to determine what people *think* are the important properties of those same concepts."[10]

Private and Shared Meanings

In psychology and semantics much research is based on the distinction between denotation and connotation. The Semantic Differential, for example, is said to measure "connotative meaning." But when we examine it closely, the distinction between denotation and connotation seems to break down. All people who speak English are members of the same linguistic community; yet within that community certain groups exist for whom even the primary associations, or denotations, of a given word are different.

Take the case of the Americans and the British. In England you take a "lift," not an "elevator"; if you ask for the "second floor," you get the "first floor." You take the "underground," not the "subway," and a "tram," not a "streetcar." You "queue up"; you don't "stand in line." You go to a "chemist's," not a "pharmacy." The list seems endless. Perhaps there is some truth in the remark that America and England are two allies separated only by an ocean and a common language.

For students of communication it may be more helpful to distinguish between private and shared meanings rather than denotation and connotation.

The concept of **private meaning** takes us back to Humpty Dumpty's declaration that a word means "just what I choose it to mean—neither more nor less." We can all use language in this way. We can assign meanings to words without agreement and in effect create a private language. We can decide, for example, to call trees "reds" or "glimps" or "haves." Schizophrenic speech is often idiosyncratic in this way, but the schizophrenic is unaware that his use of language is private: he uses the words he has re-created and expects to be understood. When one young patient was admitted to a hospital, she continually referred to her father, a lawyer by profession, as "the chauffeur." Everyone with whom she spoke found this reference bizarre. Only in treatment was it learned that when she called her father a "chauffeur," she meant that he did her mother's bidding—that he was completely under her domination.

Presumably, if we assign private meanings to words, we are aware that we can use them to communicate with someone only if we let him know what the referents of these words are. **Shared meaning** requires some correspondence between the message as perceived by the sender and the receiver. As Deese has written, "In order for communication to take place between two or more individuals, meaning must be shared."[11] Two friends, a husband and wife, an entire family, or a group of physicists may decide to use language in a way that makes little sense to others. Among themselves, however, they can communicate with no difficulty. The same phenomenon occurs among members of much larger social aggregations. For example, one article has described the extensive vocabulary associated with the San Francisco drug culture:

Glossary of San Francisco Drug Language

This glossary was compiled from information collected during interviews conducted in San Francisco's Haight-Ashbury. We believe it is representative of contemporary San Francisco drug language. This listing is entirely descriptive, and while certain inconsistencies may prove to be disturbing, they are part of this new vocabulary.

Acapulco gold—Superior grade of marijuana, somewhat gold in color, supposedly grown near Acapulco, Mexico

Barbs—Barbiturates

Blow the vein—To use too much pressure on a weak vein, causing it to rupture

Bummer, bum trip—Adverse reaction to drugs

Candy—Cocaine

Cartwheel—Benzedrine time spansules

Columbus black—Marijuana of high potency grown in Central America that is black in color

█████—Best part of vein for injection

Ditch—Inside of the elbow (which has two large veins)

Doper—Drug user

Dust—Cocaine

Freak—Anyone addicted to drugs (often combined with acid-, meth-, etc.)

Head—User of drugs (often combined with acid-, meth-, etc.)

Heat—Police

Joint—Marijuana cigarette

Key—About 2.2 pounds of marijuana (one kilogram)

Magic mushroom—Psilocybin

Miss Emma—Morphine

Narcos, narks—Narcotics agents

Panama red—Marijuana from southern Mexico and Central America

Phennies—Phenobarbital

Poppers—Amyl nitrite

Rig—Paraphernalia for injections

Roller—Vein that won't stay in position for injection

Rush—Intense orgasmlike euphoria experienced immediately after an intravenous injection

Shit—Heroin or sometimes marijuana

Silver bike—Syringe with chrome fittings

Smack—Heroin
Speed—Methamphetamine
Strung out—Condition from habitual use of a drug
Ticket agent—Dealer in hallucinogenic drugs
Uppers, ups—Stimulants, especially Benzedrine or Dexedrine[12]

For the subgroup that uses this language, the meaning of "candy" or "ticket agent" or "smack" is clear. Members of the group will have no difficulty understanding one another when they use these terms. Communication difficulties emerge only when they expect meaning to be shared by those outside the group. This is a recurring expectation, especially among members of different ethnic groups. Before reading further test yourself on the vocabulary list below taken from black American culture. Opposite each item on this list is the answer. Give yourself one point for each correct answer, and grade yourself according to the following scale: 100–90, A; 89–80, B; 79–70, C; 69–60, D; below 60, F.

1.	Ax	1.	Musical instrument
2.	Baby	2.	Friend
3.	Bag (That's my bag)	3.	Profession (what I do well)
4.	Blade	4.	Knife
5.	Blow some jams	5.	Play some records
6.	Bombed out	6.	Drunk
7.	Boo-pot	7.	Marijuana
8.	Boss	8.	The best
9.	Bread	9.	Money
10.	Busted	10.	Caught by the police; fired
11.	Check out	11.	Look over very well
12.	Choice	12.	Real fine
13.	Close-knuckle drill	13.	Fist fight
14.	Close that razor	14.	Shut the window
15.	Come outa your act	15.	Be genuine
16.	Cooker	16.	A real swinger
17.	Cop	17.	Buy; get; steal
18.	Cop a nod	18.	Sleep
19.	Cop out	19.	Explain; squeal
20.	Cut him up	20.	Give him a piece of your mind
21.	Cut me loose	21.	Leave me alone
22.	Devil	22.	Select group; finest in every way; woman
23.	Dig	23.	Listen to this; approve of something; understand
24.	Doing a bill	24.	Spending $100
25.	Doing a bit	25.	Doing jail or prison time

26.	Dough	26.	Money
27.	Dropping beans	27.	Taking pills to get high
28.	Dust	28.	Money
29.	Flaky	29.	Not too smart; dumb
30.	Flick	30.	Movie; television
31.	Fox	31.	Good-looking woman
32.	Freeze	32.	Stop
33.	From the git go	33.	Beginning
34.	Front	34.	Suit
35.	Funny changes	35.	Double-talk
36.	Get yourself together	36.	Stop acting silly or stupid
37.	Getting oiled	37.	Getting drunk; drinking
38.	Gig	38.	Date; job
39.	Grease	39.	Eat
40.	Grip	40.	Car
41.	Hawk (the)	41.	Wind (the)
42.	Heavy	42.	Good
43.	Hit on the broad	43.	Sweet-talk a woman
44.	Hog	44.	Cadillac
45.	Hump; humping	45.	Working the job
46.	I got dinged	46.	I got beat
47.	Ice it	47.	Stop
48.	I'm hip	48.	I understand
49.	Joint	49.	Marijuana cigarette
50.	Joneses	50.	Dope habit; hooked
51.	Jug	51.	Pick at or nag
52.	Knocked	52.	High from drinking
53.	Lame	53.	Square
54.	Let's make it	54.	Let's leave
55.	Lid	55.	Hat
56.	Man (the)	56.	Policeman; white man in authority
57.	Mellow	57.	Girl friend
58.	Nailer	58.	Policeman
59.	Not wired too heavy	59.	Not too smart; dumb
60.	Not wrapped too tight	60.	Not too smart; dumb
61.	Oiled	61.	Drunk
62.	Okey-dokey	62.	Got taken
63.	On the humble	63.	Innocent
64.	Outa sight	64.	Unbelievable
65.	Pad	65.	Home
66.	Peck	66.	Eat
67.	Peek your hole card	67.	Find out your secrets
68.	Piece	68.	Hand gun
69.	Popped	69.	In jail; caught

70.	Pressed	70.	Dressed up
71.	Pull	71.	Leave; go
72.	Pull a creep	72.	Slip around
73.	Put the check on	73.	To look over carefully
74.	Put the hurt on you	74.	Do you violence
75.	Rap; rapping	75.	Conversation; talking
76.	Regular	76.	All right
77.	Ride	77.	Car
78.	Run it down	78.	Tell it like it is
79.	Run it, man	79.	Explain it
80.	Run you through a thing	80.	Trick you
81.	Running game	81.	Doing something wrong
82.	Screaming	82.	Talking
83.	Shank	83.	Knife
84.	Shot a blank	84.	Sweet talk failed
85.	Show	85.	Make an appearance
86.	Smoothed out	86.	Didn't do right
87.	Something else	87.	Puzzling (can't figure out)
88.	Split	88.	Leave; go
89.	Steal you	89.	Sneak up behind you
90.	Stomps	90.	Shoes
91.	Stone fox	91.	Especially good-looking woman
92.	Stone trick	92.	Lied; didn't keep word
93.	Stump	93.	Chair
94.	Take the cut	94.	Leave; go
95.	Tap dancer	95.	Uncle Tom
96.	Tighten up	96.	Straighten up
97.	Tore down	97.	Drunk
98.	Tore up	98.	High
99.	Uptight	99.	Backed into a corner; tense
100.	Wasted	100.	Demoralized

Suppose many of these expressions are unfamiliar to you, and your test score is low. You would object violently if you were informed that this score is a measure of your intelligence. Unfortunately many intelligence tests rely heavily on the assumption that test taker and test writer use language in much the same way, a problem we shall touch on in the discussion of encoding in the next section. Interpersonal communication is equally reliant on assumptions of shared meaning. It presupposes agreement between communicators concerning the symbols they exchange and therefore some consciousness not only of language but of one another. In discussing message encoding we hope to show that who is listening is no less important than who is speaking.

MESSAGE ENCODING 123

"You're lying," "I don't think you are telling the truth," "Fibber," "I don't believe you," "You liar"—these are alternate ways of formulating a single message, and there are many others. We use "Fibber" in one context, "You're lying" in another, and "I don't believe you" in a third, and we seem to make these distinctions without effort. Occasionally we wonder how to broach a delicate subject, but most of the time we speak without deliberation. Yet **encoding a message**, or *formulating it in words,* is a complex process, however straightforward the message may be:

> Coding requires the selection of appropriate verbal and nonverbal signs to express the internal state of the sender of the message. But to be effective, this must be accompanied by an imaginative interpretation of the probable meaning to be assigned to the cues by the receiver. Without the capacity to encode and the capacity to interpret from the vantage point of the receiver, the sender would not know what to put into a message. . . .[13]

In short, when we encode a message, we must have some awareness of the listener if we want to be understood.

A look at how children use language gives us a better understanding of what takes place in the encoding process. Children astonish us with their verbal facility. The three-year-old can formulate sentences, repeat all sorts of long words and colloquial expressions, and use several tenses correctly. Some three-year-olds have a vocabulary of nearly 1,000 words. The five-year-old speaks in correct, finished sentences and even uses complex sentences with hypothetical and conditional clauses. The structure and form of his language are essentially complete.[14]

To study the functions of language in children, the Swiss psychologist Jean Piaget made exhaustive observations and analyses of the way children speak both when they are alone and when they are in the company of other children. He also devised a series of experiments to determine how objective children try to be in communicating information. A typical Piaget experiment follows this pattern. A child is shown a diagram of a water tap—sometimes Piaget uses a diagram of a bicycle—and given a precise explanation of how it works. Once it has been established that the child understands the experimenter's explanation, he is asked to repeat it (with the aid of the diagram) to another child. In another variant of this procedure, the child is told a simple story and asked to repeat it to a second child. How do children perform these communication tasks? Apparently not very well. Piaget found that though a child fully understood an explanation or story, he was not necessarily successful in communicating it to another child.

Why should this be so? It is not that the child lacks the necessary vocabulary. Nor is he by any means inarticulate. Piaget's work has led him to the conclusion that in the child under age seven or eight, language has two distinct functions and that two kinds of speech exist: egocentric and socialized speech.

As Piaget describes patterns of **egocentric speech** in the child, he gives us a perfect example of a poor encoder:

> Although he talks almost incessantly to his neighbours, he rarely places himself at their point of view. He speaks to them for the most part as if he were thinking aloud. He speaks, therefore, in a language which disregards the precise shade of meaning in things and ignores the particular angle from which they are viewed, and which above all is always making assertions, even in argument, instead of justifying them. . . . In a word, the child hardly ever even asks himself whether he has been understood. For him, that goes without saying, for he does not think about others when he talks.[15]

Piaget believes that until a child is seven or eight, egocentric language constitutes almost half his spontaneous speech, and his book *The Language and Thought of the Child* is full of amusing "conversations" between children in which virtually no communication takes place:

L.: "Thunder rolls."
P.: "No, it doesn't roll."
L.: "It's water."
P.: "No, it doesn't roll."
L.: "What is thunder?"
P.: "Thunder is . . ." (*He doesn't go on.*)[16]

In contrast to egocentric speech, **socialized speech** involves adapting information to the listener and in some sense adopting his point of view; it involves social rather than nonsocial encoding. Piaget goes beyond his findings about language to argue that the adult "thinks socially, even when he is alone, and . . . the child under 7 thinks egocentrically, even in the society of others."[17]

One team of researchers went on to a further examination of this discrepancy between the communication skills of children and adults.[18] Their strategy was to create a communication problem in the form of a game called Stack the Blocks. Two children, one designated "speaker" and the other "listener," are seated opposite each other at a table. They are separated by an opaque screen so that they cannot see each other. Before each child is a wooden dowel and a set of six blocks. A hole has been drilled through each block so that it may be stacked on the dowel, and each block is imprinted with a different graphic design. As you can see from Figure 11, the designs have **low codability**—that is, they are *difficult to describe*. The speaker's blocks are in a dispenser, and he is instructed to remove them one at a time. As he stacks each block on the dowel, he must also describe it for the listener, who must

Figure 11

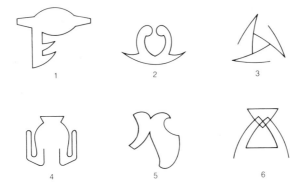

Designs on Blocks for a Communication Experiment

SOURCE: Sam Glucksberg, Robert M. Krauss, and Robert Weisberg, "Referential Communication in Nursery School Children: Method and Some Preliminary Findings," *Journal of Experimental Child Psychology,* 3 (1966), 335. Reprinted by permission.

put what he thinks is the same block on his dowel. Describing the design of the block so that the listener can identify it and stack his blocks in the same order is the communication problem.

In what terms does the speaker describe the novel design of each block to the listener? Here are the descriptions of design 3 given by five nursery schoolchildren:

Somebody running
Eagle
Throwing sticks
Strip-stripe
Wire

Their descriptions of design 4 are equally varied:

Daddy's shirt
Milk jug
Shoe hold
Coffee
Dog

There is little social encoding in these identifications. How, for example, is the listener expected to know what "strip-stripe" refers to or what "Daddy's shirt" looks like? In the role of speaker, some kindergartners and first-graders make comments such as "It goes like this," using one finger—which of course the listener cannot see—to trace the design in the air. In general, children tend to use private rather than socially shared images; as a result their messages are often idiosyncratic.

Variations of the Stack the Blocks experiment have been conducted with children of all grade levels as well as with adults. While nursery schoolchildren seem totally unable to complete this communication task, it has been found that effectiveness in communication clearly increases with age (as measured by grade level).

If we interpret these results literally, we expect all adults to have perfect encoding abilities. We know, however, that this is not the case. Some adults are better at social encoding than others. One reason for the variation in ability is suggested by the British sociologist Basil Bernstein. He proposes that different social settings can generate different modes of communication—in other words, different styles of linguistic encoding. The two codes Bernstein discusses, the restricted and the elaborated code, are based on his analysis of speech patterns in the United Kingdom.

A **restricted code** is *created by a community-based culture;* it emphasizes the community rather than the individual ("we" rather than "I," Bernstein explains). It is largely concerned with shared or context-bound meanings rather than abstractions. The speaker assumes that the listener knows what he is talking about. Therefore the message tends to be simple and relatively brief, the syntax simple and rigid, and the vocabulary undifferentiated. A restricted code creates social solidarity by minimizing the verbal elaboration of individual experience. This is the linguistic code of the working classes.

An **elaborated code** on the other hand is *person-oriented, emphasizing individual rather than group experience* ("I" rather than "we"). The speaker's view of the listener is different here. He does not know the listener's intent; nor does he take it for granted—he assumes very little. Therefore he elaborates meanings to make them more comprehensible to the listener. This linguistic code requires a more differentiated vocabulary, one suitable for making subtle distinctions. It also demands a style of speech that is analytic and abstract rather than concrete. This is the linguistic code available to the middle and upper classes, who unlike the working classes have the advantage of being able to use both codes.

Bernstein's theory has one very practical application. In many countries of the world, including our own, children of low socioeconomic status tend to get lower scores on intelligence tests, especially on the verbal tests, than do children of higher status. It has often been argued that children from lower-status families do poorly because they are less intelligent. Bernstein accounts for poor performance in another way. Intelligence tests are cast in the language of the elaborated code. Although middle- and upper-class children are fluent in both the restricted and elaborated codes, the lower-class child knows only the restricted code. Once he enters school he is caught between two radically different communication systems. Bernstein comments:

Thus the relative backwardness of many working-class children who live in areas of high population density or in rural areas, may well be a culturally induced backwardness transmitted by the linguistic process. Such children's low performance on verbal IQ tests, their difficulty with abstract concepts, their failures within the language area, their general inability to profit from the school, all may result from the limitations of a restricted code.[19]

We have seen that the speaker's expectations about the listener can have a crucial effect on how he prepares his message and on how that message is decoded by the listener. Bernstein's theory has important implications for interpersonal communication. It suggests that message encoding is a form of social learning, a part of the socialization process itself. It further suggests that to some degree each of us may be able to improve our social encoding. How this can be done on a large scale so that it offsets the inequities in our system of education is still an open question.

LANGUAGE AND THOUGHT

Language and thought are often said to be interrelated, but the nature of their relationship is far from clear. Is language a precondition of human thought? Is thinking simply inner speech? Does language shape our ideas, or is it merely an instrument of thought? There seem to be no easy answers.

Students of communication have been particularly concerned with the last question. One version of the view that our thought is shaped by the language we speak was proposed by the linguist Benjamin Lee Whorf and is often referred to as the **Whorfian hypothesis**.[20] Whorf believes that *the world is perceived differently by members of different linguistic communities and* that *this perception is transmitted and sustained by language,* which he regards as the primary vehicle of culture. In short, the language we speak determines our experience of the world.

Whorf supports his theory with findings from his studies of American Indian languages. In English, he points out, we tend to classify words as nouns or verbs; in Hopi the words tend to be classified by duration. For example, in Hopi "lightning," "flame," "wave," and "spark" are verbs, not nouns; they are classified as events of brief duration. In Nootka, which is spoken by the inhabitants of Vancouver Island, categories such as things and events do not exist; thus it is said that "A house occurs" or "It houses."

Is it the case that differences in language reflect differences in perception? An Amazon tribe called the Bororo have several different single words for types of parrots. The Hanunóo of the Philippines have

128   single words for ninety-two different kinds of rice. The Eskimos distinguish at least three kinds of snow in this way. We have only one word for parrot, one for rice, and one for snow. Does this mean that we are incapable of perceiving several types of each? Probably not. Social psychologist Roger Brown suggests that the perceptual categories we use more frequently are merely more "available" to us:

> It is proposed, really, that categories with shorter names (higher codability) are nearer the top of the cognitive deck—more likely to be used in ordinary perception, more available for expectancies and inventions. . . . [Other things being equal,] the presence in someone's vocabulary of a one-word name for a category instead of a phrase name should indicate a superior cognitive availability of the classifying principle involved. . . . The man who readily identifies a set of faces as *Jews* should be more prone to form expectancies about Jews than the man who names the same array *a lot of people, most of them are rather dark, quite a few are wearing button-down shirt collars.*[21]

Linguistic distinctions tell us something about priorities within a given culture. Eskimos have several words for snow because they need to make finer verbal distinctions than we do when communicating about it. By and large, we are unaffected by different kinds of snow and therefore expend little effort on making such distinctions. This does not mean that we are incapable of seeing or making them. In fact, members of certain subgroups within our own linguistic community make more verbal distinctions than most of us—weather forecasters, bobsled owners, ski-resort managers, and so on. We can qualify the Whorfian hypothesis by saying that as a person learns the language of a given culture or subculture, his attention is directed toward aspects of reality or relationships that are important in that context, and this focus affects the category system in his memory. Similarly, if someone tells you about several ways to view a certain painting, you will in some sense see more when you look at it—but not because the image on the retina is different.

Language may not determine thought completely, but it seems to do two important things. First, language serves as an aid to memory. It makes memory more efficient by allowing us to code events as verbal categories. Researchers have shown, for example, that we find it easier to recognize colors of low codability again if we named them for ourselves the first time we saw them.[22] It is now believed that an adult's memory is primarily verbal. Language also enables us to abstract indefinitely from our experience, which is especially important in communicating about abstract relationships (something animals are unable to do).

Ideally language is a valuable instrument of thought; yet we know that language can sometimes interfere with our ability to think critically. Although Whorf was best known for his writings on linguistics, he was trained as an engineer. It was as an accident investigator that he began to realize that a certain percentage of accidents occurred as a result of what might be called "careless thinking." For example, people would be very careful around barrels labeled "GASOLINE" but would smoke unconcernedly around barrels labeled "EMPTY GASOLINE BARREL," though the fumes in the empty barrels were more likely to ignite than the actual gasoline.[23] There are many ways in which an imprecise use of language interferes with our thought processes. In the balance of this chapter, we shall examine four that have a direct influence on interpersonal communication.

Inferences

Every day you make dozens of inferences. When you sit down, you infer that the chair will support your weight. When you go through a green light, you infer that the traffic moving at right angles to you will stop at the red light. When you drive down a one-way street, you infer that all the traffic will be going in one direction. You may have good reason to expect these inferences to be correct, but there is also some uncalculated probability that events will not go as you expect. Drivers who have been involved in traffic accidents frequently say that the accident occurred because they inferred that the other party would act in a certain way when in fact he did not. Every year we read of people who were accidentally shot with guns they inferred were not loaded.

As students of communication we are concerned with the inferences implicit in verbal messages. If you say, "It is sunny outside today," your statement can be easily verified. It is a factual statement based on an observed and verifiable event. If you say, "It is sunny outside; therefore, it is sunny 50 miles from here," you draw a conclusion based on more than what you have observed. You have made a statement based in part on an inference.

Like "unloaded" guns, inferential statements also involve a certain amount of risk. Imagine yourself as the witness in this courtroom scene:

PROSECUTING ATTORNEY:	Would you tell us in your own words what you saw on the night of December 5, 1972?
WITNESS:	First I heard yelling and then I saw a girl coming out of the defendant's apartment. She was crying, and her dress was torn. She also had a bruise on her cheek.
PROSECUTING ATTORNEY:	Would you say that it looked as if the girl and the defendant had been brawling?
DEFENSE ATTORNEY:	Objection! The question calls for a conclusion from the witness.
JUDGE:	Sustained. Would counsel please restate the question?

130   You, the witness, describe what you have seen. You have made a factual statement. The prosecutor asks whether "it looked as if the girl and the defendant had been brawling." He wants to lead you into an inferential statement, one that goes beyond what you have observed. In such a situation an incorrect inference on your part can have serious consequences for the defendant. Suppose, for example, that the girl in question had fallen, and that was why she appeared to have been beaten.

We make inferences in every imaginable context, and it is neither possible nor desirable to avoid them entirely. Nevertheless, to use language more precisely and to be more discerning when we hear others speak, we should learn to distinguish between factual and inferential statements. "You spend a great deal of time with my roommate" is a statement of fact. It involves a low level of uncertainty, it is made as a result of direct observation, and it can be verified. Add to it "I'm sure he won't mind if you borrow his coat" and you have an inferential statement that may well jeopardize a friendship. In becoming more conscious of inference making, we can at least learn to calculate the risks involved.

Dichotomies

Some semanticists classify English as a two-valued rather than a multi-valued language. By this they mean that English has an excess of polar words and a relative scarcity of words to describe the wide middle ground between these opposites. Obviously every person, entity, or event can be described in terms of a whole array of adjectives ranging from very favorable to very unfavorable. Yet we tend to say that a student is a "success" or a "failure," that a child is "good" or "bad," that a woman is "attractive" or "unattractive." Try, for example, to think of some words to describe the spots marked on the continua in the scale of dichotomies. As you search for words, you begin to see that there are a lot of distinctions for which we lack single words. The continua also illustrate how our language suggests that certain cate-

Success	___	___	X	___	___	___	___	Failure
Brilliant	___	___	___	X	___	___	___	Stupid
Handsome	___	___	X	___	___	___	___	Ugly
Winner	___	___	___	X	___	___	___	Loser
Honest	___	___	___	X	___	___	___	Dishonest
Black	___	X	___	___	___	___	___	White

gories of experience are mutually exclusive when in truth they are not.

Consider the first set of terms, "success" and "failure." Any person, no matter who he is, has undoubtedly known some success and some failure. Is Richard Nixon a success or a failure? As a political candidate Nixon won elections for the United States House of Representatives and the Senate, then lost elections for the presidency and the governorship of California, then won again to become president, and was later humiliated by the Watergate incident. Certainly he has experienced the mixture of success and failure that characterizes a lifetime. Yet our language suggests that he is either a success or a failure, that he cannot be both.

Until recently a person was thought to be either dead or alive; these two categories were considered mutually exclusive if two ever were. Medical advances being what they are, heart transplants have now become possible. And with the possibility of a heart transplant has come the problem of how to decide when a heart donor is beyond all hope himself so that his heart may be taken for another human being. We know today that there is usually a time lag between the loss of some capacities (brain functioning, for example) and others (heartbeat and respiration, for example), and that in the interval the person is not "dead." Compare this with the days when the absence of breathing and pulse alone meant that life was gone. So even the distinction between life and death now involves more than just two mutually exclusive categories.

When we use polar terms in a misleading way, we make what are called false dichotomies. We reduce experience in a way that it need not be reduced. We emphasize differences and overlook similarities, and in the process we lose a great deal of information. This is certainly true in our country at election time. During a political campaign each candidate presents his finest qualities and avoids mention of his shortcomings. At the same time he calls as much attention as possible to his opponent's shortcomings while ignoring his good qualities. Even when it does not exist, he tries to create the impression of great contrast between his own position and his opponent's. The voter is encouraged to vote a straight ticket. But must one be either a Democrat or a Republican, a Liberal or a Conservative? Don't we sometimes split our votes? Don't we vote differently in different elections?

One way to avoid making false dichotomies, as Haney has pointed out, is to make use of the questions "How much?" and "To what extent?":[24]

How much of a success am I?
How much of a change is this from his former stand on gun control?
To what extent is he honest?
To what extent is her plan practical?

With the aid of such questions, perhaps we can keep in mind that we have many options, that we need not cast our messages in black-and-white terms, and that we need not accept these either-or distinctions when they are made by others.

Word Power

In ancient Egypt a man received two names: his true name, which he concealed, and his good name, by which he was known publicly. Even today there are many primitive societies in which words are believed to have magical powers. People go to great lengths to conceal their personal names. They avoid saying the names of their gods. The names of their dead are never uttered. Presumably we moderns are far more sophisticated. Yet we have our own verbal taboos. Thus we often hear not that someone "died" but that he "passed away" or that he has "CA," not "cancer." When the airline industry switched over from propeller aircraft to jets, flight crew members whose services were no longer needed were "furloughed," not "fired." There seem to be several insidious ways in which words reflect and influence our thinking.

Let us look at what one writer has called the "semantics of color." Consider the word "white," keeping in mind that we live in a predominantly "white" society. "White" denotes the reflection of nearly all the rays of the sun. It also has many other associations: purity, chastity, freedom from stain, innocence. When we speak of "white magic," we refer to harmless magic. We even have the expression "That's very white of you" (honest or decent). The word "black," on the other hand, denotes the absorption of light, without reflection of any of the rays composing it. Like "white" this word has several other associations, but most of them are negative: gloomy, soiled, disgraceful, evil, wicked, and so on. Then there is "black magic." These are not merely lists of connotations drawn from a dictionary. Duncan has corroborated the differences in feeling evoked by "white" and "black" by asking his students to describe the associations these two words brought to mind.[25]

Another writer takes this distinction a step further by arguing that our language reflects a kind of white racism and that such connotations influence our thinking:

> We *blacken* a man's reputation, *whitewash* a political mistake. A den is a *black sink of iniquity,* war is a *black crime against humanity,* Englishmen were stuffed into the *Black Hole of Calcutta.* The loss of a football game is a *black day* for the Navy; to anticipate such a loss is to *look on the black side of things.* To fail to mow one's lawn is to receive a *black mark* in the community. We are *black-balled* at the club, *blackmailed* by our onetime friends, and *blacklisted* by our enemies.[26]

If you study our language from this angle, you may begin to see the rationale behind such expressions as "Black is beautiful."

One of the few empirical studies of word power is an examination of how a speaker's use of profane words affects our judgments about his credibility.[27] (See Chapter 11 for a discussion of credibility.) Three classes of profanity were used: religious, excretory, and sexual. The experimenters hypothesized that religious profanity would be least offensive and referred to it as "mild usage"; sexual profanity was referred to as "extreme usage." Subjects were asked to rate speakers who included various degrees of profanity in their messages. Under some conditions the speaker seemed to be provoked by the circumstances surrounding the speech; at other times the profanity seemed unjustified. Although religious profanity was less offensive when circumstances appeared to justify it, sexual profanity—whether provoked or unprovoked—always seemed to bring the speakers significantly lower credibility ratings. These results are surprisingly consistent: they are the same for males and females, older and younger women, and freshmen and graduate students.

In addition to affecting our feelings, words may have a direct effect on the way we behave. Novelist Herbert Gold was advised by one publisher that any book with the word "virgin" in the title would automatically receive an advance of $25,000—presumably because the book's sale was guaranteed. In other words, sometimes our decisions are based in part on how a thing is labeled.

Some words clearly have greater prestige than others. The same desk commands different prices when it is called "used," "secondhand," or "antique." "Doctor" is another powerful word. For years the basic law degree was called a "bachelor of laws," or "LL.B." Early in the 1960s, some law schools began to call the same degree by a more prestigious title: *juris doctor* ("doctor of law"), or "J.D." By 1969 more than 100 of the nation's 150 law schools had switched over and were granting J.D.s instead of LL.B.s. In the meantime J.D.s were getting better job offers than LL.B.s.

Diplomats and politicians are particularly sensitive to how they use words, but sometimes they slip up. In 1964 Barry Goldwater's use of the word "extremism" caused him no end of political grief. George Romney's statement about being "brainwashed" by the American military while in Vietnam had a disastrous effect on his political image. A public career can also be damaged if opponents come up with a negative label that sticks. The description of the late Adlai Stevenson as an "egghead" undoubtedly did him some harm during the presidential campaign.

Sometimes special-interest groups attempt to use words for their own purposes. Maddocks describes this well when he writes about "the monstrous insensitivity that allows generals to call war 'pacification,' union leaders to describe strikes or slow-downs as 'job actions,' and politicians to applaud even moderately progressive programs as 'revolutions.' "[28] Advertisers want to know which brand names are appealing because market research has shown that the same product often sells differently under different names.

When we are swayed by a speaker's choice of language rather than by the content of his message, we do react to words as if they had magical powers. Perhaps it is reasonable to expect that we will behave this way occasionally. Nevertheless we can learn to keep this behavior in check if we remember that when we fail to distinguish between symbols and their referents, we forfeit our ability to think clearly.

Single Meanings

A common cause of breakdown in communication is the assumption that a word, a phrase, or even a sentence has only one meaning. There seem to be two sources of confusion about words or phrases.

First, two people may assume that because they are using the same word, they agree, when in fact each of them interprets the word differently. In a comical incident a woman asks a pharmacist for a refill of her prescription for "the pill." "Please hurry," she adds, "I've got someone waiting in the car." Much humor is based on such double meanings. In daily communication this type of confusion may not be so funny. For example, one of the authors and spouse—and we're not saying which one—were drawn into a needless argument:

HUSBAND: You know, the travel literature on Switzerland that I borrowed is still in the house. Since we're not going I'd better return it to that fellow in my office. Could you get it together for me so I can take it in tomorrow?

WIFE: I don't know where it is.

HUSBAND: What kind of an answer is that? If it's too much trouble, forget it.

WIFE: What do you mean, "What kind of an answer is that?" How can I do anything with it if I can't find it?

HUSBAND: There's nothing to *do*. All I asked you to do was find it. You don't have to give me a smart answer.

WIFE: But you said "get it together." I thought you meant put it in some sort of order.

HUSBAND: I meant "find it." Don't you know what "get it together" means?

WIFE: Well, I didn't know it meant *that*.

HUSBAND: If you didn't know, why didn't you ask me?

WIFE: Because I thought I knew. I speak English too, you know.

For a time this misunderstanding created a lot of ill feeling. Both husband and wife were insulted—the husband because he felt his wife had refused to do something relatively simple for him, and the wife because she felt her husband had insulted her intelligence.

A second type of misunderstanding about the meaning of a given word occurs when two people assume that they disagree because they are using different words when actually they may agree on the concept or entity represented by those words. That is, they use different terms that have the same referent. This heated discussion between two college professors was due to just such a semantic breakdown:

PROFESSOR WILLIAMS: Are we having a meeting at lunch?

PROFESSOR ROSS: Well, it isn't exactly a meeting. It's a seminar.

PROFESSOR WILLIAMS: (a little angry) Then we are having a meeting.

PROFESSOR ROSS: No, it's a seminar.

PROFESSOR WILLIAMS: (walking away) Thanks, I call that a meeting.

PROFESSOR ROSS: (yelling after him angrily) Good for you. I call it a seminar.

As it turned out, to Professor Williams "meeting" meant getting together with other faculty members; to Professor Ross "meeting" meant solving problems as opposed to presenting research papers. Yet neither was flexible enough to ask the other what he meant by his term.

There are two ways in which we can minimize the problems just described. First, we should acknowledge that the symbols we use may or may not be meaningful to the receiver of the message—that any symbol can be interpreted ambiguously. Second, we have to grant the possibility that our own interpretation of a given word is not necessarily superior to another person's. When people cannot agree to use the same words for the same ideas, they tend to get angry with one another. Even if it becomes clear that they are talking about the same thing, each thinks that the other should switch to the word he himself prefers. Neither is likely to give in until one requests that they stop and define their terms.

Although in this chapter our attention has been given to words or phrases, most messages take the form of sentences. "It's a rainy day," remarks Jack to Jill. What could be clearer than the meaning of that sentence? Yet Laing suggests five ways in which Jack might intend his statement. Perhaps he wishes to register the fact that it is a rainy day. If yesterday Jack and Jill agreed to go for a walk instead of going to a movie, he might be saying that because of the rain he will probably get to see the movie. He might be implying that because of the weather Jill should stay at home. If yesterday the two argued about what the weather would be like, he might mean that Jill is right again or that he is the one who always predicts the weather correctly. If the window is open, he might be saying that he would like Jill to close it.[29] No doubt each of us could come up with several other interpretations. The point is that any message derives a great part of its meaning from the context in which it is transmitted. Our knowledge of the speaker and of how he uses language, our own associations with the words he chooses, our previous relationship, and the messages we have already exchanged should all play a part in how we interpret what is said.

Although all our behaviors have possible meaning for a receiver, language is by far our most explicit form of communication. In using it our desire is to facilitate thought, not to obscure it. Language is potentially the most precise vehicle we have for interpersonal communication, and few have written of this potential more eloquently than the linguist Edward Sapir:

> Everything that we have so far seen to be true of language points to the fact that it is the most significant and colossal work that the human spirit has evolved—nothing short of a finished form of expression for all communicable experience. This form may be endlessly varied by the individual without thereby losing its distinctive contours; and it is constantly reshaping itself as is all art. Language is the most massive and inclusive art we know, a mountainous and anonymous work of unconscious generations.[30]

Summary

Our analysis of verbal communication began and ended with a consideration of the concept of meaning. In discussing the symbolic nature of language, we saw that symbols and referents are associated with each other only by convention and that it is men who assign meanings to words. We reviewed the traditional distinction between denotation and connotation and suggested that it might also be useful to distinguish between private and shared meanings.

Our second subject was message encoding, which we approached through a comparison of the encoding abilities of children and adults. Piaget's research on socialized and egocentric speech and other research on social and nonsocial encoding make it clear that the speaker's perceptions and expectations about the listener affect his ability to communicate accurately.

Our last concern was the relationship between thought and language, and here we examined several ways in which language can either facilitate or interfere with our thought processes. In our discussion of inferences, dichotomies, word power, and single meanings, we stressed the direct influence that language can have on interpersonal communication.[31]

Review Questions

1. What is meant by the statement "The word is not the thing"?
2. What is the difference between denotation and connotation?
3. Explain the difference between private and shared meanings.
4. What is the distinction between egocentric and socialized speech?
5. What are the differences between a restricted code and an elaborated code?
6. What is the Whorfian hypothesis?
7. What are two ways in which language affects thought?
8. Describe four imprecise uses of language. Give an example of how each affects interpersonal communication.
9. Identify two sources of confusion about words or phrases. Give an example of each and indicate how each can be minimized.

Exercises

1. a. Construct a Semantic Differential consisting of ten bipolar adjectives. Assess the potential marketability of a fictitious product name by asking several classmates to react to the names using the Semantic Differential. The sample scale below shows two names for a Christmas wrapping paper:

	Holly Filigree			**Green Lace**	
good X _ _ _ _ _ bad			good _ _ _ _ X _ bad		
sharp _ X _ _ _ _ dull			sharp _ _ _ _ _ X dull		
active _ _ X _ _ _ passive			active _ _ _ X _ _ passive		
pretty _ _ X _ _ _ ugly			pretty _ _ _ X _ _ ugly		

   b. How do the responses on the Semantic Differential reflect the difference between denotation and connotation; private and shared meaning?

2. Construct a two-column list with proper names in one column and stereotypical occupations associated with those names in the second. Randomize the order of names and occupations in each column. Present the lists to several people and ask them to match the names and occupations. An example of a two-column list appears below:

Bubbles	Policeman
Killer	Stripper
Nick	Librarian
O'Malley	Mobster
Miss Penwinkle	Boxer
Lance	Actor

    a. To what extent do people agree in their responses? How do the results relate to the statement "The word is not the thing"?

    b. How do the results relate to the three factors that affect stereotype perceptions (see Objective 4, Chapter 4)?

    c. What implications do these results suggest about the relationship between language, stereotyping, and communication effectiveness?

3. Interview two people who are ostensibly very different—a hard-hat sympathizer and a left-wing radical, for example. Ask each of them to make a list of adjectives describing (a) himself and (b) a member of the other group. Compare the lists to see how differently each group member perceives himself from the way he is perceived by the other person. Notice how the perceptual differences are manifested in the words chosen for the descriptions.

4. Prepare an oral persuasive message in two forms. Use the most tactful language possible in one and the most inflammatory terms you can think of in the other. Give the messages to two groups, and try to assess their reactions on an attitude scale. Which message is more effective? If the audiences are similar and your messages alike except for word choice (and assuming the nonverbal cues are similar), any difference in your results should be due to the difference in the language you use.

5. In a chance conversation deliberately assume that individual words have only one meaning, and try to interpret them in a way that the other person does not intend. What are the results?

Suggested Readings

Haney, William V. *Communication and Organizational Behavior.* 3rd ed. Homewood, Ill.: Irwin, 1973. This classic book represents an excellent overview of the field of study referred to as general semantics. Although the book's slant is on the business environment, its principles apply to most everyday situations. The cases which are included make excellent class discussion starters.

Mercer, Jane R. "The Lethal Label." *Psychology Today* (September 1972), 6:44–46, 96, 97. This article is part of an issue investigating "I.Q. Abuse." The series emphasizes the importance of language in intelligence tests and of labeling children on the basis of test scores. The written IQ test is largely oriented toward the white middle class, which causes many minority children to be classed as "retarded" and placed in special-education classes. Mercer's studies, using a cross-section of children and adults in Riverside, California, result in a way to test a subject, not only for academic ability, but to see how well he gets along in everyday situations—behavioral ability.

Premack, David. "The Education of Sarah." *Psychology Today* (September 1970), 4:54–58. After a brief discussion of the function of language, highlighting its symbolic nature, the article outlines the methods for teaching Sarah, a chimpanzee, to "talk" using different shaped plastic pieces as "words." Gradually she learns a vocabulary of about 120 words, and ends up understanding enough to ask questions and give short word tests to her trainers.

Notes

[1] Lewis Carroll, *Through the Looking Glass and What Alice Found There* (New York: Random House, 1965), pp. 93–94.

[2] Thomas Long, "Tek-nol'o-ji and Its Effect on Language," *Space Digest,* March 1969, p. 87.

[3] Paul Sithi-Amuai, "The Asian Mind," *Asia,* Spring 1968, pp. 78–91.

[4] Adapted from *The Random House Dictionary of the English Language: College Edition,* ed. by Laurence Urdang and others (New York: Random House, 1969), p. 1516.

[5] Colin Cherry, *On Human Communication,* 2nd ed. (Cambridge, Mass.: M.I.T. Press, 1966), p. 71.

[6] Israel Shenker, "If hous'wif' Becomes Obs., What Is There to Take Its Place?", *The New York Times,* February 9, 1972, p. 26.

[7] William Arnold and Roger Libby, "The Semantics of Sex Related Terms" (paper delivered at the annual convention of the Speech Communication Association, Chicago, December 1970), p. 5.

[8] Loren Crane, Richard Dieker, and Charles Brown, "The Physiological Response to the Communication Modes: Reading, Listening, Writing, Speaking, and Evaluating," *Journal of Communication,* 20 (1970), 231–240.

[9] Charles Osgood, George Suci, and Percy Tannenbaum, *The Measurement of Meaning* (Urbana, Ill.: University of Illinois Press, 1957), chaps. 1–4.

[10] James Deese, *Psycholinguistics* (Boston: Allyn & Bacon, 1970), p. 106. Italics added.

[11] Deese, p. 126.

[12] Adapted from David Smith and Clark Sturges, "The Semantics of the San Francisco Drug Scene," *Etc: A Review of General Semantics,* 26 (1969), 168–175.

[13] Dean C. Barnlund, *Interpersonal Communication: Survey and Studies* (Boston: Houghton Mifflin, 1968), p. 9.

[14] For an introduction to this subject from the psycholinguistic point of view, see F. Smith and G. A. Miller (eds.), *The Genesis of Language: A Psycholinguistic Approach* (Cambridge, Mass.: M.I.T. Press, 1966).

[15] Jean Piaget, *The Language and Thought of the Child,* tr. by Marjorie Gabain (New York: Meridian, 1955), p. 60.

[16] Piaget, p. 44.

[17] Piaget, p. 60.

[18] Robert M. Krauss, "The Interpersonal Regulation of Behavior," in Dwain N. Walcher (ed.), *Early Childhood: The Development of Self-Regulatory Mechanisms* (New York: Academic, 1971), pp. 187–208.

[19] Basil Bernstein, "A Sociolinguistic Approach to Socialization: With Some Reference to Educability," in Frederick Williams (ed.), *Language and Poverty: Perspectives on a Theme* (Chicago: Markham, 1970), p. 37.

[20] Benjamin Lee Whorf, *Language, Thought, and Reality,* ed. by John B. Carroll (Cambridge, Mass.: M.I.T. Press, 1956).

[21] Roger Brown, *Words and Things: An Introduction to Language* (New York: Free Press, 1958), pp. 236–237.

[22] Roger Brown and Eric H. Lenneberg, "A Study in Language and Cognition," *Journal of Abnormal and Social Psychology,* 49 (1954), 454–462.

[23] Whorf, p. 135.

[24] William V. Haney, *Communication and Organizational Behavior,* 3rd ed. (Homewood, Ill.: Irwin, 1973), p. 374.

[25] Wm. Walter Duncan, "How White Is Your Dictionary?", *Etc.: A Review of General Semantics,* 27 (1970), 89–91.

[26] John Haller, "The Semantics of Color," *Etc.: A Review of General Semantics,* 26 (1969), 203.

[27] Charles Rossiter and Robert Bostrom, "Profanity, 'Justification,' and Source Credibility" (paper delivered at the annual conference of the National Society for the Study of Communication, Cleveland, 1968).

[28] Melvin Maddocks, "The Limitations of Language," *Time,* March 8, 1971, p. 36.

[29] R. D. Laing, *Self and Others,* 2nd rev. ed. (New York: Pantheon, 1969), pp. 139–140.

[30] Edward Sapir, *Language: An Introduction to the Study of Speech* (New York: Harcourt, Brace, 1921), pp. 219–220.

[31] See Stewart L. Tubbs, "An Introduction to General Semantics," *Kansas Speech Journal,* 29 (1967), 5–10.

Chapter 7 The Nonverbal Message

OBJECTIVES

After reading this chapter the student should be able to:

1. Distinguish between sign language, action language, and object language.

2. Identify four kinds of interpersonal distance and give an example of each.

3. State four rules about eye contact.

4. Identify three categories of nonverbal courtship behavior and give an example of each.

5. State the relationship between head and body movements in communicating emotion.

6. Describe how a person's clothes communicate messages to others.

7. Define paralinguistics and give examples of paralinguistic cues.

8. Identify four categories of emotion consistently identified by paralinguistic cues.

9. Identify three ways in which nonverbal messages relate to verbal messages.

10. Define double bind and describe how it relates to nonverbal and verbal communication.

7

In silent films wordless communication reached the perfection of an art form. Take this scene from one of Harry Langdon's movies: ". . . watching a brazen showgirl change her clothes, he sat motionless, back to the camera, and registered the whole lexicon of lost innocence, shock, disapproval and disgust with the back of his neck."[1]

Each of the silent comedians had a style all his own. Buster Keaton played every role with an absolutely blank face. Harold Lloyd portrayed a meek soul with glasses; sometimes he looked rather like a schoolboy. Charlie Chaplin was the beloved tramp: everything about him seemed comic and endearing—his shy smile, ill-fitting suit, cane, and funny gait. Without words these actors were able to communicate not only isolated ideas but complete sequences of behavior. We are not speaking here only of comic experience. The Russian film maker Sergei Eisenstein was masterful in his treatment of social and political themes, and even the silent comedians could bring their audiences to tears.

Actors and directors have to be keen observers of nonverbal communication, and mimes of course have been students of human expression for hundreds of years. But what about the rest of us? We are not actors. Yet unwittingly we are fairly skilled observers—and performers. Even though we may be unaware of much of it, nonverbal communication is going on all the time.

Jurgen Ruesch, a psychiatrist, and Weldon Kees, a film producer, were two of the first people to devote themselves to a serious study of nonverbal communication in daily experience. They suggest that we express nonverbal messages in one of three languages: sign language, action language, or object language.[2]

We are using **sign language** when we deliberately use *gestures to replace words, numbers, or punctuation marks*. The gesture can be as simple as the peace sign or the hitchhiker's signal or as complex as the system of signals motorists use while driving.

Ruesch and Kees classify as **action language** *all the movements that we do not use exclusively as signals*—walking, running, eating, and so on. Many if not most of these actions are unintentional nonverbal stimuli. For example, if while walking your head droops and your shoulders sag, your posture expresses your mood. If you slam your fist on a table during a stalemated argument, your action conveys anger and frustration very directly. Action language is the principal means of expressing emotion.

Object language is *the intentional or unintentional display of mate-*

143

144   *rial things*—art objects, machines, clothing, jewelry, and so on. A social worker who appears in a ghetto neighborhood driving a big car and wearing expensive clothes is obviously using the wrong language if he hopes to establish rapport with the residents.

Again and again we find forms of nonverbal communication described in terms of language. Thus we hear that someone "talks" with his hands or that his gesture made a powerful "statement." One writer reminds us that

> We communicate every minute of the day with others and the outside world through "speaking" gestures, peculiarities in gait and dress, a sense of touch while shaking hands, the mannerisms of another person's glance or looks, the condition and texture of his skin, the color of his eyes, his lips, his body build and a multitude of similar bodily characteristics.[3]

Haiman refers to the sit-ins, mass marches, silent vigils, black arm bands, hair styles, and clothing of the 1960s as a form of "body rhetoric."[4] One popularist has written a book called *Body Language*. Anthropologist Edward T. Hall refers to "the silent language of space and time."[5]

There are so many special studies of this sort that we can think of nonverbal communication as made up of many different languages. Regardless of how we classify them, however, these languages have at least one thing in common. They all provide us with cues for interpreting human behavior. In this chapter we are going to speak about nonverbal cues rather than languages, and we shall begin with a closer look at how the word "cue" is used.

One of the broadest dictionary definitions of **cue** is *anything that excites to action; stimulus*. In the theater a cue is "anything said or done, on or behind the stage, that is followed by a specific line or action." If you fail to respond to a cue or you miss the point someone is making, you are said to "miss a cue." You "cue someone in" by giving him news, instructions, or information. A cue is also defined as *a hint or intimation,* and this definition is important to our discussion.

Psychologists often use the word "cue" (or "sign") in place of "signal."

> We ask what "cues" a rat follows in finding his way through a maze, and we seek an answer by depriving him of visual cues, olfactory cues, etc. This convenient word has spread from the animal to the human laboratory so that we speak of visual cues of distance and of auditory cues of direction, when perhaps the word "clue" would be more in accordance with general usage. . . .[6]

This suggestion that "clue" may be a more appropriate word brings us back to the dictionary definition of cue as "a hint or intimation." Through their nonverbal messages people give us many clues, or hints, about their emotions, their intentions, their personalities, and even their social status. In this chapter we shall speak about three kinds of cues—cultural, visual, and vocal—and then about the broader issue of how we interpret these cues and what their relationship is to verbal messages.

CULTURAL CUES

Only when we meet people of other cultures (and unfortunately some of us never have) do we realize that some of our most cherished ideas about what is appropriate conduct are **norms**, or *rules about behavior*; that is, they are relative, not absolute, values. Indirectly our culture teaches us to communicate in many ways—through our voices, our hand gestures, and even our clothing. Yet each of us interprets and expresses these conventions somewhat differently. Culture has an even more subtle and pervasive influence on nonverbal communication, however. Each culture continually provides its people with input about how the world is structured. Slowly we develop preconceptions about the world. It is the cues derived from these preconceptions that we take most for granted and that imperceptibly set the limits for our style of communication.

Space

If you were to enter a restaurant with only one customer in it, chances are that you would not sit down right next to him. Hall explains that though this behavior seems natural to an American, an Arab might have a very different notion of appropriate distance between strangers. Students of nonverbal communication are indebted to Hall for his cross-cultural studies of space. Because of his work we probably know more about this dimension of cultural experience than we do about time, color, and many other factors.

Hall has given the special name of **proxemics** to *the study of space*. We spoke in Chapter 5 about the Scale of Social Distance, an instrument that uses the term "distance" figuratively, to indicate degree of liking or preference. Hall goes a step further and speaks of measurable distances between people—1½ inches, 1 foot, 3 feet, and so on. In fact, he offers a four-part classification of distances between people. There is nothing arbitrary about this classification, as he explains:

> . . . it is in the nature of animals, including man, to exhibit behavior which we call territoriality. In so doing, they use the senses to distinguish between one space or distance and another. The specific distance chosen depends on the transaction; the relationship of the interacting individuals, how they feel, and what they are doing.[7]

Human relationships are described in terms of four kinds of distance: intimate, personal, social, and public. Each of the four distance zones is further differentiated by a close phase and a far phase within

146   which different behaviors occur. Let us take a look at these four distances and Hall's findings about what they mean to most North Americans.

At **intimate distance**, which is *18 inches or less,* the presence of another person "is unmistakable and may at times be overwhelming because of the greatly stepped-up sensory inputs." In its close phase (6 inches or less) intimate distance lends itself primarily to nonverbal communication. Any subject discussed is usually top secret. The far phase (6 to 18 inches) is often used for discussing confidential matters, with the voice usually kept to a whisper. Such close proximity is considered improper for public places, though dormitories at closing hours seem to be exceptions to the rule. In general, Americans try hard to avoid close contact with one another on buses and other public vehicles.

Hall compares **personal distance**, which is from *1½ to 4 feet,* to "a small protective sphere or bubble that an organism maintains between itself and others." Topics discussed would still be personal. The close phase (1½ to 2½ feet) is still a distance reserved for very close relationships; the far phase (2½ to 4 feet) is a comfortable distance for conversing with friends.

Social distance, ranging from *4 to 12 feet,* is described as a psychological distance, "one at which the animal apparently begins to feel anxious when he exceeds its limits. We can think of it as a hidden band that *contains* the group." The close phase (4 to 7 feet) is suitable for business discussions and conversations at social gatherings. The far phase (7 to 12 feet) is appropriate for meetings in a business office. People who are in the room but outside the 7-foot boundary can be ignored without being offended. Those who violate the 7-foot boundary tend to be surprised if we do not acknowledge their presence, unless we are very busy. Man has extended social distance by means of the walkie-talkie, telephone, radio, and television.

The largest of the zones, **public distance**, denotes *12 feet or more* of space, and it exists only in human relationships. In fact, the public relationships and manners of Americans and Europeans are considerably different from those of other cultures. At the close phase (12 to 25 feet) a more formal style of language and a louder voice are required. At the far phase (25 feet or more) further accommodations to distance are usually made; experienced public speakers exaggerate body movements, gestures, enunciation, and volume while reducing their rate of speech.

Even within a culture, groups of people use space differently. Baxter's study of Anglo-, black, and Mexican-Americans shows sizable differences in how members of different ethnic groups in one culture interact.[8] Mexicans stand closest to one another, Anglos are intermediate, and blacks are most distant. Age and sex also make differences. Children interact at the closest range and adults at the greatest, with spacing between adolescents intermediate. The range in male-female groups is closest and in male-male groups greatest, with female-female groups intermediate.

Hall and Baxter are not saying that we calculate these differences while communicating. On the contrary, our sense of what distance is natural for a given interaction is so deeply ingrained in us by our culture that we automatically make spatial adjustments and interpret spatial cues. Frenchmen, Latin Americans, and Arabs, for example, stand so close to each other that if they exercise their own distance norms while conversing with an American, they arouse hostile or sexual feelings. If you want to test this concept in proxemics, the next time you converse with someone, keep inching toward him. See how close you can get before he starts backing away.

Time

Have you ever written a letter to a friend only to wait what seems an endless time for a reply? What inferences do you make about the strength of the friendship? Or have you ever received a phone call at 3 in the morning? You probably thought that it was a very important call, a wrong number, or a prank. How far in advance can a first date be arranged? Must it be several days ahead, or can one call thirty minutes before? In each of these cases, timing leads to certain expectations on the part of the people involved, and these expectations influence the interpersonal communication that subsequently occurs. A late entrance that violates standards of courtesy can have a disastrous effect, not just a dramatic one. Much of the verbal communication that ensues may have to be spent explaining away the nonverbal message that has already been conveyed.

Conceptions of what is "late" or "early" vary from culture to culture. Americans are "busy" people. We use our watches throughout the day. We like schedules and agendas. We value doing things "on time." To us five years might be a long period. To Asians a long time is more like a thousand years. (Think what differences in point of view toward the length of war must be.) It is sometimes disarming to see ourselves as others see us. Here is a Brazilian reaction to "Anglo-American" time:

> The rigid Anglo-Saxon attitude—"Time is money"—with an almost mystical cult of minutes and seconds on account of their practical, commercial value, is in sharp contrast to the Latin American attitude, a sort of "more-or-less" ("*mais ou menos*") attitude. It is easy to understand why a Nordic was so shocked in Spain to know that a Spanish or Latin American guest in a hotel asked the desk to call him next morning not exactly at ten or ten-fifteen, as an Anglo-Saxon or an Anglo-American would have asked, but at ten or eleven. . . .[9]

Hall relates an amusing anecdote about a friend of Spanish extraction whose business affairs were managed "Latino" style:

This meant that up to fifteen people were in his office at one time. Business which might have been finished in a quarter of an hour sometimes took a whole day. He realized, of course, that the Anglo-Americans were disturbed by this and used to make some allowance for them, a dispensation which meant that they spent only an hour or so in his office when they planned on a few minutes. . . . If my friend had adhered to the American system he would have destroyed a vital part of his prosperity. People who came to do business with him also came to find out things and to visit each other.[10]

Gurvitch, a French sociologist, believes that each country has its own time or tempo. This argument seems well taken. If we could just remember that "Time in France is not identical with time in Norway nor with time in Brazil,"[11] our political, economic, and social relationships with other countries would rapidly improve. Even for personal effectiveness with people of our own culture, we need to be more aware of time as an aspect of communication.

VISUAL CUES

At the end of the nineteenth century, a German horse named Hans was discovered who ostensibly knew how to add. If you asked him to add 2 and 6, for example, he pawed the ground eight times. The curious thing was that Hans could do sums only in the presence of human beings. His mysterious talent was later explained rather simply: when he unwittingly reached the answer, he saw his audience relax, and he stopped pawing.

The people who came to see Hans perform would have been shocked to learn that they were, by their body movements, transmitting the correct answers visually. Yet they were probably leaning forward eagerly to take in every aspect of the spectacle before them, for we all know how much we gain by seeing a performer, a lecturer, or any person we are speaking to. In fact, one study found that members of discussion groups interacted more frequently when seated facing each other rather than side by side.[12] In other words, the greater the visibility, the greater our potential for communicating. And as we saw in Chapter 2, the greater the number of channels we use in communication, the more information we receive.

Visual cues add to the information transmitted through other channels and at times stand alone. Specific motions of the head, for example, give the equivalents of certain brief verbal messages such as "Yes" and "No," and these movements may vary from culture to culture. Even head orientation, the direction in which we turn our heads, communicates something. Defining head orientation as the percentage of time two people direct their faces toward each other, Mehrabian found that a person who gives more head orientation to the person he speaks with conveys to the second person a more positive feeling.[13] Reece and Whitman support this conclusion in their study of how "warmth" and "coldness" are conveyed during an interview: "Leaning toward the subject, smiling, and looking directly at him enabled the subject to judge the experimenter as warm. Conversely, looking away from the subject, leaning away from him, not smiling, and intermittently drumming the fingers on the table impressed the subject as coldness."[14]

Notice that the nonverbal cues described include facial expression, eye contact, and body movements. We shall be discussing each of these sources of information. We ask you to bear in mind, however, that when you look at another person, you get a total impression. We separate various cues here only to examine the kind of information that each conveys.

Facial Expression

One of the things that made Buster Keaton's silent films so hilarious was his facial expression—or rather his lack of expression. He was the original deadpan. Film critic James Agee describes his style this way:

> He used this great, sad, motionless face to suggest various related things: a one-track mind near the track's end of pure insanity; mulish imperturbability under the wildest of circumstances; how dead a human being can get and still be alive. . . . Everything that he was and did bore out this rigid face and played laughs against it. When he moved his eyes, it was like seeing them move in a statue. . . .[15]

Keaton must have had superb control over his facial muscles. Most of us couldn't manage a poker face for very long. In fact, the human face is so mobile that it can effortlessly register boredom, surprise, affection, and disapproval one after another in a few seconds. This brief scene from *War and Peace*, for example, probably takes place in less than one minute:

> On the way to his sister's room, in the gallery that united one house to the other, Prince Andrey encountered Mademoiselle Bourienne smiling sweetly. It was the third time that day that with an innocent and enthusiastic smile she had thrown herself in his way in secluded passages.
> "Ah, I thought you were in your room," she said, for some reason blushing and casting down her eyes. Prince Andrey looked sternly at her. A sudden look of wrathful exasperation came into his face. He said nothing to her, but stared at her forehead and her hair, without looking at her eyes, with such contempt that the Frenchwoman crimsoned and went away without a word.[16]

With the exception of one sentence, almost all the communication that takes place is conveyed by means of facial cues. Yet the episode seems realistic because even in less dramatic encounters, we constantly read expressions from people's faces. In fact, facial cues are the single most important source of nonverbal communication.

It has been learned that we tend to describe faces in terms of a general evaluative dimension (good or bad, beautiful or ugly, kind or cruel, and so on) and a dynamism dimension (active or passive, inert or mobile, interesting or boring).[17] And apparently some people are much more adept than others at interpreting facial cues.

So we like a face or we don't; we think it is animated or relatively inert. These are general impressions. But what do we see that makes us judge someone to be sad or happy or frightened or angry? Isolating which facial cues specify particular emotions is more difficult. In one attempt to decipher a facial code, subjects were shown simple illustrations (pictomorphs) such as those in Figure 12. A statistical analysis of the results led to the conclusions that half-raised eyebrows indicate worry; a single raised eyebrow, skepticism; half-closed eyes, boredom; closed eyes, sleep; an upcurved mouth, happiness; and a downcurved mouth, unhappiness.[18] We are reminded of the smile button, which has become so popular; its brief suggestion of a face—pinpoints for eyes and a single upcurved line for the mouth—is enough to suggest to most people a happy face.

Figure 12

The study of facial cues as expressions of specific emotions has a long history. One of the most eminent scientists to examine this subject was Charles Darwin. Darwin set himself an even larger task: he tried to find out whether the facial behaviors associated with particular emotions are universal. One method he used was to ask subjects to identify specific emotions from still photographs of people's faces. In *The Expression of the Emotions in Man and Animals,* published in 1872, Darwin presented some of his conclusions and speculations about expressive behavior. He felt that most of man's expressive actions, like those of other animals, are instinctive, not learned behaviors:

> So little has learning or imitation to do with several of them that they are from the earliest days and throughout life quite beyond our control; for instance, the relaxation of the arteries of the skin in blushing, and the increased action of the heart in anger. We may see children, only two or three years old, and even those born blind, blushing from shame. . . .[19]

Darwin's argument about the facial expressions of blind children is given further support by several studies done more than half a century after his book was published. The facial behaviors of blind and sighted children seem to have many similarities. More recently Ekman and Friesen asked members of a preliterate New Guinea culture to judge emotions from the facial expressions of Westerners. The subjects had had virtually no exposure to Western culture either through direct experience or, because they were unable to read, through literature. Yet they made the same identifications that Westerners made, with one exception: they were not able to differentiate between fear and surprise. Ekman and Friesen conclude that, at least in some respects, emotional facial behavior is constant across cultures. They acknowledge that cultural differences exist, but they argue that the differences are reflected "in the circumstances which elicit an emotion, in the action consequences of an emotion and in the display rules which govern the management of facial behavior in particular social settings."[20]

Other experts on nonverbal communication, including Ray Birdwhistell and Weston La Barre, argue against the possibility of universal facial cues. The issue is far from settled. Experimental evidence is scarce and somewhat contradictory. Several researchers report negative results with techniques such as still photographs and illustrations that reveal only the face. Generally, accuracy in identifying emotion seems to increase with the number of cues one sees.

Eye Contact

Proper street behavior among Americans permits passers-by to look at each other until they are about 8 feet apart. At this point both parties cast their eyes downward so that they will not appear to be staring. Goffman refers to this phenomenon as a "dimming of our lights."[21] The many other rules implicit in our culture about looking at others are a tacit admission that eye contact is perhaps the single most important facial cue we use in communicating.

One psychologist estimates that in group communication we spend 30 to 60 percent of the time in eye contact with others (10 to 30 percent of the looks last only about a second). He sums up several of the unstated rules about eye contact:

a. A looker may invite interaction by staring at another person who is on the other side of a room. The target's studied return of the gaze is generally interpreted as acceptance of the invitation, while averting the eyes is a rejection of the looker's request.

b. There is more mutual eye contact between friends than others, and a looker's frank gaze is widely interpreted as positive regard.

c. Persons who seek eye contact while speaking are regarded not only as exceptionally well-disposed by their target, but also as more believable and earnest.

d. If the usual short, intermittent gazes during conversation are replaced by gazes of longer duration, the target interprets this as meaning that the task is less important than the personal relation between the two persons.[22]

Argyle's second point is corroborated by other researchers: frequent eye contact does seem to be a sign of affection or interest. One study showed that when an audience gave a speaker negative feedback (including poor eye contact), he tended to lose his fluency and to do poorly in his presentation.[23] It has also been discovered that audiences prefer speakers who give good eye contact.[24]

Why is eye contact so rewarding to others? Perhaps it is because the eyes are considered such a valuable source of information. Hess found that Chinese jade dealers watch the eyes of their prospective customers for interest in a particular stone because the pupils enlarge with increased interest; similarly magicians are able to tell what card a person is thinking about by studying his eyes. Hess' studies confirm that pupil size is indeed a sensitive index of interest.[25]

There are other popular beliefs about what can be learned from watching someone's eyes. For example, two people who exchange knowing glances at a party seem able to communicate without words. Being able to look another person in the eye traditionally implies that you are being truthful and that your intentions are not to be questioned. Conversely it is said that someone who averts his eyes is hiding something. These beliefs are not always borne out by experience, however. High Machs are able to sustain good eye contact even when telling lies.

Body Movements

If during a party you were asked to record and classify all the body movements of two people in conversation during a five-minute period, you would probably think this an impossible task. Nothing short of a film could capture the rapid, often subtle changes of the body even during so brief a time. Much of what we know about **kinesics**, Birdwhistell's term for *the study of body movements,* has come to us indirectly, from such disciplines as anthropology, psychiatry, and psychotherapy.

The work of Scheflen is a case in point. He noticed that patterns of nonverbal flirting, or "quasi-courtship," emerged during psychotherapy. After studying films of a great many therapy sessions, he was able to classify some of the typical behaviors he observed. Signs of **courtship readiness** included preening hair, pulling at stockings, adjusting the tie, and so on. **Positioning** was another source of cues about interpersonal attraction. For example, two people might face each other and lean forward eagerly. Sometimes they sat with the upper half of their torsos turned in an open position so that a third person might enter the conversation but with their legs forming a circle and thus excluding the intruder. A third category, **actions of appeal**, included flirtatious glances and head cocking. Women signaled sexual invitation by crossing the legs, exposing the thigh, exhibiting the palm of the hand, and protruding the breast. Here is an example of these behaviors in context:

> At the beginning of the sequence . . . the therapist . . . turns to watch an attractive research technician walk across the room. The patient [female] begins to preen. . . . The therapist turns back to the patient and also preens, but he then disclaims courtship by an ostentatious look of boredom and a yawn. . . . Immediately afterward, the patient tells him she is interested in an attractive male aide.[26]

Courtship behaviors occur in many other settings, such as business conferences, neighborhood parties, and other social gatherings. If we omit people's identities in the sequence just described, the scene could easily have taken place during a university seminar, an interview, or a committee meeting. Scheflen's observation that courtship behaviors tend to occur most often when a person feels he is not receiving enough attention can probably be extended to many interpersonal relationships.

An interesting question raised by Ekman is whether body movements convey information different from that given by head and facial cues. His findings suggest that the head and face tell us what emotion is being experienced and the body indicates how intense that emotion is. The hands, however, can give us information such as that we receive from the head and face.[27]

Hand Gestures

Anthropologists distinguish man from other animals by his use of language and also by his superior manual dexterity. His flexible hands have enabled him to use tools and to draw on a wide range of gestures in communicating. It is not surprising, therefore, that as a mode of nonverbal communication, hand gestures rank second in importance only to facial cues.

Although it is said that some people "talk" with their hands, it is not only broad, expansive gestures that communicate mood. Less animated people often communicate inadvertently by means of their hands. The rather reserved husband of a psychotherapist we know repeatedly drums his fingers on a table or chair whenever his wife speaks about her practice. This behavior is the only sign of his impatience with her deep involvement in her profession.

In his analysis of foot, head, and hand movements of mental patients under treatment in hospitals, Ekman was able to distinguish more than 100 different hand acts. Coding them along with the other body movements, he discovered that from the time of the patient's admission to his discharge, his hand movements corresponded with various stages of his treatment.[28]

154   Hand gestures sometimes substitute for verbal communication. For example, solely by means of his hands, one person can give another instruction on how to park a car. Deaf-mutes use a system of hand signals so comprehensive that it literally replaces spoken language. The signals themselves are arbitrary. It seems, for example, that many of our hand movements are culturally determined. Thus the same gesture can convey different things to members of different cultures. La Barre offers some interesting examples:

> Placing to the tip of the nose the projecting knuckle of the right forefinger bent at the second joint was among the Maori of New Zealand a sign of friendship and often of protection; but in eighteenth-century England the placing of the same forefinger to the right side of the nose expressed dubiousness about the intelligence and sanity of a speaker— much as does the twentieth-century clockwise motion of the forefinger above the right hemisphere of the head.[29]

Such differences in meaning are a potential source of communication difficulty. To an American, for example, making a circle with one's thumb and forefinger and extending the other fingers means "okay," but to a Brazilian it is an obscene sign of contempt. Apparently American visitors and even statesmen unwittingly offend their Brazilian hosts with this gesture.

In addition to what can be learned from observing hand gestures, the tactile cues we receive from hand contact are especially revealing. In our culture we often shake hands upon meeting, and a handshake can set the tone for the exchange that follows. A limp handshake evokes negative feelings in most Americans; we interpret it as a lack of interest or vitality. A moist hand is often considered a sign of anxiety, especially if the handshake precedes a potentially stressful situation such as an interview. Hands, it seems, disclose a great deal more than many of us would care to reveal.

Physical Appearance

Clothes may not make the man, but dress, grooming, and general physical appearance are often the basis of first and relatively long-lasting impressions. As we saw in Chapter 4, even glasses affect the way the wearer is perceived by others. When Ruesch and Kees speak about object language, they include "the human body and whatever clothes or covers it."[30]

Uniforms tell us a great deal about rank and status; many people believe that dress and grooming do too. For example, Lefkowitz, Blake, and Mouton found that people dressed in high-status clothes were more influential in getting others to jaywalk than those who wore low-status clothes.[31] Freedman's study of beards led him to the conclusion that beards make men more appealing to women and give them "more status in the eyes of other men"; he also observed that beards "may increase the social distance between two men."[32]

Sometimes people deliberately attempt to increase social distance. In colonial Brazil people of rank used a parasol to indicate their social status as well as to protect themselves from the sun; their long nails were another sign of superior social standing. Even today we sometimes dress to impress others, to be more like them, or—when we dress counter to prevailing norms—to express rejection of their values.

In our country great emphasis is placed on democratic values so that high-status clothes can be a barrier to communication; as we saw in Chapter 5, people tend to dislike those who differ from themselves. Politicians as a rule are aware of this phenomenon, for on campaign tours they often adopt signs of local dress (ten-gallon hats in Texas, for example) in an effort to be more appealing to voters. Even when worn casually, high-status clothes are noticed by others. Novelist F. Scott Fitzgerald once took a supervisory position at the Northern Pacific car barn. Told to wear old clothes on the job, he turned up wearing a blue cap, a polo shirt, a sweatshirt, and—perhaps most inappropriate— dirty white flannels. The men who worked for him must have been put off by the way he dressed, because Fitzgerald complained about not being able to converse with them. Conditions improved when he came to work in overalls.[33]

VOCAL CUES

"I hate you." Imagine these words being said to show anger or in a much different way to sound seductive. The simple sentence "I'm glad to meet you" can sound cold and insincere despite its verbal message. We make the distinction here between the verbal and the vocal message, between what is said and how it is said. Mehrabian puts it well when he explains vocal information as "what is lost when speech is written down."[34]

To give the study of vocal phenomena a special name, anthropologist George L. Trager has coined the term "paralinguistics." *"Para"* is Greek for beside, near, or beyond; hence **paralinguistics**, or **paralanguage**, refers to *something beyond or in addition to language itself.* According to Trager paralanguage has two principal components: *voice qualities,* such as pitch, range, resonance, lip control, and articulation control; and *vocalizations,* or noises without linguistic structure, such as crying, laughing, and grunting.[35] Our primary concern will be with voice qualities, but we shall touch on vocalizations in our discussion of fluency later in this section.

156   Vocal cues, as we shall see, differentiate emotions and also influence our judgments about personality and social standing. Yet though we are self-conscious about the visual impressions we make on others, we pay little attention to our vocal impressions. There is a good reason for this. If someone is staring at your face, you can look into a mirror and find out what he is staring at. And you probably look into a mirror at least once a day. On the other hand, you never hear your voice as others hear it. The first time you listen to a tape recording of yourself, you are likely to be shocked or disappointed; you may not even recognize your own voice.

Unlike most of us, actors, singers, public speakers, and others who have had voice training are keenly aware of how they sound. For example, Katharine Hepburn sued the makers of Vita Herring products for $4 million because a character named Harriet allegedly imitated her voice in a series of their radio commercials. Miss Hepburn charged that Harriet's voice sounded like her own, which she described as "distinctive with a unique, characteristic quality of sound, style, delivery, pitch, inflection and accent."[36]

In truth, every human voice is distinctive because it is a unique combination of qualities. After discussing some of the information provided by vocal cues, we shall look briefly at four significant voice qualities and their effects on interpersonal communication. Keep in mind, however, that when you speak, all these voice qualities as well as several others are interacting simultaneously.

The Information in Vocal Cues

Intuitively we feel that we can make some judgments from a person's voice about what he is communicating. Perhaps you have been in an argument during which someone said, "Don't answer me in that tone of voice!" At a point like this, tempers really begin to escalate, for an objection to someone's tone of voice is based on inferences about his feelings. Vocal cues are the sources of several kinds of inference, and those that we know most about have to do with emotion.

In contrast to the conflicting evidence about facial cues and specific emotions, studies all seem to support the notion that several distinct emotions can be accurately identified solely on the basis of vocal cues. Several different emotions can be distinguished just from hearing people recite the letters of the alphabet.[37] One study using the alphabet-recital technique shows, however, that the more similar the emotions are to each other (admiration and affection, for example), the greater the difficulty in identifying them.[38]

Much of the research on vocal characteristics and emotions parallels the studies of facial expressions; instead of photographs or illustrations, tape recordings are used. A popular instrument for isolating vocal cues from verbal messages is an electronic filter. The filter eliminates the higher frequencies of recorded speech so that words are unintelligible but most vocal qualities can still be heard. Using this method Mehrabian found that people are easily able to judge the degree of liking communicated vocally.[39] One team of researchers used a comparable filtering process for several male voice samples. They then played a tape recording of the samples for forty-nine inexperienced judges and asked them what emotions they thought each voice conveyed. Four categories of emotion were consistently and reliably identified: positive feeling, dislike, sadness, and apprehension, or fear. The results of this research confirm "the generally held view that voice sounds alone independent of semantic components of vocal messages carry important clues to the emotional state of a speaker."[40]

Other emotions can also be determined solely from vocal cues. Starkweather found, for example, that people could reliably detect aggressiveness from a tape recording of a speaker, though not from a written transcript of the speaker's message. In a later study he showed that we can also judge intensity of emotion from vocal characteristics.[41]

Vocal cues are sometimes the basis for inferences about personality traits. For example, it has been found that speakers who increase the loudness, pitch, timbre, and rate of their speech are thought to be more active and dynamic.[42] And those who use more intonation, higher speech rates, more volume, and greater fluency in their speech than others have been judged more persuasive.[43]

Despite wide agreement about certain relationships between voice qualities and personality traits, no conclusive evidence supports such inferences. These judgments seem to derive from vocal stereotypes. Even if our beliefs have no basis in fact, however, they have striking effects on our response to others, for we act on what we believe to be true. Thus when the talkies appeared several stars of the silent films were ruined because the public expected their voices to sound consistent with their screen personalities. The great lover with the high-pitched voice was too great a disappointment.

In discussing how the voice can be used to convey social status, Goffman quotes from a nineteenth-century book of etiquette. The subject—how to speak to one's servants:

> Issue your commands with gravity and gentleness, and in a reserved manner. Let your voice be composed, but avoid a tone of familiarity or sympathy with them. It is better in addressing them to use a higher key of voice, and not to suffer it to fall at the end of a sentence. The best-bred man whom we ever had the pleasure of meeting always employed, in addressing servants, such forms of speech as these—"I'll thank you for so and so,"—"Such a thing if you please."—with a gentle tone, but very elevated key. The perfection of manner, in this particular, is to indicate by your language, that the performance is a favour, and by your tone that it is a matter of course.[44]

158   Quaint perhaps but accurate in its appraisal of the impact of vocal characteristics—and not totally outdated.

A study by Harms suggests that status cues in speech are probably based on a combination of "word choice, pronunciation, grammatical structure, voice quality, articulation, and several other observable features." An interesting sidelight of Harms' research is that most subjects apparently made judgments about status (and credibility) after listening to the recorded samples for only ten to fifteen seconds even though the samples were from forty to sixty seconds long.[45] Apparently we are all highly skilled at making such inferences.

Volume

One precondition of effective verbal communication is adequate volume. The person who speaks so low that he can barely be heard is a burden to others; they rapidly become too tired or too embarrassed to ask him to repeat his last remark. Of course, adequate volume varies from situation to situation. What is appropriate in a library is useless while dancing in front of a rock band.

Aside from circumstantial differences in speech volume, appropriate sound level varies from culture to culture. In describing voice level at social distance, Hall observes that ". . . in overall loudness, the American voice . . . is below that of the Arab, the Spaniard, the South Asian Indian, and the Russian, and somewhat above that of the English upper class, the Southeast Asian, and the Japanese."[46]

Human sensitivity to unpleasant levels of sound is reflected in the present concern with noise pollution. But the noises of jet aircraft are not the only disturbing sounds. The person who speaks too loudly often offends others. In fact, most people link volume to certain personality traits; thus it is commonly thought that an aggressive person speaks in a louder voice than one who is reserved and shy. Volume, however, is not necessarily a function of personality. A person's models as a child can influence his volume level somewhat apart from his personality.

The best check on volume is the feedback from your listener. If you are not getting through or if you are coming on too strong, then you should adjust your voice accordingly.

Rate and Fluency

Your **rate of speech** is *the number of words you utter within a specified time.* The unit most often used is 1 minute, and the average speaking rate is about 125 words per minute.

Although research on rates of speech has been limited, we do know that rates are highly stable for individuals. For this reason a faster rate (as well as shorter comments and more frequent pauses) seems to be linked to fear or anger and a slower rate to grief or depression.[47] Some people are able to control their rate of speaking despite their emotions, but the strain of maintaining this control is often expressed in other vocal or facial cues.

There is no optimum speaking rate. One speed may be appropriate for a comedian addressing an audience; another is needed for talking to a foreign student, a translator, or a secretary taking dictation. Speaking quickly when explaining technical material to those unfamiliar with the subject can completely undermine a verbal message. Think of the instructor who lectures so rapidly that his students become paralyzed. They do not have time to follow what is being explained or to take notes so that they can study at home. No matter how high the caliber of this man's teaching, his students will think of him as a terrible instructor. If the same lecture were given to a group of graduate students, they might have no objection to the rapid speaking rate.

There are, of course, rates of speech that are too fast or slow for the majority of listeners. Take the machine-gun delivery. People in this category tend to speak so rapidly that they run the risk of being unintelligible; at the very least, they may make others feel tense. At the opposite extreme are people who speak so slowly that their listeners become bored or impatient. When you hear someone like this drone on and on, you almost want to finish his sentences for him.

Thus rate of speech can have a definite effect on people's responses to a communicator. And like many other vocal qualities, rate of speech is most effective when it is adapted to the verbal content of the message and to the specific listener.

The **fluency**, or *continuity*, of our speech is closely related to rate, and pauses, of course, affect fluency. Pauses are usually described in terms of three dimensions: length (from milliseconds to minutes), filled (vocalized) or unfilled (silent) time, and location (at the end of a thought or within the context of an idea, for example). A person who pauses continually, whose speech is full of vocalizations such as "um," "er," and "ah," may destroy his effectiveness as a communicator. Let us take an extreme case. If during a press conference the President pauses frequently in responding to a controversial question, we are not inclined to give credence to his answer. Instead we think he is stalling for time or is lying or he doesn't know.

Pauses that are frequent, long, and vocalized and that come in the middle of an idea are usually distressing and serve to undermine the communicator's purpose. When used selectively for emphasis and variation, pauses often enhance the verbal message—particularly if they are infrequent, short, and unfilled and are used at the end of an idea.

Pitch

When, in *My Fair Lady*, Professor Higgins speaks with distaste about someone's "large Wagnerian mother with a voice that shatters glass,"[48] he is referring to **pitch**—*the frequency level (high or low) of the voice.* Each person has a pitch range determined by the size and shape of the vocal bands within his larynx, or voice box. Optimum pitch, the level most comfortable for you, is usually one-third above the lowest pitch you are capable of producing.[49] Most untrained speakers use a pitch somewhat higher than their optimum pitch, but it has been found that lower pitches are most pleasant to listen to. You can test this statement by going into a store where hi-fi equipment is sold. Check to see how much bass and treble are used. Most demonstrators will set the bass control forward because this creates an optimum pitch for hi-fi equipment too.

Pitch is an important element in people's judgments about a speaker. A voice with unvaried pitch is monotonous and is usually disliked; in fact, a monotone seems to be as unpopular as a poker face. People expect a voice to be varied in pitch and sometimes derive information about emotions from changes in pitch. In a summary of recent research, Weick writes:

> The potential significance of pitch measures lies in the fact that they may be accurate indices of emotional states. . . . Mahl suggested that the general pitch level at which one speaks is unimportant in the English language, people receive little explicit training in it, therefore, it may be more sensitive to drive states.[50]

Apparently pitch level does not affect the amount of information a listener comprehends,[51] but it does influence his attitude toward the communicator and the content of his message. One study showed that exaggerated pitch changes are even more unpopular than the monotone.[52] A naturally expressive voice has a variety of pitch levels, which are spontaneous and unforced changes.

Quality

The primary difference between a portable record player and a console hi-fi unit is the quality of the sound reproduction. In fact, "hi-fi" stands for "high fidelity," or small loss of quality in the reproduction of sounds. Differences in the *timbre*, or **quality**, of the human voice become easier to explain if we use another musical analogy. Think of a violin, a viola, and a cello. Each has a different size and shape. The same note played on each of these stringed instruments has a different quality of sound. Similarly each of us has a distinctive voice quality. One reason for this is that resonance—which to a great extent determines quality—is a function of size and shape. Because each person's physique (as well as the size of his vocal cords) is somewhat different from everyone else's in size and shape, each person has a different resonator for his voice.

There seems to be wide agreement in responses to vocal qualities.

One study shows that judges could reliably distinguish voices described as shrill or harsh from those considered pleasant, or "resonant."[53] Although it is common practice to refer to a pleasant voice as one that is "resonant," Anderson reminds us that a voice with "a disagreeable quality or lacking in general effectiveness is not necessarily lacking in resonance—it may have too much of the wrong kind. Mere resonance alone does not make a superior voice."[54]

There are several particularly unpleasant voice qualities, and we shall mention five of them here. See if you recognize a familiar voice or two among them.

Hypernasality is talking through the nose; think of someone imitating a whining child. *Denasality* sounds as though the person has a constant head cold. *Hoarseness* will sound like perpetual laryngitis. *Harshness,* or *stridency,* results in a piercing voice. One writer comments, "Strident voices seem to be able to make themselves heard more easily than normal voices even though the effect is often unpleasant." *Breathiness* is caused by air wastage, and like *huskiness* it occurs most often in women; sometimes these have organic origins, but frequently they are due to faults in phonation (voice production), which can be relearned and improved.[55]

Through practice and training almost all of us can make improvements in our vocal quality. The use of a tape recorder is especially helpful.

INTERPRETING NONVERBAL MESSAGES

Nonverbal communication—indeed the whole process of interpersonal communication—must be viewed as a whole that is greater than the sum of its parts. Outside the psychologist's laboratory we do not depend on isolated cues. As one writer has explained,

> The still photo of a face alone is a radically reduced situation; in life there are more cues and so more accuracy. Reading an emotion from a still photograph of a face is rather like trying to identify animals from the tracks they leave in the snow. . . .[56]

In face-to-face communication, all the cues we have been discussing are available to us. Therefore it is not surprising to find some scholars estimating that at least 65 percent of all social meaning in interpersonal communication is conveyed through nonverbal stimuli.[57] Our knowledge of the setting in which the message occurs is another advantage. As we saw from Laing's example at the end of Chapter 6, meaning is, to a great degree, determined by context. Barnlund also reminds us that changes "in the speed or direction of a particular movement may carry as much meaning as does its form."[58]

We learn most about the meaning of nonverbal messages by study-ing them in relationship to verbal messages. Essentially a nonverbal message functions in one of three ways: it replaces, reinforces, or con-tradicts a verbal message.

A nonverbal message that substitutes for a verbal one is often easy to interpret. Our culture provides us with gestures and expressions that are the equivalents of certain brief verbal messages: "Yes," "No," "Hello," "Goodbye," "I don't know," and so on. Likes and dislikes can also be expressed without words. It will be a long time before anyone forgets Khrushchev pounding a United Nations table with his shoe.

When a nonverbal message reinforces a verbal message, meaning is conveyed quickly and easily, and with increased comprehension. Some-times a single cue such as a hand movement or a long pause gives special emphasis to one part of a message so that we are able to dis-cern what the speaker feels is most important.

As communicators most of our problems in interpreting meaning arise when we receive a nonverbal message that contradicts a verbal message. Let us explore this subject briefly.

You are familiar with the word "bind" as used to describe a situa-tion one cannot get out of. In 1956 the anthropologist Gregory Bateson and a group of his associates presented a theory of the **double bind** that revolutionized the study of schizophrenia. They proposed that schizo-phrenic communication—particularly within families—was character-ized by the constant exchange of contradictory messages between two or more people, one of whom was designated the "victim."

The recurrent theme in the double bind is a sequence of three injunctions or commands. The first says, "Do not do so and so, or I will punish you," or "If you do not do so and so, I will punish you." The second command contradicts the first and is often communicated nonverbally: "Posture, gesture, tone of voice, meaningful action, and the implications concealed in verbal comment may all be used to con-vey this more abstract message."[59] The third negative command makes the victim's position completely untenable by forbidding him to leave this paradoxical situation. Laing has given us this summary of a chill-ing example taken from Bateson's work:

> A mother visits her son, who has just been recovering from a mental breakdown. As he goes towards her
> a.   she opens her arms for him to embrace her, and/or
> b.   to embrace him.
> c.   As he gets nearer she freezes and stiffens.
> d.   He stops irresolutely.
> e.   She says, "Don't you want to kiss your mummy?"—and as he still stands irresolutely
> f.   she says, "But, dear, you mustn't be afraid of your feelings."

Laing notes that the description does not include the patient's double-binding behavior toward his mother. "For instance, between steps (b) and (c) above, the patient in moving towards his mother may have succeeded by minute nuances in his expression and walk, in putting into his mother *his* fear of closeness with her, so that she stiffened."[60]

Bateson's double-bind thesis explains a great deal about contradictory messages and the breakdown of interpersonal relationships that may result from them. Although the theory applies specifically to schizophrenic communication, it is relevant to more general studies such as ours because normal and so-called abnormal, or deviant, behavior exist along a continuum.

Within the normal range of experience, Birdwhistell uses the term **kinesic slips** for *contradictory verbal and nonverbal messages.* Imagine this conversation between a married couple who have just had a bitter quarrel. The wife asks the husband, "Honey, are you still angry?" "No," he replies, "it's all right." "But you *sound* as though you're still angry," she says. "I'm telling you I'M NOT ANGRY!" he answers. The husband's words give one message, his voice another. He may not even be aware of the second. Which message is his wife likely to believe?

Recall for a moment the estimate we spoke of earlier: if nonverbal stimuli account for at least 65 percent of all social meaning in interpersonal communication, verbal stimuli can account for no more than 35 percent. Nonverbal cues predominate by sheer number. It seems likely then that the nonverbal message will have the greater impact. In general, if as receivers we are caught between two discrepant messages, we are more inclined to believe the nonverbal message.

One reason for this is that nonverbal cues give information about our emotions and intentions. Another is that most of us feel that body movements, facial expressions, vocal qualities, and so on cannot be simulated with authenticity by the average person. This belief is borne out by the fact that planned gestures rarely appear spontaneous. Somehow the discrepancy between what we say and what we feel gets communicated.

Writers in several fields have proposed that the more we can reduce this discrepancy, the less often kinesic slips will occur. Two courses of action seem obvious. First, as mentioned in Chapter 2, a poor communicator transmits many unintentional stimuli; thus, if we can become more conscious of our own nonverbal messages, we can use our communication patterns more effectively. Second, we have to be honest and open about what we feel. As we shall see in Chapter 10, candor is one of the primary objectives of sensitivity training. Directness has obvious limitations. In many situations we cannot or should not reveal all our thoughts. Parents who deeply resent their children, for example, need help in changing or managing their feelings; they should not

164 necessarily be brought out in the open. For the most part, however, expressing our true feelings will dramatically reduce the number of contradictory messages we transmit and increase our effectiveness as communicators.

Summary

Nonverbal communication is going on all the time. In this chapter we have looked at three kinds of nonverbal cues.

We discussed space and time, two cultural cues that have a subtle but pervasive influence on our style of communication. Visual cues from facial expressions, eye contact, body movements (particularly hand gestures), and physical appearance were analyzed. We found that these cues give us information about human emotions and intentions; they are also the basis for some of our judgments about personality and social status. Vocal cues are another source of information. We spoke in some detail about volume, rate and fluency, pitch, and quality. Although all these cues were discussed separately for the purpose of analysis, in the actual interpersonal communication process it is misleading to speak about individual cues without considering the entire communication event.

We concluded with a look at how we interpret nonverbal messages, particularly in relation to verbal messages. The source of most communication difficulties, double or contradictory messages, was considered in terms of double-bind situations and the kinesic slips common in daily experience.

Review Questions

1. Describe the difference between sign language, action language, and object language.
2. Discuss four kinds of interpersonal distance. Give an example of each kind.
3. What are four rules about eye contact?
4. Describe three categories of nonverbal courtship behavior. Give an example of each type.
5. What is the relationship between head and body movements in the communication of emotion?
6. How can a person's clothes communicate messages?
7. What is paralinguistics? Give some examples of paralinguistic cues. What four categories of emotion are consistently identified by paralinguistic cues?
8. What are three ways in which nonverbal and verbal messages may be related?

9. What is a double bind? How does it relate to both verbal and non-verbal communication?

Exercises

1. Form several two-person teams consisting of one male and one female. Have each team select a place where several people are likely to pass by. Have both members take turns asking strangers the time of day, or some other standard question. While speaking to the stranger, slowly violate his proxemic norms until you are very close to him. The other member of the team should record his observations of the stranger's reactions. When all the teams have collected data, discuss these questions in light of the data collected:
   a. In what ways did the strangers demonstrate sign language, action language, and object language and under what conditions?
   b. How did the strangers respond to the questioner as he began to violate proxemic norms?
   c. Did male and female strangers respond differently to proxemic norm violation depending on whether a male or female did the violating?
2. Repeat the exercise just described, but this time have one questioner dress very neatly, and the other in a sloppy, unkempt manner. Discuss the differences in the strangers' reactions to the questioner.
3. Make a list of the various paralinguistic and vocal cues discussed in this chapter. Tape-record a series of short messages presented by a male and female that illustrate the various types of paralinguistic and vocal cues. Construct a Semantic Differential similar to the one suggested in Exercise 1a in Chapter 6; then ask a number of people to listen to the taped messages and rate the speakers using the Semantic Differential. How did the various paralinguistic and vocal cues affect the listeners' perceptions of the speaker? Relate the results to the concepts discussed in Chapter 4 on interpersonal perception.
4. Next time you communicate face to face with your parents or other members of your family, notice their nonverbal communication behavior, especially their facial expressions, gestures, and vocal cues. Now try—and this is hard—to observe your own nonverbal behaviors. Do you notice similarities? What differences can you detect? Can you account for these similarities and differences?
5. Try playing charades. Notice how much more aware of nonverbal communication everyone is during the game. Do all players communicate equally well? (They probably don't.) What differences can you identify between the good players and those who are less skilled?

Suggested Readings

Fast, Julius. *Body Language*. New York: Evans, 1970. This lively, popularized introduction to nonverbal communication is an entertaining treatment of the subject, including such topic areas as "To touch or not to touch," "Winking, Blinking and Nods," and "Putting it all together." The reader must be aware that this treatment is not considered to be wholly accurate.

Knapp, Mark L. *Nonverbal Communication in Human Interaction*. New York: Holt, Rinehart and Winston, 1972. This book is an excellent resource for the student of nonverbal communication. Professor Knapp writes in a readable and lively style, and he has a significant message to convey. One interesting feature of this book is the illustrative material which is included (pictures, diagrams, charts).

Mehrabian, Albert. *Silent Messages*. Belmont, Calif.: Wadsworth, 1971. Mehrabian has contributed still another of his absolutely first-rate publications to the literature in interpersonal communication. This little book synthesizes a lot of experimental and theoretical material on nonverbal communication.

Notes

1 James Agee, *Agee on Film: Reviews and Comments by James Agee*, Vol. I (New York: Grosset & Dunlap, 1967), p. 13.

2 Jurgen Ruesch and Weldon Kees, *Nonverbal Communication* (Los Angeles: University of California Press, 1956).

3 Dominick Barbara, "Nonverbal Communication," *Journal of Communication*, 13 (1963), 167.

4 Franklyn S. Haiman, "The Rhetoric of 1968: A Farewell to Rational Discourse," in Wil Linkugel, R. R. Allen, and Richard Johannesen (eds.), *Contemporary American Speeches*, 2nd ed. (Belmont, Calif.: Wadsworth, 1969), p. 159.

5 Edward T. Hall, *The Silent Language* (New York: Fawcett, 1959), p. 15.

6 Robert Woodworth and Harold Schlosberg, *Experimental Psychology*, rev. ed. (New York: Holt, Rinehart and Winston, 1954), pp. 267–268.

7 Edward T. Hall, *The Hidden Dimension* (Garden City, N.Y.: Doubleday, 1969), p. 128. Subsequent quotations are from pp. 116, 119, and 14.

8 James C. Baxter, "Interpersonal Spacing in Natural Settings," *Sociometry*, 33 (1970), 444–456.

9 Gilberto Freyre, *New World in the Tropics: The Culture of Modern Brazil* (New York: Random House, 1963), p. 264.

10 Hall, *The Silent Language*, pp. 19–20.

11 Georges Gurvitch, *The Spectrum of Social Time*, tr. by Myrtle Korenbaum (Dordrecht, Neth.: Reidel, 1964), p. 14.

[12] B. Steinzor, "The Spatial Factor in Face-to-Face Discussion Groups," *Journal of Abnormal and Social Psychology*, 45 (1950), 552–555.

[13] Albert Mehrabian, "Orientation Behaviors and Nonverbal Attitude Communication," *Journal of Communication*, 17 (1967), 324–332.

[14] Michael Reece and Robert N. Whitman, "Expressive Movements, Warmth, and Verbal Reinforcement," *Journal of Abnormal and Social Psychology*, 64 (1962), 250.

[15] Agee, I, p. 13.

[16] Leo Tolstoy, *War and Peace*, tr. by Constance Garnett (New York: Modern Library, n.d.), p. 93.

[17] Frederick Williams and John Tolch, "Communication by Facial Expression," *Journal of Communication*, 15 (1965), 17–21.

[18] Randall Harrison, "Nonverbal Communication: Explorations into Time, Space, Action, and Object," in Jim Campbell and Hal Hepler (eds.), *Dimensions in Communication* (Belmont, Calif.: Wadsworth, 1965), pp. 158–174.

[19] Charles Darwin, *Evolution and Natural Selection*, ed. by Bert James Loewenberg (Boston: Beacon, 1959), p. 398.

[20] Paul Ekman and Wallace V. Friesen, "Constants Across Cultures in the Face and Emotion," *Journal of Personality and Social Psychology*, 17 (1971), 129.

[21] Erving Goffman, *Behavior in Public Places* (New York: Free Press, 1963), p. 84.

[22] Michael Argyle, *The Psychology of Interpersonal Behavior* (Baltimore: Penguin, 1967), pp. 105–116.

[23] Jon Blubaugh, "Effects of Positive and Negative Audience Feedback on Selected Variables of Speech Behavior," *Speech Monographs*, 36 (1969), 131–137.

[24] Martin Cobin, "Response to Eye Contact," *Quarterly Journal of Speech*, 48 (1962), 415–418.

[25] E. H. Hess, "Attitude and Pupil Size," *Scientific American*, 212 (April 1965), 46–54.

[26] Albert E. Scheflen, "Quasi-Courtship Behavior in Psychotherapy," *Psychiatry*, 28 (1965), 252.

[27] Paul Ekman, "Differential Communication of Affect by Head and Body Cues," *Journal of Personality and Social Psychology*, 2 (1965), 726–735.

[28] Paul Ekman, "Communication Through Nonverbal Behavior" (Progress Report, Langley Porter Institute, San Francisco, 1965).

[29] Weston La Barre, "The Language of Emotions and Gestures," in W. Bennis and others (eds.), *Interpersonal Dynamics*, 2nd ed. (Homewood, Ill.: Dorsey, 1968), p. 204.

[30] Ruesch and Kees, p. 189.

[31] Monroe Lefkowitz, Robert R. Blake, and Jane Srygley Mouton, "Status

168   Factors in Pedestrian Violation of Traffic Signals," *Journal of Abnormal and Social Psychology*, 51 (1955), 704–706.

[32] Daniel G. Freedman, "The Survival Value of Beards," *Psychology Today*, 3 (October 1969), 38.

[33] Arthur Mizener, *The Far Side of Paradise: A Biography of F. Scott Fitzgerald* (New York: Random House, 1949), p. 94.

[34] Albert Mehrabian, "Communication Without Words," *Psychology Today*, 2 (September 1968), 53.

[35] George L. Trager, "Paralanguage: A First Approximation," *Studies in Linguistics*, 13 (1958), 1–12.

[36] "Notes on People: Herring Ad Irks Miss Hepburn," *The New York Times*, August 12, 1971, p. 39.

[37] Joel R. Davitz and Lois Jean Davitz, "The Communication of Feelings by Content-Free Speech," *Journal of Communication*, 9 (1959), 6–13.

[38] Joel R. Davitz and Lois Jean Davitz, "Correlates of Accuracy in the Communication of Feelings," *Journal of Communication*, 9 (1959), 110–117.

[39] Mehrabian, "Communication Without Words," p. 54.

[40] William F. Soskin and Paul E. Kauffman, "Judgment of Emotion in Word-Free Voice Samples," *Journal of Communication*, 11 (1961), 78.

[41] John A. Starkweather, "Content-Free Speech as a Source of Information About the Speaker," *Journal of Abnormal and Social Psychology*, 52 (1956), 394–402; and "Vocal Communication of Personality and Human Feelings," *Journal of Communication*, 11 (1961), 63–72.

[42] Joel R. Davitz and Lois Jean Davitz, "Nonverbal Vocal Communication of Feeling," *Journal of Communication*, 11 (1961), 81–86.

[43] Albert Mehrabian and Martin Williams, "Nonverbal Concomitants of Perceived and Intended Persuasiveness," *Journal of Personality and Social Psychology*, 13 (1969), 37–58.

[44] Anonymous, *The Laws of Etiquette* (Philadelphia: Carey, Lee, and Blanchard, 1836), p. 188; quoted in Erving Goffman, *Interaction Ritual* (Garden City, N.Y.: Doubleday, 1967), p. 62.

[45] L. S. Harms, "Listener Judgments of Status Cues in Speech," *Quarterly Journal of Speech*, 47 (1961), 164–168.

[46] Hall, *The Hidden Dimension*, p. 121.

[47] Dean C. Barnlund, *Interpersonal Communication: Survey and Studies* (Boston: Houghton Mifflin, 1968), p. 529.

[48] Alan Jay Lerner and Frederick Loewe, *My Fair Lady*.

[49] Jon Eisenson and Mardel Ogilvie, *Speech Correction in the Schools* (New York: Macmillan, 1963), p. 283.

[50] Karl E. Weick, "Systematic Observational Methods," in Gardner Lindzey

and Elliot Aronson (eds.), *The Handbook of Social Psychology,* 2nd ed. (Reading, Mass.: Addison-Wesley, 1968), Vol. II, *Research Methods,* p. 392.

[51] Charles F. Diehl, Richard C. White, and Paul H. Satz, "Pitch Change and Comprehension," *Speech Monographs,* 28 (1961), 65–68.

[52] Barbara J. Eakins, "The Relationship of Intonation to Attitude Change, Retention, and Attitude Toward Source" (paper delivered at the annual convention of the Speech Association of America, New York, December 1969).

[53] Ned Bowler, "A Fundamental Frequency Analysis of Harsh Vocal Quality," *Speech Monographs,* 31 (1964), 128–134.

[54] Virgil A. Anderson, *Training the Speaking Voice,* 2nd ed. (New York: Oxford University Press, 1961), p. 435.

[55] Charles Van Riper, *Speech Correction,* 4th ed. (Englewood Cliffs, N.J.: Prentice-Hall, 1963), pp. 174, 172.

[56] Roger Brown, *Social Psychology* (New York: Free Press, 1965), p. 624.

[57] Harrison, p. 161.

[58] Barnlund, p. 525.

[59] Gregory Bateson and others, "Toward a Theory of Schizophrenia," *Behavioral Science,* 1 (1956), 254.

[60] R. D. Laing, *Self and Others,* 2nd rev. ed. (New York: Pantheon, 1969), p. 127.

Contexts
of Interpersonal
Communication

part
four

Chapter 8 Two-Person Communication

OBJECTIVES

After reading this chapter the student should be able to:

1. Describe the relationship between disruptive power and norms in dyadic communication.

2. Distinguish between expected roles and enacted roles.

3. Define intrarole and interrole conflicts and give a example of each.

4. Describe two ways in which involvement on the part of communicators is related to dyadic communication.

5. State the relationship between one's level of arousal and the ability to perform effectively.

6. Describe the relationship between need for dominance, need for achievement, and self-concept.

7. State the relationship between need for affiliation and need for dominance.

8. Describe at least two ways in which status affects dyadic communication.

9. Describe the MUM effect.

10. Identify ten different types of interview objectives.

11. Distinguish between standardized interviews and unstandardized interviews.

12. Distinguish among five types of interview questions and give an example of each type.

13. Identify five types of inadequate responses to interview questions and describe a strategy that may be used to handle each type.

14. Describe three responsibilities of the interviewer at the beginning of an interview.

15. Describe the funnel sequence as it is used in the body of an interview.

16. Describe three steps in terminating an interview.

17. Identify four responsibilities of an interviewer.

18. Identify four responsibilities of a respondent.

8

In preceding chapters we have developed several elements of our model illustrated in Figure 1: the psychological makeup of the individual communicator, his perception of other human beings, the bases of his interpersonal choices, the components of his verbal and nonverbal messages. In this chapter we finally bring communicator 1 and communicator 2 together, and we raise two basic questions concerning their encounters: What if anything do we know about two-person communication? What predictions can we make about how two people will interact?

You will recall that our model focuses on the **dyad**, or *two-person group*. The dyad is the smallest unit of interaction, and in many ways it is a microcosm of all larger groups. Certainly dyadic communication is no less complex than any other form of interpersonal communication. Like members of larger groups, the members of a dyad may differ in any number of ways—age, sex, status, motivation, attitude, and so on. In fact, small-group and public communication cannot be studied without an understanding of what takes place within the dyad. Yet in some respects two-person communication differs from other forms of interpersonal communication. In this chapter and the three that follow, these similarities and differences should become more apparent.

THE SOCIAL SETTING

When we consider communicator 1 and communicator 2, we find that we have set our actors on a rather bare stage. We have already discussed some of the variables that make them unique and others that influence their responses to one another. Now we must place them within a social setting.

Norms

Interpersonal attraction, we have seen, is in part based on perceived similarity of relevant or salient characteristics. We tend to like others whom we view as resembling ourselves. We find it comfortable to believe that they share our attitudes, beliefs, or values. In effect, these similarities confirm us: they suggest that we must be right because others think the way we do.

When we speak of attitudes, beliefs, or values that are shared by several people, we approach the subject of social norms. **Norms,** as we saw in Chapter 7, are *rules about behavior,* rules from which we develop certain expectations about how people should act. We have norms for sex, eating, grading exams, tipping, and child rearing—in fact, for every aspect of human life. Even in casual encounters there are norms for how to communicate: "There are rules for taking and terminating a turn at talking; there are norms synchronizing the process of eyeing the speaker and being eyed by him: there is an etiquette for initiating an encounter and bringing it to an end."[1]

The word "norm" refers to a standard or average, and it often implies that the standard or average is acceptable. Behaviors that violate a given norm are called "deviant," the implication being that deviant behaviors are in some way unacceptable or even abnormal. Of course, extremely deviant behavior is more likely to elicit strong negative responses than behavior that deviates only slightly from any given norm. A man who eats with his hands in an elegant restaurant will get more disapproving glances than one who uses the wrong knife.

Norms develop at a number of social levels. Some norms are shared by almost all members of a given culture. Some are specific to countries, regions of a country, communities, smaller social groups, or families. Certain norms are transferred from one relationship to another. Thus when two people meet, each already has a great many expectations about how the other will behave. Both will be strongly influenced by the norms they have already adopted. As they interact, however, they may also establish some norms of their own—rules, whether implicit or explicit, by which they agree to behave. During courtship, for example, a couple decides on a number of acceptable and unacceptable behaviors concerning love-making, use of profanity, topics of conversation, places to go on dates, and so on.

An interesting question that has been raised is whether certain dyads establish more norms than others. Suppose that Will and Barbara are friends. When Will can keep Barbara from doing something she wants to do, Will may be said to have **disruptive power** over her. In some dyadic relationships one person has more disruptive power than the partner. In others both members may have relatively high or low disruptive power. One team of researchers reports that the frequency with which norms are established in dyads is linked to the disruptive power each person has over the other. When both members have high disruptive power, they tend to establish more normative agreements—perhaps, it has been suggested, because both are conscious that "the overuse of their power can be self-defeating."[2] When disagreements between two people are a common occurrence, normative agreements will often reduce the level and frequency of conflict. If Will always prefers films and Barbara always favors hockey games, they can decide to alternate these activities. If Barbara has greater disruptive power than Will, they may end up always going to hockey games. Either arrangement would be considered a normative agreement.

Norms then are guidelines that limit and direct behavior. We accept them because they allow us to establish standard operating procedures—ground rules, if you will—that make the behavior of others more predictable and decrease the need for communicating about that behavior. If a married couple reaches an agreement about where to spend Christmas and Easter holidays each year or about who handles the finances, there is no need to renegotiate these decisions repeatedly. Thibaut and Kelley put it well when they write that effective norms "can reduce the costs of interaction and eliminate the less rewarding activities from a relationship. They can act to improve the outcome attained by members of a dyad and to increase their interdependence." They also point out that a conformity agreement tends to become rewarding in and of itself.[3]

Not all normative agreements are rewarding. Some are inappropriate for a given relationship. Some restrict communication in an unhealthy way. Others are too rigid. For example, if a normative agreement exists between father and son that the son will never question the father's judgments or decisions, the son may forfeit his own good judgment simply because it conflicts with his father's opinion. Ellis believes that a great deal of psychological damage can be attributed to attempts to live by norms that we are virtually unaware we have assumed, standards inappropriate for our own well-being.[4] He bases his rational-emotive school of psychotherapy on the premise that norms can best serve us if we know that they exist and can periodically evaluate their appropriateness.

Roles

In public places adults are expected to use cutlery when eating certain foods. People who borrow library books are expected to return them. In any given culture some norms apply to all members. Others apply only to some of its members. A **role** is a *set of norms that applies to a specific subclass within the society*. The term itself is unsettling. Actors play roles. What have they to do with us? If a college student is expected at various times to play the role of son, student, friend, lover, employee, grandson, Catholic, and tennis player, how seriously can he assume these roles without becoming an automaton or sacrificing his individuality?

To answer this question a distinction must be made between **expected roles** and **enacted roles**. For example, in parent-child relationships the parent is expected to minister to the needs of the child, to provide for him financially, and so on. The enacted role of parent may in fact be quite different. A father who is an alcoholic or an invalid may be tended to and even supported by his child. Even if such an

"Why don't you get dressed, then, and go to pieces like a man?"

obvious reversal of roles does not take place, different men will interpret the role of father differently—one as a stern disciplinarian, one as a completely permissive companion, one as a firm but loving teacher. Granted, we "enact" roles. We shall not say, however, that we are "actors" in a completely theatrical sense but rather that some roles are more central to us than others. Thus the intensity with which a person takes on various roles differs; some will be enacted casually, with little or no involvement, and others with great commitment.

We are, of course, more comfortable in some roles than in others. The roles we do not enjoy playing are those that create conflict. There are two types of role conflict, and both tend to lead to communication difficulties.

A person is likely to experience **interrole conflict** when he occupies *two (or more) roles that represent contradictory expectations about a given behavior.* Suppose that a student who is proctoring an exam sees his friend cheating during the test. As a proctor he feels obliged to report the cheating. As a friend he may feel that out of loyalty he should overlook what he has just seen. The options in interrole conflicts seem clear. The demands of role 1 and role 2 are known. They conflict. One must be chosen over the other.

What about **intrarole conflict**—*conflicting expectations concerning a single role?* Let us consider an example that concerns us all: the conflict in sex roles.

Much has been written about redefining the traditional female role, especially as it relates to marriage. Must a woman assume the roles of wife and mother to be totally feminine? And what after all are her obligations as wife and mother? Are housework and child rearing exclusively female responsibilities? No, say many women— and some men.

For the moment the Women's Liberation Movement has focused attention on the female sex role. But male and female roles are complementary; a redefinition of the female role will, of necessity, require changes in the male role. Some men are already aware of this possibility. Recently a group of husbands whose wives had committed themselves to instituting some change in their marriages discussed some of the problems entailed by redefinition of roles and the confusion that often results. For example, Dick, one of the participants, commented that he had "a hard time calling a waiter or a cab" and that his wife's ability to do these things well made him even less effective.[5]

Trivial as it may seem, Dick's concern over not being able to get the attention of a waiter or a cab driver illustrates some of the problems of intrarole conflict. Is success in getting a cab or calling a waiter essential to fulfilling a masculine role? Do others expect him to do this? Does he expect it of himself? He is not sure. The issue is complicated by the fact that as a result of her consciousness-raising sessions, Dick's wife wants him to change some of his expectations about her behavior. Yet the roles of male and female are complementary. Would she be flexible enough to change some of her expectations about his behavior? How would she react when he said, "If you want the waiter, call him yourself"?

Role conflicts and the misunderstandings to which they give rise illustrate the interdependence of role, self-concept, and communication. When we enact a role with any measure of intensity, we communicate from within that role—that is, we take on a certain stance. We also internalize certain expectations about how we should respond and how other people should respond to us. Most communication takes place within the boundaries of these expectations.

UNSTRUCTURED TWO-PERSON COMMUNICATION

Much of the day-to-day interaction between members of dyads is casual and spontaneous. We can describe their encounters as relatively unstructured if we contrast them with more structured two-person exchanges such as interviews. We emphasize the word "relatively." Daily interactions do have some structure; conversely some more formal encounters have only the barest minimum of structure. With this qualification in mind, we turn to some elements of unstructured two-person communication.

Involvement and Arousal

Researchers have known for some time that as the number of people interacting increases, the individual satisfaction of each member of the group decreases. Thus the dyad is potentially the most satisfying social context within which communication can occur, partly because there is likely to be more opportunity to participate than there is in larger groups. Also there is convincing evidence that the opportunity to talk is in itself satisfying. Consequently members of dyads are more deeply involved than members of larger groups.

There is another side to the coin of **involvement**. Although experiences in a dyad tend to be satisfying, they may also be intensely unsatisfying. Because of the depth of involvement, members of a dyad are likely to have more intense negative feelings about an unpleasant experience in the relationship than are members of a larger group. For example, everyone acknowledges the importance of listening in communication. Yet when tempers begin to flare, less listening occurs. Sereno and Mortensen found that dyads consisting of slightly involved members were able to reach effective compromises more often and with a more favorable private attitude change than were highly ego-involved members of dyads.[6] (They point out, however, that a number of variables are probably relevant to the communication process that may in time help us negotiate conflict with maximum effectiveness.) It is known that in open-ended or unstructured situations, high Machs, who have greater emotional detachment than low Machs, seem to "direct the tone and content of interaction—and usually also the outcome."[7] Low Machs, who are more open to emotional involvements, are less effective strategists but more sensitive to the feelings of others. It is particularly interesting that the differences between high Machs and low Machs show up most in face-to-face interactions.

Another concept relevant to dyads as well as to larger groups is **arousal level**. It is well known that one's ability to behave efficiently may be activated by a certain level of physiological arousal. Athletes as well as entertainers are better able to perform if they can first get "psyched up" for the effort. In fact, all of us need a minimum level of arousal in order to use cues efficiently; otherwise we fail to perceive them. But arousal level works against us beyond a certain point— overexcitation can make us unable to organize the stimuli we receive. This is what seems to happen when a person is overcome by stage fright or when he becomes so deeply involved in an argument that he is virtually unable to communicate. As Figure 13 illustrates, the rela-

Figure 13

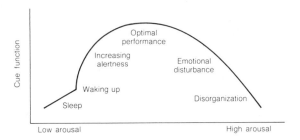

Arousal Level and Performance

Source: Donald Hebb, *A Textbook of Psychology*, 3rd ed. (Philadelphia: Saunders, 1972), p. 235.

tionship between the ability to perform effectively and one's level of arousal seems to follow an inverted U curve. We need a minimum arousal level to function and in fact a moderate level of arousal facilitates communication, but we reach a point of diminishing returns, beyond which high arousal level results in poor performance.

Some Dimensions of Interpersonal Relations

The dyad, like all social units, presupposes certain norms and roles. This means that we need not start afresh in analyzing the behaviors of the two communicators; we have at least some basis for prediction. Another variable that will qualify any predictions we make will be motivation.

Certain dimensions of motivation have more relevance for communication than others. One important predictor of how two people will interact is the strength of their affiliative needs, discussed in Chapter 3. For present purposes the **need for affiliation** may be seen as a continuum from highly affiliative to antisocial behavior. The high affiliater prefers being with others to being alone. He enjoys and seeks out their company. He may be described as friendly, gregarious, and generally sociable. The person who is low in his need for affiliation probably prefers being alone. He has much less desire for companionship and is not very reinforcing to other people. In fact, he is usually described as unfriendly or unsociable.

Given a knowledge of two people's affiliative tendencies, we can make some predictions about how they will respond in a face-to-face encounter. But suppose that we add to this knowledge some information about a second important dimension of interpersonal relations: the **need for dominance**. Like the need for affiliation, the need for dominance can be imagined as a continuum: at one end we have the person who wants control over others and at the other the person with a relatively submissive style of communication. Need for dominance seems to have some correlation with need for achievement—those who rate high in the first also tend to rate high in the second.

A correlation also seems to exist between dominance and self-concept. A person with an unfavorable self-concept, chiefly measured by level of self-esteem, tends to be low in his need for dominance, and he is likely to defer to the other dyad member. For example, in one of your authors' classes, students were assigned two-person projects. Student A on one team complained to the instructor that his partner, B, was bossing him around and preventing him from taking part in planning. Yet each time the instructor observed the two at work, he noticed that A made no attempts to get B to let him participate in the planning. This submissive behavior seems typical of the person with low self-esteem: he is unable to influence others, but he is not satisfied with the role he must play when others try to influence him. Furthermore his hesitancy tends to bring out the dominating tendencies of others who are less submissive.

When we combine what we know about behaviors associated with the needs for affiliation and dominance, as in Figure 14, we see some communication patterns possible in a dyad as well as in a larger group. Allowing for the individuality of each member of the dyad, we can still make some predictions about how the two will interact if we know something about the strengths of their needs for affiliation and dominance. If Will (communicator 1) has a high need for dominance but a low need for affiliation, we expect him to be analytic, to make many judgments, to be resistant, and so on; if Barbara (communicator 2) has a low need for dominance but a high need for

Figure 14

Some Behaviors Associated with Needs for Dominance and Affiliation

	High dominance	Low dominance
High affiliation	Advises Coordinates Directs Initiates Leads	Acquiesces Agrees Assists Cooperates Obliges
Low affiliation	Analyzes Criticizes Disapproves Judges Resists	Concedes Evades Relinquishes Retreats Withdraws

SOURCE: Adapted from David W. Johnson, *Reaching Out: Interpersonal Effectiveness and Self-actualization* (Englewood Cliffs, N.J.: Prentice-Hall, 1972), p. 35. By permission of Prentice-Hall, Inc.

affiliation, we expect her to acquiesce much of the time, to cooperate with Will, and so on. But if, like Will, Barbara has a high need for dominance, it is likely that a power struggle will ensue, or as we suggested in discussing norms, the two will work out some satisfactory normative agreements that regulate their behavior—at least for a time.

No discussion of power or dominance would be complete without some mention of **status**. Potter has written at length about a familiar strategy for achieving higher status in human relationships; he calls it "one-upmanship." No doubt the popularity of his tongue-in-cheek descriptions of how to gain the upper hand stems from their authenticity. In one guise or another, the one-upper is known to you all. He is always busier than you are. He goes to more expensive places. He knows more important people. And most telling of all, he is a name dropper. A remark such as "When I was talking to Skinner at the A.P.A. meetings last week . . ." may leave a colleague or graduate student duly impressed. An undergraduate who doesn't know that A.P.A. stands for the American Psychological Association but who has seen B. F. Skinner's name in his psychology text may be even more impressed.

Potter comes through with one-upmanship techniques for all of us: doctor and patient, businessman, artist, sportsman, wine lover. And he has not forgotten the college student. If you want to be one up before exams have started or after they are over, you might give either of two impressions: that you spend all your time studying or that you never open a book. For example, "to Harvard," the second strategy, is "to seem, even when the examination is only two days off, to be totally indifferent to the impending crisis, and be seen walking calmly and naturally about, out of doors, enjoying the scenery and taking deep breaths of air."[8] Efforts to outdo another person or group clearly take place on both verbal and nonverbal levels.

Status has marked effects on the form of all communication, no matter how unstructured. It makes a great difference, for example, whether the status of members of a dyad is the same. If two people are unequal in status, there is a good chance that the one with higher status will control the topics of conversation as well as the length of the discussion. His higher status may even enable him to avoid the discussion entirely if he so chooses. If the president of a bank and one of his tellers are engaged in conversation, for example, and the teller asks a question that seems too personal, it is likely that the bank president can respond in such a way that the teller will feel uncomfortable pursuing the subject.

Perceptions of status are immediately reflected in greetings as well as in form of address. Thus "Hi" may be permissible for some encounters; "Hello" or "Good morning" may be more appropriate

184   for others. The higher-status person is often addressed by his title and last name and the lower-status person by his first name or even a briefer version of his name: "Hi, Mike." "Good morning, Dr. Jones." One sociologist observes that greetings may also affirm a subordinate's willingness to maintain his lower status. American military practice, for instance, requires that the subordinate salute first and hold the salute until it is returned by the person of higher rank.[9] Observe people of different status greeting one another and see whether these behavior patterns are borne out by your own experience.

Status differences between members of a dyad affect not only communicative style but the actual content of the communication. For years we have known that in larger social systems those interested in achieving higher status tend to distort what they say to their superiors in order to create the most favorable impression possible. In other words, they create a filter through which only the more pleasant information passes. This phenomenon has been called the **MUM effect** (*Mum about Undesirable Messages*).[10]

No doubt the status filter operates at a number of levels within the federal government. One Vietnam veteran observed that the South Vietnam military efforts appeared to be more successful than they were because combat officers were eager to report considerable progress to their superiors each month. We also expect this filtering process to exist in all sorts of institutions and businesses—hospitals, schools, legal firms, department stores. And some of us can personally attest to the presence of the MUM effect within our own families.

It is not surprising therefore that the MUM effect is also present in dyads—even when the two people are relatively similar in status. Each tries to communicate so that he either maintains his existing status level or achieves a higher one. And though each enters the relationship with a certain status, it may change as a result of his interaction with the other.

The MUM effect can be thought of as a form of interference. In a dyadic relationship the temptation to distort messages and thus put himself in a favorable light is especially great for the person who occupies the lower-status position. He can keep this tendency in check by becoming more conscious of the tendency and by considering the consequences that distortions will undoubtedly have on his future encounters. On the other hand, the higher-status person must be aware that he may be receiving slanted messages.

Sound communication depends upon accurate information, and this is true not only of informal communication but communication in groups of all sizes, including large organizations. One writer has identified ten characteristics of a healthy organization; at least three of them depend on minimal distortion of information not only between superiors and their subordinates but between peers.[11] And clearly there is less message distortion when people communicate within an atmosphere that encourages feedback.

We could carry this discussion still further by examining other dimensions of interpersonal relations—Machiavellianism, for example —but we shall have more to say about unstructured communication in Chapter 12. For the moment let us shift our attention to a more structured form of two-person communication: the interview.

STRUCTURED TWO-PERSON COMMUNICATION: THE INTERVIEW

If you associate interviews only with job hunting, your definition of "interview" is too narrow. The interview encompasses many of the elements of all two-person communication. When you consult a doctor, canvass door to door for a political candidate, or ask a stranger for detailed instructions on how to get to a particular place, you are in some sense involved in an interview, or a "conversation with a purpose," as it was once defined.[12] The interview has also become a popular form of entertainment: witness the television talk shows as well as the more formal interviews on press-panel programs.

Interviews serve a number of functions, as can be seen from the table of interview objectives. The interviewer may gather or convey information; he may influence people's attitudes; at times he may

Ten Interview Objectives

Objective	Description	Example
Getting information	Interviewer gathers facts, opinions, or attitudes from respondent	Census taker collects data
Giving information	Interviewer presents facts, opinions, or attitudes to respondent, often as a form of instruction	Doctor explains to his patient how to maintain a balanced diet
Persuading	Interviewer attempts to influence respondent's attitude and ultimately his behavior	Student tries to convince his instructor to give a make-up exam
Problem solving	Interviewer and respondent attempt to identify causes of a problem and together seek a possible solution	Parent and teacher discuss child's reading difficulties

Ten Interview Objectives (*cont.*)

Objective	Description	Example
Counseling	Respondent seeks advice from interviewer on a matter of personal concern (closely related to problem-solving interview)	Client requests legal advice from his attorney
Job seeking or hiring	Interviewer and respondent exchange information on which to base an employment decision	Campus recruiter meets with senior students
Receiving complaints	Interviewer tries to minimize the respondent's dissatisfaction	Store manager speaks with customer about defective merchandise
Reviewing performance	Interviewer offers feedback on respondent's performance and helps him establish specific goals to be met by next appraisal interview	Editor in chief of newspaper gives periodic evaluation of each of his editors
Correcting or reprimanding	Interviewer and respondent, usually in the roles of superior and subordinate, meet to discuss respondent's need to improve his performance (ordinarily most effective when handled informally and with a helpful rather than critical tone)	Maintenance supervisor of airline discusses with mechanic areas in which he must improve his technical competence
Measuring stress	Interviewer determines how respondent acts under pressure	Personnel director of large corporation selects a top executive
	Interviewer gathers information from a respondent who does not wish to divulge it	Army officer questions a military prisoner

affect their behavior. An appraisal interview, for example, often exercises a major influence on an employee's morale. The interview is also a valuable research tool. It allows the interviewer to gather more complete information than he could in a questionnaire or a telephone conversation and to make full use of nonverbal as well as verbal cues. It also enables him to interpret or explain questions more easily so that he is more likely to get answers than he would if he simply used a questionnaire.

Standardized and Unstandardized Interviews

Whatever his objectives, the interviewer may use one of two approaches: standardized or unstandardized. The **standardized interview** consists of *a set of prepared questions from which the interviewer is not allowed to deviate.* He poses the questions precisely as they are worded on his form. He does not even have the option of changing their order. The standardized interview has one distinct advantage: uniform responses over a large number of interviewers and respondents. An inexperienced interviewer may still be able to conduct a fairly successful interview. As a rule more skill is required as the interview becomes less structured.

The **unstandardized interview** *allows the interviewer as well as the respondent considerable latitude.* He may deviate from any of the prepared questions. He may follow up a prepared question with one of his own to obtain a more complete or appropriate answer. He may drop a question he feels is unsuitable or one that might put the respondent on the defensive. If he discovers an interesting subject that he had not originally anticipated, the interviewer has the freedom to pursue this line of questioning as far as he is able. In short, the unstandardized interview gives him considerable flexibility and potential for discovery.

As we have described them, the standardized and unstandardized interviews are extremes. In fact, some standardized interviews allow some departure from the prepared questions; some unstandardized interviews do not permit the interviewer unlimited freedom. No matter how the interview is structured, however, some feedback must flow between interviewer and respondent. In the discussion that follows, let us assume that the interviewer is conducting an unstandardized interview in which he can make maximum use of feedback from the respondent by departing where necessary from his list of questions.

Questions and Answers

Interviewing is essentially dialogue, dialogue in which one party, the interviewer, guides the direction of the conversation by means of a series of questions. A skillful interviewer knows a great deal about the art of questioning. He responds to the answers he is receiving by modulating his subsequent responses—particularly the kinds of questions he asks. We can illustrate by first looking at several categories of questions.

The **open question** resembles an essay question on a test; it *places no restrictions on the length of the respondent's answer.* It also

188   allows the respondent more latitude in interpreting the subject to be discussed. Examples of open questions would be, "Would you please summarize your work experience?" and "What are your feelings about your marriage?" The interviewer may want to use open questions early in the interview to get the respondent to relax and reveal more about himself in general.

The **closed question** is more specific and *usually requires a shorter, more direct answer.* Contrast the following with the two open questions just given: "How many years of work experience have you had in this field?" and "What aspect of your marriage seems to trouble you most?" Closed questions may restrict the respondent still further by requiring a simple yes-or-no answer. "Would you like to work for a small corporation?" or "Do you feel you have a happy marriage?"

Another alternative is the **probing question**, which *encourages the respondent to elaborate on what he has been saying.* Such remarks as "I see. Can you tell me more?" or "Why don't you go on?" tend to bring about further comment on a previous statement. Short pauses may elicit the same reaction, allowing the respondent to express his thoughts more completely.

A more volatile and often annoying type of question is the **loaded question**, which *stacks the deck by implying the desired answer.* This is a form of the closed question that may be used to back the respondent into a corner. In effect, the interviewer poses and answers his own questions: to a left-wing militant, "Isn't it true that violence can only make matters worse?"; to the Secretary of Defense at a press conference, "Hasn't your new policy been tried in the past with no success?" Such questions are emotionally charged, and they immediately put the respondent on his guard. Undeniably, loaded questions are sometimes used to advantage, especially in the news media. Thus a reporter can ask a politician questions that are on the lips of many voters, forcing him to meet the issues head on. Nonetheless, if we are interested in getting information, the loaded question is a doubtful technique. A better way, for example, to question the Secretary of Defense might be, "Would you explain the advantages and disadvantages of your new policy?"

Another type of question to steer clear of is the **obvious answer question**, which by its phrasing *implies the expected response.* For example, if during an employment interview a college professor is asked, "You wouldn't be opposed to teaching freshmen, would you?", he knows that the expected answer is something on the order of "I don't mind at all" or "No, I enjoy teaching freshmen." If he wants the job, our professor is likely to give the "right" answer, regardless of his preferences.

Regardless of the kinds of questions the interviewer chooses, he is never completely sure of obtaining the number and quality of answers he would like to have. Interviewing is a dynamic process, not a programed event. It cannot move forward without the participation of the respondent. Thus another aspect of interviewing skill involves handling inadequate responses. Let us look at five that the interviewer can anticipate and try to avoid.

First, suppose that the respondent gives **no answer**—that is, he either refuses to answer (the familiar "No comment" or "I'd rather not say") or he says nothing at all. A sufficient number of such responses will bring the interview to a dead end. The interviewer might follow up such a response with a second, related question, or if necessary he might drop the line of inquiry altogether.

Imagine instead that the respondent gives a **partial answer**. The interviewer might then restate the part of the question that has not been answered. If he gets a good many partial answers, he should review the questions he has asked. Perhaps some could be subdivided and posed individually. In general, it is best to avoid asking more than one question at a time.

Reacting appropriately to an **irrelevant answer** is more complex because there are two reasons the respondent may have gone off on a tangent: he may not have understood the question completely, or he may be making a conscious effort to avoid answering it. Politicians, it seems, frequently evade questions by offering irrelevant answers.

Often a respondent who does not wish to disclose information will offer an **inaccurate answer**, especially if he is embarrassed about revealing the truth. Unfortunately an inaccurate answer is often difficult for the interviewer to detect, especially in an initial interview. Of course, the accuracy of the information he receives is determined in part by the respondent's motivation. A person who feels threatened by an interview is more inclined to provide data within what he perceives to be the interviewer's expectations. And as we saw in discussing the MUM effect, people sometimes respond inaccurately in an attempt to maintain their status level or achieve a higher one. It has been found, for example, that people (particularly those with high incomes) overestimate the number of plane trips they have made but play down any automobile loans they have taken out.[13]

Whether they are intentional or not, inaccurate responses are damaging not only to the interviewer but to the respondent. If he will be seeing the interviewer again—as is probable after an employment, appraisal, or counseling interview—it is likely that some of these distortions will be revealed at a later date. If the interviewer finds that over a series of meetings the respondent has been giving inaccurate answers, he should consider possible reasons for this behavior. The interviewer has much to gain from establishing greater rapport with the respondent, putting him at ease so that he feels it will not be personally damaging for him to tell the truth.

If the respondent tells the interviewer much more than he wants to know, his is an **oververbalized answer**. Sometimes lengthy answers contain a great deal of irrelevant information. A high percentage of oververbalized responses will severely limit the number of topics that an interviewer can cover in the time allotted. He should try as tactfully as possible to guide the respondent back to the heart of the question, and to do this he may wish to increase the number of closed questions.

As if these difficulties were not enough to contend with, it now seems that there are people who have a response set to agree (yeasayers) or to disagree (naysayers). Couch and Keniston, two psychologists who have analyzed response tendencies as a personality variable, describe yeasayers as impulsive people who respond easily to stimuli. Naysayers, on the other hand, inhibit and suppress their impulses and tend to reject emotional stimuli.[14] The language in which statements are cast also affects response bias. Yeasayers are particularly attracted to statements that are enthusiastic and colloquial in tone. On the rare occasions when naysayers do agree, they are inclined to go along with statements that seem guarded, qualified, or cautious. Further research findings will be needed, however, before the interviewer can attempt to offset response bias by the way he constructs his questions.

Interview Structure

In addition to developing his skill in the art of questioning, the interviewer is sometimes responsible for giving the meeting structure. Much of what we have said thus far can be applied to relatively unstructured communication as well as to interviews. But in most cases an interview should have an apparent structure—an opening, body, and closing—and the interviewer will have specific responsibilities during each part.

In beginning an interview, an interviewer has three basic responsibilities. The first is to introduce the objectives of the interview to the respondent. Although these usually seem obvious to the interviewer, a brief statement of purpose is reassuring to the other party: an employee who is called in for a routine appraisal, for example, may perceive it as a reprimand interview unless the purpose is made clear. A second task for the interviewer is to establish rapport with the respondent, to get him to feel that he can trust the interviewer and that the meeting does not present a threatening situation. The interviewer's third and most important responsibility is motivating the respondent to answer his questions. Sometimes the respondent's interest seems assured. If he is applying for a job, he will probably do his utmost to answer questions. But what if you are conducting some research interviews? Typically, door-to-door canvassing is considered a nuisance, and respondents may be reluctant to talk. An interviewer should never assume that a potential respondent is just waiting to be interviewed. Instead he should act as though the person is busy and try to show briefly why it is important that he take a few moments of his time.

The body of the interview constitutes the major portion of time spent with the respondent, and it should be carefully planned for best results. If at all possible, it should be free from interruptions, phone calls, and other distractions so that both parties remain as relaxed as possible. We have seen that a number of different types of questions can be used in an interview. Each has advantages and disadvantages; the student of interviewing should at least be familiar with them. In addition, the sequence of questions used is important.

The first step in interview planning is to determine the topics to be covered. What, for example, is the typical content of the employment interview? One analysis of twenty employment interviews lists the topics shown in the accompanying table as the most frequently discussed.

Themes of Twenty Employment Interviews

Theme	Percentage*
Information about the company:	
General organizational orientation	100
Specific job area	90
Promotion policies	60
Information about the candidate:	
Job expectations	80
Academic background	75
Prepared for the interviews	75
Scholastic record	70
Military status	70
Work experience	60
Geographical preference	60
Interviewing for other jobs	50
Marital status	50
Information about the interviewer:	
His job	25
His background	25
Where he lives	10

* Refers to the percentage of observed interviews in which this theme occurred.

Source: Adapted from Cal Downs and Wil Linkugel, "A Content Analysis of Twenty Selection Interviews" (paper delivered at the annual conference of the International Communication Association, Phoenix, Ariz., April 1971), p. 3.

Once the interviewer has selected the topics, he then determines the actual sequence of questions. At this point a strategy known as the **funnel sequence** is often useful: he *begins with broad questions and gradually makes them more specific.*[15] Here is a funnel sequence that was used in a discussion of population control:

1. What are your views about increasing population growth in the United States?
2. What are your feelings about controlling our population growth?
3. Do you think legalized abortion should be used to help control the U.S. population?
4. Should there be restrictions on abortions?
5. What restrictions should there be?

Because each question in the sequence is more specific than the preceding one, the interviewer can reconstruct a more complete picture of the respondent's attitudes and at the same time evaluate specific answers in relation to the general issue. The funnel sequence may be used for any number of individual topics within the body of the interview.

The funnel sequence is just one of several ways of organizing the exchange. In their discussion of the research interview, Cannell and Kahn offer some advice about selecting the sequence of topics that might well apply to almost any type of interview:

> The sequence of topics themselves should be planned to make the total interview experience as meaningful as possible, to give it a beginning, a middle, and an end. More specifically, the early questions should serve to engage the respondent's interest without threatening or taxing him before he is really committed to the transaction, and to exemplify and teach him the kind of task the interview represents. The most demanding of questions might well be placed later in the interview, when respondent commitment can be presumed to have peaked—and fatigue has not yet set in. Sometimes the riskiest of questions may be put very late in the interview, so that if they trigger a refusal to continue, relatively little information is lost. This procedure seems prudent, but it risks also the possibility of an unpleasant leavetaking.[16]

The possibility of an unpleasant or at least an unsatisfying conclusion points to the importance of skillfully terminating the interview. All too often interviews end abruptly because of a lack of time, and both parties are left feeling the need for closure, or resolution. Almost any interview profits from a summary of the ground covered. It can range from a brief statement to a review of all the major points discussed. Then, if some action is to be taken as a result of the interview (hiring a person, for example), the nature of the next contact should be agreed on. If each person thinks the other will initiate the contact, both may wait too long before following up. More than one job has been lost this way. Finally, a written summary may be sent to the respondent. In appraisal interviews this procedure is especially helpful: both parties then have a written record of the agreed-upon objectives for the employee's future job responsibilities. The summary will also serve as a record of the employee's progress.

We have seen various ways in which the interviewer can introduce or reinforce interview structure, but the **nondirective interview** demands skill of a different order. In this approach, often associated with psychotherapeutic treatment, *the interviewer merely restates the respondent's answers* without making value judgments about them or guiding the conversation along any prescribed lines. The aim is to induce the respondent to elaborate on previous statements in greater depth and realize the implications of what he has said. In this excerpt from the M.I.T. MAD Doctor computer program we see an exchange between computer and patient that reads like a parody of the nondirective interview:

HOW DO YOU DO. I AM THE DOCTOR. PLEASE SIT DOWN
    AT THE TYPEWRITER AND TELL ME YOUR PROBLEM.
I am unhappy.
I AM SORRY TO HEAR YOU ARE UNHAPPY.
What shall I do about it?
WHY DO YOU ASK?
I don't like being unhappy.
YOU SAY YOU DON'T LIKE BEING UNHAPPY.
Yes, I don't like it.
YOU SEEM QUITE POSITIVE.
Of course I am.
IS IT BECAUSE YOU ARE THAT YOU CAME TO ME?
Because I am what?[17]

To elaborate on the skills needed to conduct a nondirective interview would go beyond the limits of this chapter. We shall simply note in passing that such an interview requires great restraint and sensitivity on the part of the interviewer and that this is not a technique to be exploited by the amateur psychologist.

Responsibilities of the Interviewer and the Respondent

Although numerous responsibilities must be shared by the two participants in any interview, a few stand out as specifically those of the interviewer. First, as we mentioned earlier, he should choose a suitable physical setting—one that is relatively free from distractions and interruptions. Second, he should create a psychological atmosphere conducive to successful communication so that the respondent is not placed in a defensive position. This requires that the interviewer take the initiative in introducing himself and maintain a friendly and encouraging manner. He should be well prepared so that the interview attains its original objectives. Usually the interviewer is also responsible for summarizing the discussion and for keeping an accurate record of any pertinent information that develops out of the interview. And to fulfill the last two requirements, he must be a willing and active listener. Finally, he should terminate the interview in a way that lets the respondent know what to expect as a result of the meeting. If action is to be taken, the interviewer is responsible for making sure there is agreement on what that action will be.

The responsibilities of the respondent vary according to the type of interview. In an employment interview he makes the encounter what he wants it to be—at least to some extent. In an information-giving interview, he has fewer responsibilities than the interviewer and is ordinarily more passive.

There are some general responsibilities, however, that the respondent should assume in almost any type of interview. First, he should be willing to communicate. If the interview requires it, he should prepare any information that must be conveyed to the interviewer. He should dress and act appropriately. He should try to give adequate and accurate responses that are relevant and not overlong, and he should avoid being arrogant or belligerent. Finally, he should be willing to clarify himself if he feels that he has been misinterpreted. He shares the responsibility for making the interview a success, for interviewer and respondent are complementary roles.

Summary

The dyad is in many ways a microcosm of all larger groups. In the present chapter we have seen that even two-person communication must be viewed within a social setting. Members of a dyad are strongly influenced by the norms they have already adopted, and they also establish some normative agreements of their own as they interact. In addition, the roles they enact affect how they will respond to each other; we examined some consequences of conflicts within and between roles.

Our second topic was the dynamics of unstructured two-person communication. We found that given certain norms and roles, several other variables affect interaction. For example, greater emotional involvement is possible within the dyad than in a larger group and this involvement is usually satisfying; such involvement can have negative consequences, however. Arousal level is another correlate of performance. Need for affiliation and need for dominance—two important dimensions of motivation—were also seen to be predictors of face-to-face interaction.

The final section of the chapter examined a more structured form of communication: the interview. Interview objectives, various kinds of questions and responses, and ways of structuring the interview were all discussed, largely in terms of the interviewer's role. In conclusion we reviewed some responsibilities of both interviewer and respondent.

Review Questions

1. How are disruptive power and norms related to dyadic communication?
2. What is the difference between expected and enacted roles?
3. Explain the distinction between intrarole and interrole conflict, and give an example of each.
4. What are two ways involvement of communicators is related to dyadic communication?
5. How is one's level of arousal related to one's ability to perform effectively?
6. How are need for dominance, need for achievement, and self-concept related?
7. How are need for affiliation and need for dominance related?
8. Describe two ways in which status affects dyadic communication.
9. Define the MUM effect.
10. Identify ten different types of interview objectives.
11. How do standardized and unstandardized interviews differ?
12. What are five different types of interview questions? Give an example of each.
13. What are five inadequate responses to interview questions? What strategy or strategies may be used to handle each?
14. Discuss three responsibilities of the interviewer at the beginning of an interview.
15. What is the funnel sequence? How might this technique be used in the body of an interview?
16. Describe three steps recommended in terminating an interview.
17. What are four responsibilities of an interviewer?
18. What are four responsibilities of a respondent?

Exercises

1. Select one of the role-playing situations listed in the Appendix. Determine what norms appear to operate in the specific role-playing situation selected. How might these norms be adhered to and violated in terms of the expected and enacted roles of the interviewer and respondent?
2. Write a short paper in which you analyze some communication difficulties that might arise for a college student as a result of his role conflicts.
3. Create two or three different role-playing situations similar to those listed in the Appendix. Select members of the class to role-

play the situations in which the players have different dominance and affiliation needs. How do differences in these needs affect the communication patterns in the interview?

4. After observing a conversation between two people, try to determine what specific messages (nonverbal as well as verbal) reveal the dominance or submissiveness of each communicator. Make the same observations with respect to affiliative or antisocial behaviors. Do the characteristic roles shift from time to time?

5. Videotape an interview conducted by your classmates. Play back the interview and have the class evaluate it in terms of the suggested procedures for conducting the beginning, body, and end of an interview.

6. Role-play as respondent to a classmate, providing inadequate responses to develop his ability to probe for better answers. Then switch roles and let him put you to the test.

Suggested Readings

Bach, George, and Wyden, Peter. *The Intimate Enemy: How to Fight Fair in Love and Marriage.* New York: Morrow, 1968. This book attempts to show constructive ways to resolve conflicts between the sexes. Numerous people have found it to be a useful guide to problem-solving communication in the love relationship.

Gorden, Raymond. *Interviewing: Strategy, Techniques, and Tactics.* Homewood, Ill.: Dorsey, 1969. This comprehensive text has both depth and breadth and covers both theory and application well. If you are interested in an extensive sourcebook, this would be a good one.

Goyer, Robert, Redding, W. Charles, and Rickey, John. *Interviewing Principles and Techniques.* Dubuque, Iowa: Brown, 1968. This useful little project text has an inventory of classroom exercises in interviewing. In addition, it offers guidelines for conducting and evaluating the interviewing exercises.

Notes

1 Erving Goffman, *Relations in Public: Microstudies of the Public Order* (New York: Basic, 1971), pp. 3–4.

2 Peter Murdoch and Dean Rosen, "Norm Formation in an Interdependent Dyad," *Sociometry,* 33 (1970), 273.

3 John W. Thibaut and Harold H. Kelley, *The Social Psychology of Groups* (New York: Wiley, 1959), pp. 147, 128.

4 Albert Ellis, *Reason and Emotion in Psychotherapy* (New York: Lyle Stuart, 1962).

5 Robert E. Gould, "Some Husbands Talk About Their Liberated Wives," *The New York Times Magazine*, June 18, 1972, p. 47.

6 Kenneth Sereno and C. David Mortensen, "The Effects of Ego-Involved Attitudes on Conflict Negotiation in Dyads," *Speech Monographs*, 36 (1969), 8–12.

7 Richard Christie and Florence L. Geis, *Studies in Machiavellianism* (New York: Academic, 1970), p. 313.

8 Stephen Potter, *One-Upmanship* (New York: Holt, Rinehart and Winston, 1952), p. 22.

9 Goffman, p. 74.

10 Sidney Rosen and Abraham Tesser, "On Reluctance to Communicate Undesirable Information: The MUM Effect," *Sociometry*, 33 (1970), 253–263.

11 Richard Beckhard, *Organizational Development: Strategies and Models* (Reading, Mass.: Addison-Wesley, 1969), pp. 10–11.

12 Walter Van Dyke Bingham and Bruce Victor Moore, *How to Interview* (New York: Harper & Brothers, 1924), p. 3.

13 J. B. Lansing and D. M. Blood, *The Changing Travel Market*, Monograph No. 38 (Ann Arbor, Mich.: Survey Research Center, 1964).

14 Arthur Couch and Kenneth Keniston, "Yeasayers and Naysayers: Agreeing Response Set as a Personality Variable," *Journal of Abnormal and Social Psychology*, 60 (1960), 173.

15 Robert L. Kahn and Charles F. Cannell, *The Dynamics of Interviewing* (New York: Wiley, 1957), pp. 158–160.

16 Charles F. Cannell and Robert L. Kahn, "Interviewing," in Gardner Lindzey and Elliot Aronson (eds.), *The Handbook of Social Psychology*, 2nd ed. (Reading, Mass.: Addison-Wesley, 1968), Vol. II, *Research Methods*, p. 578.

17 Quoted in Michael Argyle, *Social Interaction* (London: Methuen, 1969), p. 169.

Chapter **9**

The
Small
Group:

Problem-
Solving
Communication

OBJECTIVES

After reading this chapter the student should be able to:

1. Distinguish between primary, learning, and therapeutic groups.
2. Describe the concept of conformity in terms of the autokinetic effect.
3. Distinguish between private acceptance and public compliance.
4. Identify four conditions under which private acceptance is likely to occur.
5. Identify four characteristics of people likely to conform to group pressure.
6. Describe two theories that have been used to explain compliance to social pressure.
7. Explain the risky shift phenomenon.
8. Describe the relationship between group cohesiveness and the effectiveness of the brainstorming technique.
9. List twelve types of group member roles and give an example of each.
10. Identify four characteristics of group cohesiveness.
11. Describe the relationship between group size, member satisfaction, and group performance.
12. Draw five types of communication networks and describe their relative effectiveness in relation to group performance.
13. Distinguish between the trait and function views of leadership.
14. Distinguish between task and consideration leadership functions.
15. Identify six common difficulties that small groups encounter in developing ideas and solving problems.
16. Distinguish between the standard agenda, ideal solution, and single question formats for group discussion.
17. Describe four phases of group interaction during the decision-making process.
18. Identify four strategies that may be used to resolve group conflict effectively.
19. Describe four ways of arriving at a decision in a group.

9

A camel, it's been said, is a horse that was built by a committee—the implication being that group solutions are far less effective than those made by individuals. Whether or not this statement is true (and we shall examine it further in this chapter), all of us spend at least some of our time as members of problem-solving groups. A student council, a parent-teacher's committee on sex education in the public schools, a commission investigating the causes of prison riots, a fund-raising committee for a political party, and a tenants' association organized to fight rent increases have much in common. Despite the diverse issues that concern them, each group consists of several human beings with different ideas, skills, and levels of interest. Each group has a problem to solve and must determine the best way to go about solving it—ideally by making use of the resources of all its members.

This chapter is about the kind of communication that takes place in small groups, particularly in **problem-solving,** or *task-oriented,* groups. We shall focus first on the ways in which such groups typically function and second on the ways individual members can improve their effectiveness in them. In doing so, we begin to extend the two-person communication model outlined in Chapter 2 and developed in Chapter 8. The dyad is sometimes referred to as a two-person group, and often two people will engage in problem solving. But in discussing the small group, particularly the problem-solving group, we shall follow Bales' definition. That is, we shall consider the **small group** to consist of *three to fifteen people* or a number small enough so that "each member receives some impression or perception of each other member distinct enough so that he can . . . give some reaction to each of the others as individual persons, even though it be only to recall that the other was present."[1]

Small-group experience is by no means confined to problem solving. Each of us is simultaneously a member of many small groups. The first and most informal are **primary groups,** *the basic social units to which we belong.* Our first primary group is our family. Our childhood friends constitute another. In the company of adult friends, neighbors, and others with whom we socialize, we continue and extend our primary-group relationships. Occasionally members of primary groups solve problems together or counsel one another, but much of their communication is spontaneous and unstructured.

Most of us are also members of **learning groups.** Here we *come together* in an attempt *to teach or to learn something about a given* *subject,* whether it is yoga, politics, or cooking. Quarterback clubs meet to learn more about football. Film buffs get together to share their interpretations of movies. Seminars and courses involving group interaction also constitute learning groups.

At one time or another, some of us will also belong to **therapeutic groups,** whose members *come together to learn about themselves and to improve their interpersonal relationships* (especially primary-group relationships). Unlike learning groups, which focus on mastering a given subject, therapeutic groups are consciously concerned with process, with small-group experience itself. Therapeutic groups usually take one of two forms: the psychotherapeutic group or the encounter group. The first usually meets over a longer period of time than the second and is largely conducted in conjunction with individual therapy. Encounter groups, sometimes described as "therapy for normals," are the subject of Chapter 10.

Homans has described membership in small groups as "the first and most immediate social experience of mankind." Even his definition of a group is linked to the concept of interpersonal communication: "We mean by a group a number of persons who communicate with one another often over a span of time and who are few enough so that each person is able to communicate with all the others, not at secondhand, through other people, but face-to-face."[2] As you read about groups in the next three chapters, you might give some thought to this definition.

GROUP DYNAMICS

One of the major complaints about committees and other problem-solving small groups is that they take up too much time and seldom accomplish as much as they should. To make better use of the time spent in small groups, we have to know something about how people ordinarily behave in them.

Conformity

One night several restless upperclassmen in a small dorm at the University of Wisconsin decided to persuade a fellow student that it was time for class. It was about 1 A.M. As the girl lay sleeping, they reset her alarm clock so that it went off at 1:15 but read 8:15. A few people were stationed in the bathroom, towels and toothbrushes in hand. Others were strategically placed along the corridor, ready to go through the motions of bustling off to class.

When her alarm rang the poor victim stumbled out of bed to see her roommate in the process of getting dressed. She couldn't believe that it was morning, despite the activity. "You can still see the stars. There's something wrong with the alarm. It's pitch dark outside," she protested, only to be told that it was "a dark morning." The sight of two students on their way to have breakfast was the final touch. It was spring, and there aren't many dark mornings in the spring. Nonetheless other people seemed to think it was morning, and despite the evidence of her own senses, the weary girl started to dress for breakfast.

This is a common prank, not only in college but in summer camps and military barracks. It works often enough to suggest the potent influence of group opinion on individual judgment. In the 1930s a psychologist named Sherif designed a series of experiments on social influence in which he made use of a phenomenon called the **autokinetic effect**. The autokinetic effect is an optical illusion that was first pointed out by ancient astronomers: when a stationary point of light is viewed in total darkness, the light seems to move because no frame of reference exists against which the observer can localize it.

Individual estimates of autokinetic movement vary a great deal. To one person it might seem that the light has moved 2 inches; to another the distance might seem to be 6 inches. Yet Sherif found that a person who first views this phenomenon when he is isolated from others and observes it several times under these conditions will develop a standard of his own so that all his subsequent estimates of distance fall within this range. On the other hand, when he witnesses the autokinetic effect for the first time as a member of a group, the group establishes a norm; if he is then exposed again to the autokinetic effect when he is alone, he will make his estimates in terms of the group norm. Moreover, if a person who has made his initial judgments in isolation is put in a position where he overhears others estimate the distance, he will correct his own estimate so that it tends to converge with that of the others. The autokinetic effect is thus also a measure of the effect of prestige on conformity:

Miss X and I (Assistant in Psychology, Columbia University) were subjects for Dr. Sherif. I was well acquainted with the experiment, but Miss X knew nothing whatsoever about it. Since she was a close friend of mine, and I carried some prestige with her, Dr. Sherif suggested that it would be interesting to see if we could predetermine her judgments. It was agreed beforehand that I was to give no judgments until she had set her own standard. After a few stimulations it was quite clear that her judgments were going to vary around five inches. At the next appropriate stimulation, I made a judgment of twelve inches. Miss X's next judgment was eight inches. I varied my judgments around twelve inches and she did the same. Then I changed my judgment to three inches, suggesting to Dr. Sherif that he had changed it. She gradually came down to my standard, but not without some apparent resistance. When it was clear that she had accepted this new standard, Dr. Sherif suggested that I make no more judgments lest I might influence hers. He then informed her on a subsequent stimulation that she was underestimating the distance which the point had moved. Immediately her judgments were made larger and she established a new standard. However, she was a little uneasy with it all, and before the experiment had progressed much farther, whispered to me, "Get me out of here."[3]

There could be no right or wrong answers in Sherif's experiments; yet norms developed. In another work Sherif tries to explain why social influence is so strong:

> . . . when a group of individuals faces a new, unstable situation and has no previously established interest or opinions regarding the situation, the result is not chaos; a common norm arises and the situation is structured in relation to the common norm. Once the common norm is established, later the separate individuals keep on perceiving it in terms of the frame of reference which was once the norm of the group.[4]

We discussed the concept of norms in Chapter 8. Suffice it to say that in the small group, social influence is even more powerful than it is in the dyad. Moreover, as we know from our discussion of balance theory, the judgments of other people affect our attitudes, beliefs, and values as well as our perceptions.

One of the criticisms of conformity research has been that subjects rarely get to argue their point of view against the majority opinion. Yet even in studies that allow dissenting members to present their arguments, considerable conformity behavior still occurs.[5] These studies distinguish between **private acceptance** of a judgment or opinion and **public compliance**—that is, between whether one changes his

"Well, heck! If all you smart cookies agree, who am I to dissent?"

Drawing by Handelsman; © 1972 The New Yorker Magazine, Inc.

thinking as a result of hearing opinions different from his own or whether he says he agrees with the group when in fact he disagrees.

Private acceptance is more likely to occur when (1) the individual greatly values his membership in the group, (2) opinion is unanimously against him, (3) the issue in question is ambiguous to begin with, or (4) the group is under pressure to achieve an important goal.[6] Public compliance usually stems from the desire to avoid the unpleasantness of conflict. After maintaining a dissenting opinion for a long time, a person may be made so uncomfortable by social pressures that as a peace-keeping gesture he gives the impression that he goes along with the rest of the group. A number of studies have shown that the person who conforms readily tends to be (1) more submissive or dependent, (2) high in his need for social approval and low in his need to be outstanding, (3) more often female than male, and (4) lacking in self-confidence.[7]

Sometimes, of course, compliance is forced. For example, during the Korean War the so-called confessions of American prisoners to Chinese participants holding them captive often included remarks or emphases that undercut their own statements of contrition:

> . . . the prisoners found numerous ways to obey the letter but not the spirit of the Chinese demands. For example, during public self-criticism sessions they would often emphasize the wrong words in the sentence, thus making the whole ritual ridiculous: "I am sorry I called Comrade Wong *a no-good son-of-a-bitch.*" Another favorite device was to promise never to "get caught" committing a certain crime in the future. Such devices were effective because even those Chinese who knew English were not sufficiently acquainted with idiom and slang to detect subtle ridicule.[8]

The prisoner of war and the compliant group member both pretend to go along with the expectations of the group in order to spare themselves certain undesirable consequences. For the prisoner of war, these consequences are often physical—solitary confinement, lack of food, torture. For the member of a group, the consequences, while perhaps more subtle, are no less real—social pressure, loss of esteem, even ostracism by the group.

Social Influence

We have looked at conformity behavior in terms of the individual member. Now let us examine the behavior of the group. We know that the group tends to exert most pressure to conform on newcomers, who have not yet earned the right to deviate from group norms. Fraternities and sororities often deal out harsh criticisms when rushees and pledges dress or act differently from other members of the group. Yet a great many of the same deviations are tolerated when they exist in fraternity members who are upperclassmen.

Groups with a high level of cohesiveness tend to exert strong conformity pressures. It seems that the more closely knit the group, the more the members resist allowing anyone to become a member who does not share their values. Members with the greatest prestige tend to be "super representatives" of the attributes that are highly valued by the group. The typical football team captain is usually one of the best athletes on the team. Similarly the gang leader is often one of the toughest members of his gang. In each case the person who best represents the qualities esteemed by the group has the most prestige.

How does the cohesive group behave when one of its members takes a stand quite different from that of the rest? Schachter found that initially the deviant gets most of the group's attention. Each member will probably say or do something to persuade the lone dissenter to come around to the position held by the rest of the group. These efforts may go on for some time. Eventually the deviant either gives in— there is no way of knowing of course whether this is simply public compliance—or is ignored or rejected.[9]

Newcomb has tried to account for the group's behavior in terms of balance theory. He predicts that in groups of three or more people, the need for balance (or symmetry) will operate to reduce the discrepancy between the deviant's attitude and the attitudes of the other group members. Thus, in an effort to change the deviant's mind, the group will direct a greater proportion of its communicative acts toward him than toward any other member for a considerable length of time.[10] There is a point of diminishing returns, however, after which the deviant receives little or no communication from other group members, who for the most part ignore him.

An explanation of what makes most of us yield to social pressure is offered by Festinger's **social comparison theory**.[11] Festinger believes that *each human being has a need to evaluate his opinions and abilities and that when he cannot do so by objective nonsocial means he compares them with those of other people.* How do you tell, for example, whether you are a good driver? Clearly by comparing your performance with that of other drivers. Similarly you find out whether you are liberal in your political views by comparing them with those of others. In other words, in the absence of objective criteria, you rely on the opinions of others to determine the validity of your own.

In the Schachter experiment a discrepancy existed between the opinions of one group member and the rest of the group. Social comparison theory predicts that in such a situation group members will act to reduce the discrepancy and that the person with the discrepant opinion will tend to change his position so that it is closer to that of other group members. We saw this to be the case not only in the Schachter experiment but in some of the studies of the autokinetic effect, where individual judgments tend to converge with group norms. However these phenomena are explained, the tendency to conform seems clear. In the following section we shall examine conformity as it affects group decisions.

The Quality of Group Problem Solving

In studying group dynamics, a reasonable question to ask is how groups compare with individuals in problem solving. Will the number of people in the group affect the quality of the decision? Will people meeting together generate a greater number of novel ideas than they would working in isolation? In short, how does the presence of others influence the way we think?

Acceptance of Risk. It has been established that members of groups tend to conform. As yet, however, nothing has been said about the direction of that conformity. When we call someone a "conformist," we usually think of him as somewhat conservative. A conformist doesn't rock the boat. He doesn't create dissension. He goes along with group norms. He probably goes along with group decisions. It would seem then that because he conforms he takes few risks, and from this we might guess that the decisions of the group would also tend to be conservative or at least cautious.

Suppose you are on your way to a meeting in which your group will advise Mr. A, an electrical engineer, about the pros and cons of a certain career choice. Should he remain in the large electronics corporation for which he works, where he is assured a high level of security and moderate financial rewards; or should he accept an offer from a small, recently founded company that will offer him a higher starting salary and a share in the firm's ownership but whose future is highly uncertain? What odds will you give—1 in 10, 3 in 10, and so on—that the new company turns out to be financially sound and thus that Mr. A will do better joining it than remaining where he is? Whatever the odds you choose, chances are that if a group discussion follows, it will significantly increase your estimate of Mr. A's chances for success.

The risky shift phenomenon is the name given this *tendency for people to increase their willingness to take risks as a result of group discussions.* It is by no means confined to decisions about careers. Here, for example, are summaries of a few of the experimental problems that have demonstrated a shift toward risk after group communication:

> A man with a severe heart ailment must seriously curtail his customary way of life if he does not undergo a delicate medical operation which might cure him completely or might prove fatal.

> A captain of a college football team, in the final seconds of a game with the college's traditional rival, may choose a play that is almost certain to produce a tie score, or a more risky play that would lead to sure victory if successful, sure defeat if not.

An engaged couple must decide, in the face of recent arguments suggesting some sharp differences of opinion, whether or not to get married. Discussions with a marriage counselor indicate that a happy marriage, while possible, would not be assured.[12]

Several explanations of the risky shift phenomenon have been proposed; we shall consider three of them in brief fashion. The first is that within a group no member feels totally responsible for the decision, as he would if he were alone. This might explain the actions of lynch mobs: a person who might never dare commit a murder on his own suddenly helps carry out a lynching. The second possibility is that those who argue in favor of risky positions are more persuasive than those who are conservative and that they therefore influence others in favor of riskier decisions. The first two hypotheses have little experimental support. A third and more likely possibility is that Western culture tends to value risk taking over conservative behavior. Witness the American idea that any newborn child has some chance of one day becoming president of the United States. In this country we hold success and achievement in high esteem, and both are linked to a good extent with a willingness to take risks. In contemplating a decision each person may feel that the course of action he favors involves a reasonable amount of risk, but as the group begins to communicate about the problem, more arguments for both the risky and the conservative side become apparent. The result, as Wheeler puts it, is that

> Just as an individual practices his tennis game because there is a cultural value placed on being slightly better than other people, he changes his risk level in the direction valued by the culture so that he can feel he is slightly "better" than his peers. This does not mean that the individual automatically changes his risk level but that he reinterprets elements in the situation and focuses on arguments favoring risk.[13]

As you find yourself participating in task-oriented groups, it is important to realize that the group decision is likely to be riskier than the average of the positions taken by individual group members before their interaction.

Level of Creativity. A second issue concerning the kinds of solutions groups reach has to do with creativity. Consider this problem. The Lang Advertising Agency has five writers on its staff. It is bidding for the Hudson's Bay Scotch account and must submit a sales presentation and advertising program to the prospective client. Should each of the five writers work independently and submit his own program to the advertising director, or should the five be brought together to tackle the problem? Which procedure will generate a greater number of original ideas?

In essence we are asking whether **brainstorming** is an effective problem-solving technique. This approach, first introduced in the advertising firm of Batten, Barton, Durstine & Osborn in 1939, was designed to offset tendencies of group members to be inhibited by pressures to conform. Brainstorming had several rules. There was to be no criticism of ideas. "Freewheeling" was encouraged: the more way out the idea, the better. Quantity was desired: the greater the number of ideas, the better. Taking off on other people's ideas—either by improving one or by showing how two different ideas could be combined—was also encouraged.[14]

Brainstorming sessions became extremely popular not only in large corporations but in the military and in various government agencies. No one seemed to challenge the belief that people worked more effectively in groups than in isolation until 1958. At that time a study at Yale University found that people who worked alone on a problem rather than as part of a group produced almost twice the number of ideas and twice the number of unique ideas.[15]

Yet brainstorming is still a widely practiced technique. Are we to conclude from the Yale study that groups will always solve problems less effectively and creatively than individuals? We cannot answer this question as easily as we can the issue of whether groups make more or less conservative decisions than individuals. There is evidence that when the group is a cohesive one and when members have had previous training in brainstorming techniques, the results can be highly successful.[16] It has been suggested therefore that the effectiveness of brainstorming will depend on several variables, including the relationships among group members, the nature of the problem to be solved, and the type of leadership the group has.[17]

The Role of Group Member

Nine psychotherapists have formed a group to help block the passage of mental health legislation that they consider repressive. Ostensibly the group's members are equal in status. No leader has been appointed. In this context each of the therapists has the same role—that of group member. Because of your interest in small-group communication and your friendship with one of the therapists, you are allowed to attend the meeting as an observer.

After attending a few meetings, you begin to notice that Bob knows a lot about existing mental health laws. He also makes a number of suggestions for actions the group might take: contacting legislators, raising funds for a series of broadcasts on the issue, distributing handbills about the implications of the new law. Matt, another member of the group, has few ideas of his own and tends to go along with any concrete proposals for group action. "I'm for that. Why not try it?" he often says. Frank, on the other hand, has more ideas than he knows what to do with. He proposes solutions, one after another—some sound, others extreme. Initially he is very enthusiastic, but he never seems to carry through any of his suggestions. To the chagrin of most of the group, Kay usually punches holes in other people's arguments. "It will never work," she chides. "What do we use for money? People aren't going to contribute. They don't understand the issue."

Here are four people in the role of group member. Each interprets it somewhat differently. You think you see some individual patterns of interaction emerging, but to be accurate you need a method of describing various behaviors.

One of the more important accomplishments of small-group research has been the development of several such systems. Undoubtedly the most widely known is Interaction Process Analysis (IPA), developed at Harvard University by Robert Bales. The twelve categories of IPA are virtually self-explanatory (see Figure 15), and they offer a valuable framework from which to view the functions and patterns of communication. Each interaction is assigned to one of the categories, and when the scoring has been completed, certain behavior patterns become apparent.

Figure 15

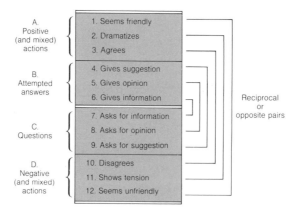

Categories for Interaction Process Analysis

SOURCE: *Personality and Interpersonal Behavior* by Robert Freed Bales. Copyright © 1970 by Holt, Rinehart and Winston, Inc. Reprinted by permission of Holt, Rinehart and Winston, Inc.

In the group we have been discussing, Bob's statements would tend to fall in categories 4 (gives suggestion) and 6 (gives information), Matt's in 3 (agrees), Frank's in 4 (gives suggestion), and Kay's in 10 (disagrees). The responses of other members of the group may be more diversified so that no single category or set of categories predominates, but over an extended period we could probably identify the characteristic behaviors of each member. In any case Bales' method of classifying human interaction gives us a systematic way to analyze group communication. By means of these categories, we can classify each communicative act regardless of its content.

As you look at the list in Figure 15, you might ask yourself which categories describe your own actions in small groups. There is a good chance that you will find yourself performing only a limited number of these behaviors. For example, one friend of ours summed up his participation in groups by saying, "I often like to play the devil's advocate and give people a bit of a hard time." If his statement is accurate, we would expect that most of his interactions (like those of Kay in the group we described) would fall in category 10 of the IPA. There are groups that need at least one critical member, someone willing to challenge others, but the last thing in the world some groups need is another devil's advocate. In general, it seems foolish to assume that any behavior or set of behaviors is appropriate in all situations; there is much to be said for developing some degree of role flexibility. Increasing one's sensitivity to the needs of the group is a first step in this direction. Cameron speaks to this point when he writes:

> To the extent that an individual, in the course of his personality development, learns to take social roles skillfully and realistically, acquires an adequate repertory of them, and becomes adroit in shifting from one role to another when he is in difficulty, he should grow into a flexible, adaptive social adult with minimal susceptibility to behavior disorders.[18]

Cohesiveness

Probably one of the most important by-products of group interaction is the emotional commitment that may evolve from having worked on a problem with others. In a classic study conducted during World War II, it was found that women who participated in group discussions on how best to cook unpopular cuts of meat (and thus leave favored cuts for the troops overseas) were much more likely to try out new recipes than were women who simply listened to a speech intended to persuade them to do so.[19]

This kind of emotional commitment seems to increase as attraction to the group increases. **Cohesiveness** has been defined as *"the total field of forces acting on members to remain in the group."*[20] It may also be considered in terms of the loyalty and high morale of group members. Think of groups you have either been in or observed that were closely knit. Two groups that are not necessarily problem-solving groups but that illustrate high levels of cohesion are the so-called Kennedy clan and the Green Bay Packers of the 1960s. Cohesiveness, which connotes pride of membership, often intensifies as a group becomes more successful. We are all familiar with the popular chant of crowds at sporting events, "We're number 1, we're number 1."

In general, cohesive groups have interested and committed members who enjoy each other's company. The group is not always highly productive, but its members do tend to help each other with problems, to adapt well to crisis situations, and to ask questions openly. We referred earlier to the conformity demands made by a cohesive group on its members. It is true, however, that they may sometimes feel free to disagree more openly than members of less cohesive groups.

In discussing emotional reactions to groups it is only fair to acknowledge that things do not always turn out so positively. Working with others can also be frustrating, boring, and unsettling. The point is that the socioemotional dimension of group interaction constitutes a very real and powerful part of group behavior. Many people think that feelings have no place in a problem-solving group. On the contrary, feelings are very much involved in group behavior and should be studied as vigorously as its logical and rational aspects.

GROUP STRUCTURE

The distinction between group structure and group dynamics is somewhat arbitrary, for the way a group is constituted has considerable influence on how it functions. In our discussion of structure, we shall be concerned with three variables as they affect interpersonal communication: group size, networks, and leadership.

Group Size

Think back to the groups you have belonged to that ranged in size from three to fifteen members. As the group got larger, what did you notice about the quality of the communication? How did you feel about your part in the discussions? How satisfied were you with them? It has been known for a number of years that as group size increases, the satisfaction of each member decreases. In larger groups a few people account for almost all the talking; the rest do very little. If you remember larger groups as boring and slow-moving, you probably were among the more silent members. We have seen a number of student groups fail to develop into effective decision-making bodies because a great many people spent most of their time listening to a few long, complicated speeches made by a handful of members.

Group size affects performance as well as satisfaction. For example, larger groups tend to take more time to reach decisions, particularly if unanimity is required. We also know that as group size increases a number of subgroups may form and that these factions tend to polarize and to distract members from the problems at hand.

You can get some idea of the subgroups that may develop by looking at the potential communication relationships within groups of various sizes. In a dyad, for example, Bostrom shows that only two relationships are possible—A to B or B to A, but in a triad, or three-person group, there are nine possibilities:

1. A to B	6. C to A
2. A to C	7. A to B and C
3. B to A	8. B to A and C
4. B to C	9. C to A and B
5. C to B	

To show how rapidly complexity increases as groups gain in size, he also calculated all the communication relationships possible within groups of three to eight people:[21]

Number in Group	Interactions Possible
2	2
3	9
4	28
5	75
6	186
7	441
8	1,056

Small wonder that to most people, belonging to a large group is less satisfying than belonging to a small one.

For our purposes the most practical question we can ask is: What size group seems best for problem solving? In a tongue-in-cheek discussion of government cabinets, the world's most powerful committees, Parkinson reasons that ideally a cabinet should consist of five members. Nevertheless membership usually increases to seven or nine and then from ten toward twenty. In addition to the obvious difficulty of assembling all these people at one time, writes Parkinson,

> . . . there is a far greater chance of members proving to be elderly, tiresome, inaudible, and deaf. Relatively few were chosen from any idea that they are or could be or have been useful. A majority perhaps were brought in merely to conciliate some outside group. The tendency is therefore to report what happens to the group they represent. All secrecy is lost and, worst of all, members begin to prepare their speeches. They address the meeting and tell their friends afterward about what they imagine they have said. . . . Internal parties form and seek to gain strength by further recruitment. . . .

As membership expands beyond twenty, the whole quality of the committee changes so that "the five members who matter will have taken to meeting beforehand."[22]

214   While not to be taken literally, Parkinson's amusing description of the life cycle of the committee has essential validity. Although it is true that a greater variety of ideas tend to be expressed in large groups, they have several limitations we have already mentioned. Generally, the optimum size for a problem-solving group is five to seven members. This figure seems to have the greatest number of advantages.

Communication Networks

In *Up the Organization* Robert Townsend, the man who revitalized Avis Rent a Car and has headed numerous other business enterprises, has some provocative things to say about how management should be organized. One of his proposals is that all positions with "assistant to" in the title be abolished. In making his point Townsend presents three charts; these are reproduced in Figure 16. Unlike the regular assistant, who is given authority to make decisions, the assistant-to "moves back and forth between the boss and his people with oral or written messages on real or apparent problems—overlapping and duplicating efforts and make-working." Further on in his book, the author makes this observation about structure:

> In the best organizations people see themselves working in a circle as if around one table. One of the positions is designated chief executive officer, because somebody has to make all those tactical decisions that enable an organization to keep working. In this circular organization, leadership passes from one to another depending on the particular task being attacked —without any hang-ups.[23]

Figure 16

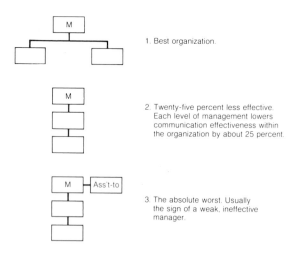

1. Best organization.

2. Twenty-five percent less effective. Each level of management lowers communication effectiveness within the organization by about 25 percent.

3. The absolute worst. Usually the sign of a weak, ineffective manager.

Three Types of Management Organization

SOURCE: Robert Townsend, *Up the Organization* (New York: Knopf, 1970), pp. 22, 23.

Townsend is talking about **communication networks,** *patterns of*
human interaction. As you read on try to decide for yourself whether
his recommendations have merit. You might reserve your judgment,
however, until after you have read the section on leadership.

In Figure 17 we see several frequently used communication networks: the Wheel, Chain, Y, Circle, and All-Channel networks. Note
that in this illustration each is a five-person group. In the Wheel one
person—who usually becomes the leader—is the focus of comments
from each member of the group. As the central person in the network,
he is free to communicate with the other four, but they can communicate only with him. In the Chain network three people can communicate with those on either side of them but the other two with only
one other member of the group. The Y network resembles the Chain:
three of the five people can communicate with only one person. Unlike
these systems, which are centralized and tend to have leaders, the Circle
and All-Channel patterns are decentralized and sometimes leaderless.
In the Circle each person may communicate with two others, those on
either side of him. In the All-Channel network, sometimes called
Concom, all communication lines are open; each member is able to
communicate with all the other members.

In studying small-group communication, we want to know how the
type of network used affects group performance in problem solving
and how given patterns affect interpersonal relationships within the
group. Much of the research on networks is based on an experiment by
Leavitt in which five subjects were each given different information
essential to the solution of a problem in symbol identification.[24] By
using various networks (the Y, Wheel, Chain, and Circle), Leavitt
manipulated the freedom with which information could be transmitted

Figure 17

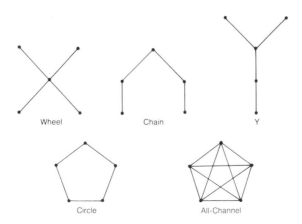

Five Types of Communication Networks

from one member to another, and he then compared the results. The Wheel, the most centralized of the four networks, produced the best-organized and fastest performance; the Circle group, the least centralized, was the most disorganized and unstable, and proved slowest in solving the problem. The biggest drawback of the Circle network, as another researcher has observed, is that it tends to generate a large number of errors as members try to communicate information around it.[25]

Numerous studies of networks have been patterned after the Leavitt experiment, but the results are not easy to summarize. It is sometimes argued, for example, that certain networks are inherently more effective because of their structure, but Guetzkow and Simon believe that there are other factors to be considered. A particular network may handicap a group not in its ability to solve a problem but in its ability to organize itself so that it can solve the problem.[26] This is an interesting hypothesis, especially in the light of Leavitt's original finding that Y, Wheel, and Chain groups were able to organize themselves so that each eventually established one procedure it used over and over, whereas members of Circle networks did not. Guetzkow and Simon believe that once a group has established a procedure for working together, it can perform efficiently regardless of its type of network.

The nature of the problem to be solved also affects performance. Groups with centralized networks are better at identifying colors, symbols, and numbers, and solving other simple problems. Decentralized networks have the edge over centralized when the problems are more complex—arithmetic, word arrangement, sentence construction, and discussion problems.[27]

Because most of the communication we are concerned with relates not to symbol identification and the like but to more complex issues, decentralized networks will usually be most desirable. For example, the Wheel, though efficient in its use of time, tends to lower the cohesiveness of a group, reduce its inventiveness, and make it too dependent on its leader.[28] Another advantage of decentralized networks is that they tend to provide the most satisfaction for individual members. The All-Channel network seems desirable for a number of reasons. Although initially it tends to be more inefficient and time-consuming, it maximizes the opportunities for corrective feedback, which ultimately should result in greater accuracy. Furthermore freedom to speak to anyone else in the group creates high morale. These findings are important to keep in mind in the event that group discussions you participate in are characterized by inaccuracy or low morale.

Leadership

For many years people believed that leaders were born, not made, and a search was conducted to determine the traits of the "born leader." The quest has been largely unsuccessful. We do know that usually a leader is more self-confident and more intelligent than other members of his group. Some studies suggest that he is better-adjusted and more sensitive to the opinions of other group members. Nevertheless these traits are by no means reliable predictors of leadership. No single set of traits seems important in all situations. The successful commander of an air force squadron is not necessarily effective in an administrative post at the Pentagon. The outstanding teacher is not always a worthwhile dean or department chairman.

Recent studies have led us to view leadership not as a quality but as a series of functions that groups must have performed. The leader then becomes the person who successfully performs a number of these functions, and sometimes leadership will pass from one person to another or be divided among group members. Thus far two major leadership activities have been identified: task functions and consideration functions. Neither set is in itself sufficient to satisfy all the group's needs.

Task functions are *activities that help the group achieve its goals.* In terms of the IPA categories in Figure 15, the activities might include giving and asking other members for suggestions, opinions, and information (categories 4–9). Other task functions might be orienting the group on how best to proceed, clarifying the remarks of others, and summarizing group progress.

Consideration functions have to do with morale. They include *any activities that improve the emotional climate or increase the satisfaction of individual members:* showing agreement, support, or encouragement; gatekeeping (that is, allowing members who might otherwise be ignored to speak); and so on.

It is often difficult for one person to perform task and consideration functions simultaneously. Suppose that an emergency meeting of a school board is called to prevent a walkout of the teachers and that two board members monopolize the discussion in an unconstructive way. Someone will have to steer the conversation back to the problem at hand, which requires immediate action, and in doing so he may bruise a few egos. It takes considerable skill for the person who has done the offending to also conciliate the offended. For this reason the group often develops two or more leaders: a task leader, whose primary concern is that the job be done and the group perform well, and a social leader, whose first interest is in maintaining the group's high morale. Nevertheless the most valuable leaders are those able to perform both task and consideration functions successfully.

Support for the concept that leaders are made, not born, comes from the Leavitt study of communication networks. Leavitt found that whereas in decentralized networks there was little agreement among members as to the identity of the group's leader, in centralized networks such as the Wheel, Chain, and Y, people who occupied central positions and were thus able to channel communication were considered leaders. (Leadership and popularity are by no means synonymous, however, as we saw in the sociograms in Chapter 5, Figures 5 and 6.)

Although we have stressed leadership functions rather than traits, there are specific behaviors often characteristic of leaders. If we compare those who get weeded out with those who emerge as leaders, we see some clear-cut differences. The first tend to be quiet, uninformed or unskilled, inflexible, and bossy or dictatorial; they also spend a great deal of time socializing. In contrast, emergent leaders tend to speak up, to have good ideas and state them clearly, to care about the group, and to make sacrifices and build cohesiveness. In sum, leadership functions include a number of behaviors that can be learned.

CORRELATES OF EFFECTIVE GROUPS

Anyone who has participated in problem-solving group discussions knows that they can be time-consuming, boring, and sometimes infuriating. Furthermore the decisions groups make may be of poor quality and may be ignored by those who must carry them out. Yet even committees that design horses which look like camels are not that easily disbanded. There are countless situations in which we cannot make decisions on our own; we must work within a group. As we have already seen, group structure—the size of a group, for example—can influence the effectiveness of problem-solving communication. In this section we shall be looking at some other correlates of small-group effectiveness.

It would be nice if we could automatically improve our communication behaviors by reading about what makes small groups successful. Unfortunately improvement is not so easily attained. It does come, however, with participation. In summarizing several studies, McGrath and Altman comment, "The adage 'Practice makes perfect' seems to be fairly well substantiated by small group research. The more task training and experience groups and group members have, the better they perform as individuals and as groups."[29]

The process by which improvement takes place is probably that of social learning. Behaviors that are productive tend to be reinforced by other members of the group, and those that are unproductive tend to be extinguished because they go unrewarded. Granted that no amount of reading can replace the experience of being part of a group, there are still some lessons we can learn from reading about communication. We can learn what the behaviors are that make for successful groups and then try to practice them when we do participate. In some situa-

tions we may be able to do no more than improve our own performance
within the group. In other cases we may be in a position to design as
well as engage in more effective group activities.

Idea Development and Problem Solving

If you were to interview members of several different kinds of small
groups about the difficulties they encounter in developing ideas and
solving problems, you would find at least six recurring complaints: (1)
Group objectives are not clearly stated or agreed upon; (2) Group
members do not come up with enough ideas; (3) The group does not
carry through discussion of each issue until it is resolved; (4) Members
rarely help one another; (5) Conflict between members becomes so
intense that it is counterproductive; and (6) Conclusions are not
reached or agreed upon.

In an attempt to correct some of these shortcomings, many groups
try to follow an agenda or schedule that will help them make better
use of their time and resources. One of the most widely known group
agendas is that adopted from a problem-solving sequence of questions
developed several decades ago by John Dewey. This approach has
often been called the Standard Agenda because, as you can see below,
the questions are broad enough to be applied to just about any problem.

Standard Agenda

1. What are the limits and specific nature of the problem?
2. What are the causes and consequences of the problem?
3. What things must an acceptable solution to the problem accomplish?
4. What solutions are available to us?
5. What is the best solution?

Although groups have been aided by the Standard Agenda for years,
experimental evidence shows that two other problem-solving sequences
—the Ideal Solution Form and the Single Question Form—result in
greater accuracy.[30] Like the Standard Agenda both these instruments
involve a series of questions intended to stimulate the thought of group
members and to keep them from reaching an impasse. In the Ideal Solution Form notice the realistic emphasis on approximating ideal goals:

Ideal Solution Form

1. Are we all agreed on the nature of the problem?
2. What would be the ideal solution from the point of view of all
   parties involved in the problem?
3. What conditions within the problem could be changed so that
   the ideal solution might be achieved?

4. Of the solutions available to us, which one best approximates the ideal solution?[31]

The Single Question Form has a slightly different emphasis. By constantly referring the group back to a single objective, it attempts to concentrate their energies on the problem and keep them from going off on a series of tangents:

Single Question Form

1. What is the single question, the answer to which is all the group needs to know to accomplish its purpose?
2. What subquestions must be answered before we can answer the single question we have formulated?
3. Do we have sufficient information to answer confidently the subquestions? (If yes, answer them. If not, continue below.)
4. What are the most reasonable answers to the subquestions?
5. Assuming that our answers to the subquestions are correct, what is the best solution to the problem?[32]

Several researchers have been interested in analyzing the group decision-making process itself, regardless of whether an agenda was used. In one study it was found that ideas were proposed, dropped, picked up again, then dropped, and so on. A forward progression of ideas did occur but in a sporadic, spiral-like fashion.[33] More recently an analysis of groups that reached consensus showed that group interaction during the decision-making process tends to have four somewhat distinct phases.[34]

Phase 1, **the orientation phase**, is characterized by a high level of agreement on anything and everything. It seems that early in the life of a group, members are interested in building a working relationship that is psychologically comfortable. Balance theory would certainly predict this. Group members may engage in small talk about weather, movies, sports, or any other topic that is relatively nonthreatening. Unsure of their social position within the group, they make assertions tentatively and are slow to express their opinions. Therefore, the orientation phase can be described as a period of ambiguity.

During phase 2, **the conflict phase**, substantive issues arise over which a decision must be made. The testing period is over. Members become much more definite about their opinions, and two opposing coalitions usually form. This period of dissent and controversy is ripe for communication failures: the more emotionally charged the discussion, the more prone group members are to jump to conclusions, lose their tempers, or interpret the comments of others as threats or criticisms.

Phase 3, **the emergence phase**, is a period of ambiguity like the first phase, but now that ambiguity serves a different function. It is a modified form of dissent. During this time members begin to yield—that is, they take more ambiguous positions in relation to the developing group decision. Conflict dies down, and the two coalitions disintegrate. This phase, during which the group tends to reach its decisions, appears to be a bridge between conflict and its resolution.

The final stage in the group's life cycle is called **the reinforcement phase**. It is the time during which group decisions that have been reached are confirmed. An atmosphere of group solidarity emerges. Few negative or unfavorable comments are expressed, and a great deal of mutual backpatting takes place. The group seems pleased with itself. Apparently it is uncomfortable for most of us to end small-group relationships on a hostile note. Because feelings of antagonism are unlikely to be resolved late in the life of the group, we tend to play down unpleasant issues when the group is disbanding, just as a family tries to suppress conflict when one of its members is leaving for a long trip (to attend college or to join the military, for example).

These four phases—orientation, conflict, emergence, and reinforcement—may not apply to each and every problem-solving group. For example, in permanent units decision making may follow a different pattern. Nonetheless it might be of interest to observe some of the groups to which you belong and see if you can recognize a similar sequence of stages.

Resolution of Conflict

One value of the four-phase model of decision making is that it enables us to see conflict as a legitimate part of small-group experience. Should we avoid conflict or meet it head on? Some group members try to avoid it at all costs; others seem to thrive on it. Somewhere between these extremes is a realistic attitude toward conflict, one that will result in maximum gain for all parties concerned.

If several approaches to conflict, along with their outcomes, are plotted on a grid, our alternatives become clear. In the model of conflict resolution in Figure 18 (page 222), these outcomes are related to the task and consideration functions that each group must have performed. The horizontal axis, "Concern for production of results," measures task functions; the vertical axis, "Concern for people," measures consideration functions.

The 1,1 position on the grid is the laissez-faire approach. It represents complete neutrality. The person with this attitude avoids pushing for the resolution of any issue that might introduce dissension; yet he shows no regard for other members of the group. The 1,9 position is person-oriented. Its goal is surface harmony, accomplished by subordinating task to consideration needs. The person who takes this position strives for the appearance of good feeling by suppressing conflicts

Figure 18

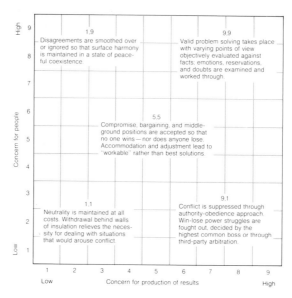

The Conflict Grid

SOURCE: Robert Blake and Jane Mouton, "The Fifth Achievement," *Journal of Applied Behavioral Science*, 6 (1970), 418.

wherever possible. The 5,5 position represents the desire for compromise. Although it seems effective this midway point leaves conflict unresolved; no one loses, but no one gains either. The hard-nosed or exclusively task-oriented approach is represented by the 9,1 position. This attitude is typified by such remarks as "Let's get the ball rolling and the job done." But the job often remains undone because of the lack of concern for group feelings.

Each of these positions has disadvantages when compared with the 9,9 approach. Here the point of view is that we must allow conflicts to be expressed openly while working vigorously at the tasks confronting the group. This means keeping the conflict directed at the problem before the group rather than at the personalities of dissenting members. Comments such as "Anyone who thinks that must be crazy" are taboo. In this view task and consideration needs are both met. Conflict is not suppressed, but it is not allowed to disrupt the progress of the group or to undercut morale.

On a grid, things look simpler than they are. Perhaps the biggest stumbling block in conflict-resolving communication in our society is the high value we place on "winning." We often cling tenaciously to our position or even move to a more extreme one just to avoid giving the other person the satisfaction of having "won." In a small group the win-or-lose mentality can only be destructive.

Clearly there are more effective behaviors for resolving conflict. First, we should try to agree on a definition of what actually constitutes the problem. Sometimes people swept away in an argument do not realize that they may not even be arguing about the same point. Second, we should explore possible areas of agreement. Two parties rarely disagree completely on a given issue, and their goals may not be mutually exclusive. Next, we can determine what specific changes each faction must make to resolve the issue satisfactorily. Most conflicts are resolved by some modifications in the original preferences of both sides. And fourth, we must not resort to personal attacks but must keep the conflict directed at the issue.

Patterns of Decision Making

Decisions can be avoided, demanded, or agreed on. Assuming that decisions will actually be made, let us briefly examine four rather different ways of carrying out the process.

One writer goes quite far in stating that "Achieving consensus is the essential purpose of interpersonal communication."[35] Although this position fails to account for several other important communication goals, we heartily agree that consensus is one of the most desirable outcomes of interaction in small groups. The term can mean a majority opinion, but we use **consensus** to denote *agreement among all members of a group concerning a given decision.* Juries must reach consensus, and those that cannot—hung juries—are ultimately dismissed.

Few groups are as concerned as they should be about trying to reach consensus on decisions. We tend to forget that the people who help make a decision are often those who are also expected to carry it out. And given a choice, most people who disagree with a decision will resist enacting it. Therefore problem-solving groups should try to reach consensus to ensure maximum satisfaction and commitment to the decision by all members.

Although not nearly as satisfying as is consensus, the **majority vote**, representing *the wishes of at least 51 percent of a group's members,* allows some group harmony in decision making. After as much deliberation on the problem as time permits, there may still be a substantial split in opinion. The majority vote allows the group to proceed despite this. The major limitation of the majority vote is that the dissenting members may be numerous and may be bitterly opposed to the decision. If so, they may be expected to resist carrying it out. When feasible the majority vote can be used to establish whether a group is near consensus. If a split still exists and time allows, deliberation should continue. If continued discussion does not prove fruitful, the majority vote may be used to reach the decision.

A still less desirable method of arriving at a decision is **handclasp-**

ing. This term applies when various *minority members within a group form a coalition to help each other achieve mutually advantageous goals*. Their decision may not represent common sentiment in the group, but they overpower the majority by dint of their collective numbers. This pattern seems characteristic of political life. It is a common practice for legislators to vote for each other's bills in order to compel support for their own. In the short run, coalitions may be quite successful, but ultimately they can have disastrous effects on group morale. Furthermore members of coalitions sometimes forget that these bargains exact obligations.

Most groups have at some time been the victim of **railroading**, which occurs when *one or a few group members force their will on the group*. This technique is used most frequently by a leader or particularly influential member, and of course it is the one most likely to produce resentment and resistance. All that we know about Machiavellianism leads us to expect that it is the high Machs who will be most inclined to engage in this sort of manipulating.

Since reaching consensus is the most desirable method of decision making within the small group, it is instructive to turn to a few of the research findings on the subject. Gouran compared the conversation of groups that were able to reach consensus with that of groups who were not. He found that the discussion in the first groups had a greater proportion of "orientation statements," statements explicitly directing the group toward the achievement of its goal or helping it resolve conflict.[36] A follow-up study reported that orientation statements contained fewer self-referent words and phrases—"I," "me," "my," "I think," and so on—and that highly opinionated statements, which were characteristic of groups that had difficulty reaching consensus, contained more self-referent words.[37]

Findings about orientation statements bear out our common-sense expectations, but we cannot always follow our hunches. We might predict, for example, that if group members expressed their ideas clearly and briefly (in one to two minutes), they would facilitate the group's progress. It has been found, however, that clarity and length of statements are not significantly related to the group's ability to reach consensus. These data need to be substantiated by further research.

Testing the Group's Effectiveness

It is to be hoped that in the near future we shall have more experimental findings pinpointing the communication behaviors that help discussion groups achieve their goals. For the time being, however, we have to agree with the writer who commented that ". . . far more is known about the dynamics of groups than about the distinctive communicative properties, functions, and outcomes in groups."[38] Thus we learn most about what goes on in groups from firsthand experience as members. Sometimes this knowledge can be increased through special exercises. One frequently used technique is called the "fishbowl discussion." Two groups form in concentric circles, one outside the other. The inner group carries on a discussion; the outer comments on what it has observed. The two groups then switch positions and repeat the procedure. Each member is allowed to remove himself from the discussion long enough to observe the behavior of the others in the group. He may be aided by a list of pointers about what he should be looking for.

Summary

In the present chapter we began to extend our two-person model by looking at the dynamics of small-group communication, with special emphasis on problem-solving, or task-oriented, groups. We observed the strong influence of social pressure on individual group members, and in discussing the risky shift phenomenon, we examined the direction of conformity behavior. The larger question we raised was how the quality of problem solving is affected when people work together instead of singly. Role behavior, another aspect of group dynamics, was also surveyed. Although role flexibility is desirable, most people interpret the role of group member rather narrowly, performing only a few of the behaviors described by the IPA categories.

After touching on some characteristics of cohesive groups, we considered three aspects of the structure of a group that affect its functioning: size, communication network, and leadership. Limiting the size of the group to five to seven members seems to assure maximum performance and satisfaction. Among communication networks the All-Channel pattern offers the greatest opportunity for corrective feedback and high morale though the centralized systems are more efficient. Two concepts of leadership were discussed, and analysis of leadership functions rather than traits was recommended.

The last question raised was practical: How can the small group be made more effective? First, the use of an agenda makes the most of time and resources. Second, an awareness of various attitudes toward conflict allows group members to resolve conflicts in a way that respects both task and human concerns. A third correlate of small-group effectiveness is an approach to decision making that ensures commitment to the decision by all members of the group.

Review Questions

1. How do primary, learning, and therapeutic groups differ?
2. How does the concept of conformity relate to the autokinetic effect?

3. What is the difference between private acceptance and public compliance?

4. Identify four conditions in which private acceptance is likely to occur.

5. What are four characteristics of people likely to conform to group pressure?

6. Discuss two theories that have been used to explain compliance to social pressure. How does each explain this phenomenon?

7. What is the risky shift phenomenon?

8. How does group cohesiveness relate to the effectiveness of the brainstorming technique?

9. Identify twelve types of group member roles. Give an example of each.

10. What are four characteristics of group cohesiveness?

11. What is the relationship between group size, member satisfaction, and group performance?

12. Draw diagrams representing five types of communication networks. Describe the relative effects of each on group performance.

13. How do trait and function views of leadership differ?

14. How do task and consideration leadership functions differ?

15. What are six common difficulties that small groups encounter in developing ideas and solving problems?

16. How do the standard agenda, ideal solution, and single question formats for group discussion differ?

17. What are four phases of group interaction during the decision-making process? What type of communication is characteristic of each phase?

18. Identify four strategies that may be used to resolve group conflict effectively.

19. What are four ways of arriving at a decision in a group? What are some relative advantages and disadvantages of each?

Exercises

1. Have five people solve the "sinking ship" exercise in the Appendix independently. After individual solutions have been reached, ask these people to solve the same problem in a group. Compare the individual solutions with the group solution. In what ways is the risky shift phenomenon illustrated?

2. Ask several people to complete a sociogram as described in Chapter 5. Use the results to form a cohesive group and a noncohesive group. Ask the groups to use a brainstorming technique in discussing one of the case studies listed at the end of the book. Observe the groups' interaction using Bales' IPA categories. What differences emerge in the two groups?

3. Conduct an in-depth study of a group of which you are a member. Keep a journal of the group's interaction patterns and activities and write a paper in which you analyze: (1) the communication network(s) of the group, (2) the leadership functions, (3) the group's cohesiveness, (4) members' satisfaction, and (5) methods of conflict resolution.
4. Observe a group discussion and examine the group in terms of the four phases of group interaction discussed in this chapter. How does the group's performance change from phase to phase?
5. Analyze the most successful group discussion that you have ever participated in. What specific factors were present that accounted for its success?

Suggested Readings

Fiedler, Fred E. "Style or Circumstance: The Leadership Enigma." *Psychology Today* (March 1969), 3:38–43. What makes a good leader? Using questionnaires and studies the author identifies three types of leaders and the group situations these leaders could handle best. Fiedler also suggests methods for improving a leader's performance. You will be able to identify types of people you know from the descriptions in this article.

Janis, Irving L. "Groupthink." *Psychology Today* (May 1971), 5:43–46, 74–76. Janis examines the infamous "Bay of Pigs" disaster of the Kennedy administration. After analyzing documented accounts of the problem-solving-group decision making of former President Kennedy and his top advisors, Janis concludes that group conformity was largely responsible for this political disaster.

Shaw, Marvin E. *Group Dynamics: The Psychology of Small Group Behavior*. New York: McGraw-Hill, 1971. This book is somewhat more challenging than most we have suggested. However, it synthesizes the findings of a large number of research studies in a meaningful way. It also lists several propositions at the end of several chapters that specifically capture those "rules" of small group behavior that are supportable by empirical research.

Notes

[1] Robert Bales, *Interaction Process Analysis* (Reading, Mass.: Addison-Wesley, 1950), p 33.

[2] George C. Homans, *The Human Group* (New York: Harcourt, Brace, 1950), p. 1.

[3] Quoted in Muzafer Sherif, *Social Interaction: Process and Products* (Chicago: Aldine, 1967), p. 150.

[4] Muzafer Sherif, *The Psychology of Social Norms* (New York: Harper & Brothers, 1936), p. 111.

5 Theodore Grove, "Attitude Convergence in Small Groups," *Journal of Communication*, 15 (1965), 226–238.

6 Dorian Cartwright and Alvin Zander, *Group Dynamics*, 3rd ed. (New York: Harper & Row, 1968), pp. 139–151.

7 A. Paul Hare, *Handbook of Small Group Research* (New York: Free Press, 1962), p. 33.

8 Edgar H. Schein, "The Chinese Indoctrination Program for Prisoners of War," *Psychiatry*, 19 (1956), 159–160.

9 Stanley Schachter, "Deviation, Rejection and Communication," *Journal of Abnormal and Social Psychology*, 46 (1951), 190–208.

10 Theodore M. Newcomb, "An Approach to the Study of Communicative Acts," *Psychological Review*, 60 (1953), 393–404.

11 Leon Festinger, "A Theory of Social Comparison Processes," *Human Relations*, 7 (1954), 117–140.

12 Michael A. Wallach, Nathan Kogan, and Daryl J. Bem, "Group Influence on Individual Risk-Taking," *Journal of Abnormal and Social Psychology*, 65 (1962), 77.

13 Ladd Wheeler, *Interpersonal Influence* (Boston: Allyn & Bacon, 1970), p. 106.

14 Alex F. Osborn, *Applied Imagination* (New York: Scribner, 1957), Chapter 26.

15 Donald W. Taylor, Paul C. Berry, and Clifford H. Block, "Does Group Participation When Using Brainstorming Facilitate or Inhibit Creative Thinking?" *Administrative Science Quarterly*, 3 (1958), 23–47.

16 David Cohen, John W. Whitmyre, and Wilmer H. Funk, "Effect of Group Cohesiveness and Training upon Creative Thinking," *Journal of Applied Psychology*, 44 (1960), 319–322.

17 Harold H. Kelley and John W. Thibaut, "Group Problem Solving," in Gardner Lindzey and Elliot Aronson (eds.), *The Handbook of Social Psychology*, 2nd ed. (Reading, Mass.: Addison-Wesley, 1969), Vol. IV, *Group Psychology and Phenomena of Interaction*, p. 73.

18 N. Cameron, *The Psychology of Behavior Disorders* (Boston: Houghton Mifflin, 1947), p. 93.

19 Kurt Lewin, "Group Decision and Social Change," in Eleanore Maccoby, Theodore M. Newcomb, and Eugene Hartley (eds.), *Readings in Social Psychology* (New York: Holt, Rinehart and Winston, 1958), p. 202.

20 Schachter, p. 191. Italics added.

21 R. Bostrom, "Patterns of Communicative Interaction in Small Groups," *Speech Monographs*, 37 (1970), 257, 258.

22 Cyril Northcote Parkinson, *Parkinson's Law* (New York: Ballantine, 1964), pp. 54–55.

23 Robert Townsend, *Up the Organization* (New York: Knopf, 1970), pp. 24 and 134.

[24] Harold J. Leavitt, "Some Effects of Certain Communication Patterns on Group Performance," *Journal of Abnormal and Social Psychology,* 46 (1951), 38–50.

[25] Alex Bavelas, "Communication Patterns in Task-Oriented Groups," *Journal of the Acoustical Society of America,* 22 (1950), 725–730.

[26] Harold Guetzkow and Herbert A. Simon, "The Impact of Certain Communication Nets upon Organization and Performance in Task-Oriented Groups," *Management Science,* 1 (1955), 248.

[27] Marvin E. Shaw, "Communication Networks," in Leonard Berkowitz (ed.), *Advances in Experimental Social Psychology* (New York: Academic, 1964), Vol. I, pp. 111–147.

[28] Guetzkow and Simon, p. 250.

[29] Joseph McGrath and Irwin Altman, *Small Group Research* (New York: Holt, Rinehart and Winston, 1966), p. 58.

[30] Carl Larson, "Forms of Analysis and Small Group Problem Solving," *Speech Monographs,* 36 (1969), 452–455.

[31] Larson, p. 453.

[32] Larson, p. 453.

[33] Thomas Scheidel and Laura Crowell, "Idea Development in Small Discussion Groups," *Quarterly Journal of Speech,* 50 (1964), 140–145.

[34] B. Aubrey Fisher, "Decision Emergence: Phases in Group Decision-Making," *Speech Monographs,* 37 (1970), 53–66.

[35] Gerald Phillips, *Communication and the Small Group* (Indianapolis: Bobbs-Merrill, 1966), p. 39.

[36] Dennis Gouran, "Variables Related to Consensus in Group Discussions of Questions of Policy," *Speech Monographs,* 36 (1969), 387–391.

[37] John Kline, "Indices of Orienting and Opinionated Statements in Problem-Solving Discussion," *Speech Monographs,* 37 (1970), 282–286.

[38] C. David Mortensen, "The Status of Small Group Research," *Quarterly Journal of Speech,* 56 (1970), 309.

Chapter

10

The Small Group: Therapeutic Communication

OBJECTIVES

After reading this chapter the student should be able to:

1. Describe briefly the "typical" encounter group.

2. Describe a focused exercise and state its purpose.

3. Explain what is meant by the "here and now."

4. Discuss the six stages of Bennis and Shepard's theory of group development.

5. Discuss Schutz's theory of group development.

6. Explain how the principles of reinforcement and extinction operate in the encounter group to produce learning.

7. Identify three ways in which the encounter group setting leads to unfreezing.

8. Describe four possible reasons why people seek encounter group experiences.

9. State at least two positive and two negative aspects of sensitivity training.

10. Describe four goals of sensitivity training.

10

In a scene from Eugene Ionesco's play *The Bald Soprano,* a man and woman meet and engage in polite conversation. Before long they discover they have both come to New York on the 10 o'clock train from the same town in New Jersey. They even discover they have the same address on Fifth Avenue. Not only that—they both have a seven-year-old daughter. Finally to their astonishment they realize that they are man and wife.

For many of us this bizarre situation strikes a responsive chord. We find it by turns sad and amusing because it reflects our own growing feelings of loneliness and social isolation. Yet alienation from others and confusion about personal identity are closely linked, for we are also haunted by a diminishing sense of self—a loss that results in part from the breakdown of our significant interpersonal relationships. These feelings are shared by people of all ages, people with very different commitments: the student, the corporation executive, the veteran teacher, the middle-aged housewife.

Growing out of the need for more meaningful personal encounter has been the tremendous popularity of the therapeutic group. Although there are many kinds of therapeutic groups, a discussion of many of these presupposes some familiarity with the literature of psychotherapy. Therefore we shall confine our discussion to sensitivity training, which has been used not only by private individuals but by the staffs of business organizations, hospitals, the military, religious groups, and government agencies. In this chapter we shall view training as an intensified form of social learning—a context of interpersonal communication with much to teach us about small-group behavior and communication styles.

We begin by trying to make some sense out of the bewildering number of forms sensitivity training can take. It goes by a host of other names. It may be a T-Group (T for training), an encounter group, a process group, therapy for normals, an interpersonal skills group, or a Gestalt group. Depending on its focus, it may be a personal growth lab, a group dynamics lab, a couples lab, or an organizational development session. And it may vary in length from a minilab or a microlab to a marathon. It may be a group with one or more leaders, or it may be a leaderless, or self-analytic, group that uses taped instructions for each of its meetings.

Because of such popular sources as the film *Bob and Carol and Ted and Alice* and the best-seller *Please Touch,* by Jane Howard, the public is becoming aware of sensitivity training. But it seems to be the sensational types of training that draw the most attention—for example, nude bathing, dance exercise, and massage, which are being offered by some groups conducted at Big Sur, California. These activities represent one kind of sensitivity training, but they are not typical of the vast majority of groups.

In the following pages we shall attempt to describe the development of that nonexistent animal, the typical encounter group. Of necessity our account will oversimplify the great diversity that exists in sensitivity training. We shall do our best, however, to describe some elements that are shared by numerous types of groups.

THE GROUP EXPERIENCE

Our group will be conducted at a cultural island, a place where group members are out of contact with family, friends, and business associates. The setting may be as luxurious as a resort or as simple as a room in an office building. The twelve members of the group (groups usually have from six to fifteen members) have never met each other before. They are seated in chairs that form a rough circle.

The group leader begins by explaining that he will play a rather unusual role. He may caution group members that at some point whatever they disclose about themselves—their motivations, feelings, behavior—will probably be discussed within the group. He may briefly explain some of the goals the group should be trying to achieve. But he will offer no suggestions about how to approach these goals; he has no agenda, no plan for the meetings. In short, he will not provide structure for the group as leaders in most situations do. Perhaps he pauses for a moment, looking expectantly at the participants. "Well," he asks, "what are we here for?"

Someone giggles. Several people light cigarettes. One man accuses the leader of being "unprofessional." A young woman puts down her pen and notebook in astonishment: she had assumed she would be taking notes. Someone else comments that the leader is stranding the group. An awkward silence follows. People are angry, embarrassed, confused; they feel betrayed by the leader, who has disclaimed his traditional role. They may (and frequently do in our experience) attack him, insult him, bribe him—anything to get him to take over and show them some direction. The leader, however, is acting on the assumption that if he allows the group to, they will eventually overcome their need to depend on him.

Some leaders start their groups with a brief introduction and immediately guide them into a **focused exercise**, which is *a technique for*

shifting attention from interaction with the leader to mutual expe-
riences with group members. For example, each member in turn steps
into the middle of a circle of standing people, closes his eyes, folds his
arms, and falls forward. The group members catch him to keep him
from hitting the floor. They then pass him back and forth among themselves in an attempt to show him the support and trust they can offer.

After any focused exercise it is essential for group members to share
their thoughts and feelings about what is going on in *this* group at *this*
time. The focus is thus on increased awareness of what has come to be
called the **here and now**, or *present experience.* Whatever his approach,
the leader waits for people to reach this level of awareness, for the here
and now is the subject at the heart of all sensitivity training. In a group
in which interaction is primarily verbal, as in the one we are describing,
the here and now is the basis of the most productive discussion. In
effect, the group will be conducting an ongoing analysis of its own
behavior. Unlike more traditional educational or therapeutic settings,
which focus on a body of knowledge or on the past experience of the
individual, the encounter group stresses learning from direct, personal,
and shared experience.

How is such direct communication sustained? First, through emphasis on responses to personalities rather than to categories or stereotypes.
In an encounter group people are encouraged to step out of their social
roles. The leader's initial behavior sets the tone for what follows. Whatever their roles outside the sessions—priest, housewife, business executive, surgeon, college student—all members have equal status within
the group. No one is unapproachable. First names are used, and the
barriers are down—at least most of the time. If you turn back to the
communication networks discussed in Chapter 9, you will see that an
All-Channel network best describes this kind of communication.

Emphasis on personalities rather than social roles leads to the more
candid expression of personal feelings. In fact, the group's progress
depends on constant open feedback between members. At first many
find this startling. A woman who wants to talk about how her husband
ignores her when she speaks is asked whether she feels that the group
is listening to her. A middle-aged man who looks upset but sits quietly
may be surprised to hear the woman next to him say, "You look mad
at the group right now. Are you mad?"

Often the feedback a person receives does not agree at all with the
way he perceives himself. Just as his expectations about the leader were
disconfirmed, his self-concept is sometimes disconfirmed. "It really
bothers me when you wink at me like that," someone says. "It seems
insincere." "I like what you say, but I wish you could be briefer." A
man who has not been invited to a group party is told that the others
did not think he would be interested in going because he seems so busi-
nesslike and "antisocial." Yet this man has always thought of himself

as fun-loving. As a result of such comments, group members grow more aware of how they are coming across to others, and they are able to begin minimizing the unintentional messages, both verbal and non-verbal, that they are sending.

Oddly enough, the first personal feelings to be expressed are usually negative. Rogers suggests some possible reasons:

> Why are negatively toned feelings the first to be expressed? One speculates that this is one of the best ways to test the group's freedom and trust-worthiness. Is it *really* a place where I can be and express myself, even negatively? Is this really a safe situation, or will I be punished? Another quite different reason is that deeply positive feelings are much more diffi-cult and dangerous to express than negative ones. The person who expresses affection is vulnerable and open to rejection that can be devastating. A person who attacks another is at worst liable to be attacked, and he can usually defend himself. . . .[1]

As more current feelings are revealed, positive reactions will also be expressed, but they tend to come out at later stages in the group's development.

We cannot say that the movement of the group is strictly linear. Its momentum varies. Sometimes the group moves quickly into sub-stantive issues; at other times it slows down, and conversation may digress to less personal topics. Inconsistent tempo is typical of encoun-ter groups.

Intensity of reaction also varies from time to time. The majority of the participants may feel the need to concentrate on what is hap-pening within the group, to trust the group and reveal themselves, but one or more people may not be ready to move forward with the rest, fearing betrayal. "This is far enough," they seem to say. "No more probing." Whitman uses the term **focal conflict** to describe this con-frontation between the group and reluctant individual members.[2] Con-flict may be expressed by defensive comments such as "You can't trust people—the more they know about you, the more power they have over you," or "I've been hurt before; I'm not going to get burned again." Focal conflicts exist for all members of an encounter group. How well a conflict is resolved depends on the willingness of the person to disclose it, the ability of the group to deal with it, and the ability of the leader to maintain an atmosphere supportive enough to allow self-disclosure.

No matter how far from the group a person tries to retreat, how-ever, it is likely that the other participants will make some effort to draw him back into the present. For as one writer explains, the partici-pant finds himself in a unique social situation:

> In the business world he can rationalize his failings to achieve desired positions—his competitor is married to the boss's daughter; went to the right school; is comfortable with devious practices, etc. His difficulties

within the family are viewed as resulting from his wife's hysterical personality or his son's incorrigibility. . . . This kind of rationalizing distorts his
social comparative perceptions and masks how he influences and contributes to what happens to him.

In the process group such rationalizations are not easily tolerated. The
group is generally committed to have no rocks upright in its quest for
honesty. . . . Participants use group feedback of their behavior to discern
what it is that they contribute to their own failings. Participants who attempt to ignore these feedbacks do not get away easily.[3]

Again and again the center of all discussion returns to what is going
on within the group, and this is one reason that it is almost impossible
to describe a typical group. To plot the course of the group's development, one has to step back for a moment—away from the here and now.

THEORIES OF GROUP DEVELOPMENT

It has been said that like a human being, each encounter group has
a life cycle: it has a birth, childhood, and maturity, and ultimately it
ceases to exist. A number of theories have arisen about what growth
typically occurs in an encounter group. We shall examine two that
seem representative.

The Two-Phase Theory

One of the best-known group development theories is that proposed by
Bennis and Shepard.[4] They believe that the life of the group evolves
in a sequence that is fairly predictable. It has two phases, each working
out a major area of uncertainty in human relationships. Phase I is concerned with power, role, and authority and phase II with interdependence, intimacy, and love. The conflicts of the first phase must surface
and be resolved before those of the second phase can be worked out.
This theory is particularly interesting to students of communication
because the groups Bennis and Shepard describe have as their explicit
goal the improvement of internal communication systems. From this
vantage point, the two areas of conflict or uncertainty—dependence
and interdependence—can be thought of as the major obstacles to
valid communication.

Phase I, **dependence**, has three stages, or "subphases" as the authors
term them. It begins as members try to gain approval from authority—
in this case, the leader—as they have in past experiences. A great deal
of anxiety exists during these first days, and many futile attempts are
made to come up with some shared goal as a means of allaying the
anxiety. People are trying to keep their hostile feelings in check. Subphase 2 is an unpleasant period in which two opposing subgroups usually form. Structure or leadership is the issue that is raised most

frequently. Hostility to the leader is now expressed openly. The group is polarized. Even those uncommitted to either subgroup are unable to resolve the conflict. Bennis and Shepard feel that this stage "brings the group to the brink of catastrophe": instead of turning directly on the leader, members now become involved in "mutually destructive behavior."[5] Subphase 3 is often a turning point in the life of the group, for it is the time when the group symbolically removes the leader and becomes autonomous. The members begin to feel like a group, and their resolution of the dependency issue marks the transition to phase II.

Phase II, **interdependence**, also has three stages. At the beginning of subphase 4, the group feels quite pleased with itself. Probing and confrontation are temporarily brought to a halt as members relax. They are taking a "psychological breather." Although eager to maintain harmony at all cost, their sense of solidarity soon proves an illusion. New anxieties about their total involvement with the group emerge, and disenchantment sets in. In subphase 5 some people begin to fear the loss of individuality and self-esteem through further interaction with the group. Others demand total commitment and forgiveness. The group is polarized as it was in subphase 2. Only in subphase 6 are the issues of interdependence or intimacy resolved. In the groups Bennis and Shepard write about, two forces hasten this resolution: first, the approaching end of the training course, and second, the requirement that members evaluate one another. It is at this point that people begin to allow themselves to give and receive honest feedback and to deal with such task issues as how to evaluate what they have learned during the group sessions. Characteristically it is a time when group members are more willing and able to "validate their self-concepts with other members" and to make explicit their own assumptions about human behavior.

Thus Bennis and Shepard theorize that the life of the group evolves from an emphasis on power and role to a concern with affection and personality. Although they consider these the dominant themes of group life, they acknowledge that several minor themes are also present, that "lower levels of development coexist with more advanced levels," and that groups do not always resolve the dependency conflicts and move on to a second phase.[6] In this connection Slater makes an interesting comment: "Groups that are never able to verbalize their anger toward the group leader in a sustained and truly collective manner are in my experience generalized failures."[7]

Obviously not every group will develop precisely along the lines described above. Many groups, for example, do not require that members evaluate one another as the sessions draw to a close. We can gain some insight into group development, however, by being aware of its recurring themes.

The Three-Phase Theory

A theory quite different from that of Bennis and Shepard is proposed by Schutz.[8] His experience with groups has led him to the conclusion that there are three major phases in the life of a group—inclusion, control, and affection—and that they correspond with three basic interpersonal needs in every human being.

Inclusion involves *the process of group formation*, and it usually occurs first. Personal contact, or encounter, is the basic interaction of this first stage. Each member must decide whether and when to become an active participant. Conflicts here are typically those between wanting to become part of the group and fearing rejection or the loss of personal identity.

The issues of the **control** period are *power, influence, and authority,* and they usually follow the resolution of inclusion problems. This is a time of confrontation and ultimately of decision making among the participants. They are all involved in the struggle for control, even those who do not seek power for themselves. "The need for control," Schutz writes, "varies along a continuum from the desire for power, authority, and control over others . . . to the need to be controlled and have responsibility lifted from oneself."[9]

Affection is the last stage to emerge in the life of the group. Here the concern is with *interpersonal distance—how close people will become.* In this period members work out the relationships established in the control phase, and several people may form lasting ties. Whereas inclusion and control relationships can involve more than two people, affection relationships are dyadic. The basic interaction of this phase is embracing, whether it be literal or symbolic.

Schutz points out that though each person varies in terms of his needs for inclusion, control, and affection, he can find satisfaction in his interpersonal relationships only when he can maintain a balance in each of these three areas.

PERSONAL EXPERIENCE

Describing trends in group development increases our understanding of sensitivity training, but it tells us little about what takes place within an individual during the course of an encounter group. One way to get some idea of personal development within the group is to read the thoughts of someone who is going through this experience for the first time. The next few pages contain excerpts from the personal log of an encounter group member. Let us call him Philip. Philip is a married graduate student. The group he attended met for an hour a day five days a week for a period of eight weeks. Although the group was given as a college course during summer school, its twenty participants were quite diverse in interests and background. They ranged in age from nineteen to fifty-five.

A Case Experience: Philip's Log

Day 1

I was suspicious when the older man didn't take over the class. I thought he was the professor (he wasn't), and I thought he was sitting quietly to force the rest of us into uneasy conversation. Since he was writing something, I thought he was taking notes on what was happening to use later as examples of relations between strangers. Then Professor Markham [the trainer] started to speak. He seemed so young. He has a Ph.D. from Stanford—I was impressed. He asked why were we taking this class. One guy said he was in the course because the ones he wanted were closed. Markham responded, "There's an honest man." I thought this showed his tolerance of honesty.

The girl Johanna sounded very harsh, masculine, and dogmatic. When the trainer pronounced her name, she said condescendingly, "That's close enough." I didn't like her attitude.

I didn't like the Texan who said he was "6 feet 4 and still growing." I thought he was acting the expected part of the typical Texan; he just sounded egotistical to me.

The guy in Elementary Education (Larry) talked too long, and I found my mind wandering.

Day 2

Today we discussed the prospect of having grad students and under-grads in the same classes. Mack said grads like to hear themselves talk in classes, often saying nothing (I silently agreed and thought of myself as an example at times).

I said I wore a tie because it made me feel more professional. A rousing discussion followed, and I began to feel as though I had to defend the position that wearing a tie made you a good teacher (which is ridiculous). I felt myself getting nervous, very much like before giving a speech. After class I felt I had gone overboard trying to make a point and probably had created some bad impressions.

Day 3

To show that I didn't need a crutch, I decided not to wear a tie today.

Day 4

We had to solve the problem of which of the five project groups to be in. All went smoothly. Several people commented favorably about the fact that I didn't have a tie on. I was glad I hadn't worn one. The whole controversy has become a joke and is funny to refer to.

Day 5

Today we discussed leadership. Six of us did most of the talking. I keep wishing some of the shyer people would enter in. How can we learn more about human relationships if some of us don't relate?

Day 6

I felt that Larry helped get the discussion off the ground today. I like him more now than I did at first. I agreed with Mack: we should share our observations, even if they aren't too profound.

Day 7

Today we filled out a sociogram. I chose people who I thought would not be chosen by everybody. I thought the talkers would be chosen more—so I chose others. I really can't decide whom I would like the least.

Day 8

I'm getting more at ease in the group and find myself looking forward to class. I hate to have to miss tomorrow because I am anxious to know the results of the sociogram.

Day 9

I missed class.

Day 10

Sol [the trainer] looks at the ceiling often rather than into people's eyes. It bothered me until today in his office—he looked me right in the eye. It seems more direct to me, and I like it (from anyone, not just him).

Day 11

We got off to a slow start today, and I wished again that some *new* people would help by contributing something. I felt a strong need for Sol to give us some direction today.

Day 16

Jim has really quieted down, and so has Larry. I haven't been talking so much either. . . . Also Sue made me feel good when she said she thought I was considerate. I'll bet Rhonda doesn't feel that way.

Day 20

I was pretty quiet again today, and several people mentioned the fact. Barry gave an analysis of how my behavior has varied during the term. I felt under pressure while he was saying this. Whenever I know the focus is on me, I feel that every move or reaction I make is communicating something. I don't know whether to remain stone-faced or to let my reactions show, to move my hands or to fold them, and so on. It is an interesting feeling, and it points out to me what the quieter ones must feel when I try to draw them into the discussions.

Day 24

Sol and I had a short discussion on whether to talk about things that happened before today in the group or only the here and now. Some strain was noticeable in our voices, but the comment "That isn't what we are arguing about, *if we are arguing"* really broke the tension. I felt this was a good thing to remember—the release of tension allowed us to agree more easily, and there was less emphasis on winning the point.

Day 27

I really got mad at Barry today. He seemed to say, "Do as I say, not as I do." I literally wanted to punch him in the mouth. This is the first time in years I've felt that kind of reaction to someone. To be completely honest I sort of admire some of the things he says, but as a person I think he's an ass.

Day 29

We're getting more depth of discussion and less superficiality now. This is good.

Day 32

Today Sol read his log to the group and really got things off with a bang! I spoke about my earlier feelings toward Barry. Actually now I don't think he's an ass at all! I realize that Larry was right: I was jealous of Barry and his rivalry as a leader of the group. It was a good meeting.

Day 34

I noticed yesterday that I feel much less nervous about speaking to the group. I also think that I notice fewer and fewer attacks on people's ideas, and I am becoming (I think) less vehement about presenting my ideas. I tend to try to persuade people by overpowering them with a loud voice. I'm beginning to think this is largely ineffective as a way of communicating.

Day 35

Today we looked at the results of the second sociogram. I felt pleased at some of the people who chose me for things. I wonder what hurt feelings may have arisen in those who were not chosen?

Day 36

We seemed to have a hard time getting going today. I felt like I didn't have much of anything to say; or I guess I have been thinking things but don't feel like saying them to the group.

Day 37

We talked about grading, having a party, feelings about parents, etc., and we have gotten away from how we feel in the group at the here and now. I am becoming more inhibited about saying what I feel because it is more intimate than talking about other people, places, and so on.

Day 38

Today I think we got down to the point quite early. I was interested in Don's comment about Barry succeeding in life. I thought it was good of Don to help reduce Barry's feelings of vulnerability.

We discussed last night's party. As I was talking I got quite nervous and my voice was trembling. I was expecting a lot of negative feedback for letting myself get emotional about the subject. When I got aggressive with Jennifer [*the co-trainer*] I realized that I had been harboring a disagreement with her about reaching consensus. I guess that is part of why I became so assertive at that point. In general, I thought we had a good meeting. Afterward several people came up and we walked across campus together, which made me feel that they weren't resentful about my getting emotional.

Day 40

I thought we had a good meeting. I was glad I got further feedback telling me that they could see how I felt about the party. I guess I am beginning to realize that I can disagree with people and still have them respect my opinion. This makes me want to respect and allow their opinions too.

On the whole, I am feeling happier about myself in the group.

Case Analysis

By its very nature the group setting seems to precipitate certain conflicts. Philip's reactions to these are typical of many encounter group participants. One problem with which he grapples is his relationship to authority figures. Our first authority figures, our parents, are symbolized in later life by teachers, employers, experts, politicians, and so on —and specifically in the group by the leader. Establishing rapport with the leader is a problem that must be faced by every group member.

Philip's comments on days 1 and 11 reflect his suspicion and disappointment with the lack of conventional leadership. Even more revealing is the way in which he remarks on the trainer's behavior. Although the participants wrote their logs for submission to Sol, Philip addresses personal remarks to him as if he were discussing a third person. On day 10 Philip tells him that he was not direct in his visual behavior. But he doesn't write, "Sol, I notice you don't look into my eyes." Instead he writes as if Sol were some third person. His evasive style points up how difficult it is for him to accept and respond to Sol as a person rather than an authority figure. One member of a group given at Harvard University expressed this problem well when he commented, "I think most people in this group feel that they could talk to any other person, person to person; with him [the leader] you have to use the long-distance operator."[10]

An issue closely related to authority relationships is leadership, or control, as Schutz would refer to it. Once the leader casts off his traditional role, some members of the group try to rush in and take over; less aggressive members seem more willing to be led. Philip is apparently one of the former, and his log reflects this struggle for leadership

244   (see days 2, 5, 6, 11, 27, 32, and 39). From the discussion of motivation and personality in Chapter 3, you might be able to make some predictions about who would want control of a group such as this one. Certainly there would be some Machiavellians among them.

Philip's log also reflects his concern with participation and self-disclosure. Notice that Philip makes several references to the uneven participation of various members (see days 5, 11, and 20, for example). Members who hold back are often deeply resented by the rest of the group, as are those who try to monopolize the meetings. On days 20, 36, and 37, we see Philip wondering how much to reveal of his inner thoughts when others in the group seem reluctant to reveal theirs. Self-disclosure, of course, depends on trust (recall Whitman's concept of focal conflict). Although self-disclosure is common in encounter groups, it is only poorly handled groups that resemble what some have called an "emotional striptease." This is not what takes place in a well-conducted group.

Despite these conflicts Philip's log is a record of personal growth through learning. Let us look at how this learning occurs.

THEORIES OF PERSONAL DEVELOPMENT

At the beginning of this chapter, we suggested that sensitivity training could be considered an intensified form of social learning. But how can learning take place in so short a time? Some learning theorists explain it as modeling. Short-term learning can also be explained in terms of extinction and reinforcement principles.

As we saw in Chapter 3, to extinguish a pattern of behavior, we have to stop reinforcing it; to change it we must not only stop reinforcing it but also reward a different behavior pattern. For example, in most social situations people are reinforced for being polite to others. There are several possible rewards for politeness—social acceptance, job promotions, popularity, and so on. In many cases, however, being polite means being less than candid, so that people may learn that frankness can be undesirable. Take the case of Ann, who is extremely polite and well-mannered. She has learned to keep her own counsel and never ventures comments that are in the least critical of others. This is her first experience in an encounter group. As the group progresses she is surprised to find that politeness is valued much less than candor—that, in fact, ultimately it is candor, not politeness, that is regarded as appropriate social behavior. If from her training experience, Ann learns to be more candid in her responses to others, we could explain this change as the extinction of ineffective behavior and the reinforcement of new, more desirable behavior within the group.

Some theorists prefer to discuss personal development in an encounter group in terms of change or influence rather than learning or growth. Their model is an elaboration of Lewin's conception of change: a sequence of three distinct but overlapping processes—unfreezing, changing, and refreezing.

We know that changes in behavior and attitude tend to be resisted. **Unfreezing** breaks down this resistance by creating the motivation to change. It is a time of disequilibrium. Values are shifting. Ideas about oneself and what is appropriate behavior are suddenly challenged. The encounter group seems to promote unfreezing. Many responses to people that have been effective in the past do not work in this new setting; the ground rules, the norms, of the encounter group are different. The encounter group setting can activate the desire to change in three ways: first, through the lack of confirmation or actual disconfirmation of some part of one's self-concept; second, through fostering a sense of guilt or personal inadequacy; and third, through offering a safe psychological environment and removing barriers to change. If we look back at Philip's log, we see that the unfreezing process begins when Sol does not take over the group. Even on day 11 the group is still groping for direction. As conversation begins to focus on the here and now, the unfreezing process continues. Philip is still getting some feedback from others that does not agree with his own perception of himself. His indecision about whether to wear a tie is a good example of unfreezing.

Changing takes place when a person assimilates new information from his social environment. His search for this information grows out of the desire, created during the unfreezing period, for more effective behaviors or attitudes. He can acquire new information by identifying with a single source (that is, person) or by scanning a number of sources. Because the encounter group exposes each member to many different sources, it offers an excellent environment for change. Although changing is not always a conscious process, some of the changes in Philip seem to be—for example, his growing awareness that "to persuade people by overpowering them" vocally is not a good method. On day 40 Philip writes, "I guess I am beginning to realize that I can disagree with people and still have them respect my opinion. This makes me want to respect and allow their opinions too."

During **refreezing** a new response is integrated into one's personality and long-term relationships with others. How stable this change will be depends on "how well the new response fits in with other parts of the personality and whether or not it will be accepted and confirmed by . . . significant others."[11] In an encounter group some refreezing takes place as group members give support to new behaviors. But reinforcement in the daily setting is crucial. If the new behavior accords with one's life outside the group or if others can also learn to respond in new ways, there is a good chance that this change will be permanent.

WHY SENSITIVITY TRAINING? SOME REASONS, OUTCOMES, AND EVALUATIONS

As you read about sensitivity training, you may be asking yourself why anyone should pay money to become intimate with a group of strangers when he already has so many involvements with family, friends, and colleagues or business associates. There seems to be something pathetic about a society in which groups have to be set up to teach its members how to become more human. For several reasons, some yet undetermined, this is exactly what is happening. One well-known group leader, Leland Bradford, has been quoted as saying, "People come as lonely people—we're all lonely people—and find they can finally share with somebody. One statement I've heard 300 or 400 times from T-Group members is, 'You know, I know you people better than people I've worked with for 30 years.' "[12]

What causes this widespread loneliness and alienation? Some believe that living under the threat of nuclear holocaust has given us a feeling of desperation and with it a growing sense of urgency about improving the quality of our lives. Others speculate that the emphasis on self-actualization grows out of our affluence and increased leisure time: no longer required to worry about providing such basic necessities as food and shelter, we have become concerned with personal growth and improvement.

According to Reich part of the alienation that people—especially young people—are experiencing is the result of a shift in values to what he calls Consciousness III.[13] Those who subscribe to the beliefs of Consciousness III no longer value material possessions, as did the older generations (Consciousnesses I and II); they reject what they consider to be the cold impartiality of science and argue instead for the rights and importance of the individual in our society—that is, for more humanistic values.

Another possible explanation of our growing feelings of social isolation is suggested by Toffler in *Future Shock*. He observes that our age, with its industrial advances, faster modes of travel, and continuing urbanization, brings with it an increase in the number of human relationships and "as a likely corollary" of that increase a decline in their average duration: "The average urban individual today probably comes into contact with more people in a single week than a feudal villager did in a year, perhaps even a lifetime."[14] Toffler goes on to say that although the urbanite will have sustained relationships with a core group of people, he will also interact with hundreds, perhaps thousands of people whom he may see only once or twice. Thus in our lifetime the average interpersonal relationship is growing shorter and shorter. Perhaps it is in part the pressure of this overwhelming number of short-term associations that makes people reach out and try new ways of communicating with one another.

For whatever reasons, hundreds of thousands of people have turned to sensitivity training in an effort to make their lives more meaningful. Although it seems unlikely that sensitivity training alone can meet this need, we shall try to make some assessment of its results.

On the value of sensitivity training, we find a broad spectrum of opinion. Rogers has hailed it as "the most important social invention of our time," but many have criticized it as dangerous, destructive, worthless, or at least overrated. Until recently sensitivity training received little or no academic support. Some research projects have been conducted in an attempt to evaluate its outcomes, but the issue remains controversial. The primary obstacle seems to be the tremendous diversity in the kinds of training people are experiencing. Miles points out several other problems: separating the effects of training from those of normal change, choosing criteria of change that are meaningful and quantifiable, and finding comparable control groups.[15]

Positive Opinions

A few studies show significant changes in those who go through a sensitivity training experience. Miles conducted a study of thirty-four high-school principals who had attended a two-week training laboratory. Three months and again eight months after the experience, the participants and members of two control groups were each rated by several people with whom they worked. Coworkers were asked to state whether the subject or control had "changed his/her behavior in working with people over the last year as compared with the previous year in any specific ways" and if so to describe how. Changes were perceived in each of the thirty-four people who had had sensitivity training. Miles summarizes these changes as follows:

> . . . increased sensitivity to others, equalitarian attitudes, skills of communication and leadership, and group and maintenance skills. Personal traits such as "more considerate" and "relaxed" account for about a quarter of the reported changes . . . , with organization-relevant changes (such as "delegates more") and group-relevant changes (such as "aids group decision-making") making up the remainder. This rough balance also occurred in the participants' self-reported learnings at the close of the treatment period, and is congruent with the laboratory staff's statement of objectives.[16]

In another study Bunker asked the same question of people at the back-home setting.[17] He reports findings very similar to those of Miles. When compared with control group members, people who had undergone sensitivity training showed three kinds of changes: (1) increased openness, receptivity, and tolerance of differences; (2) increased skill in interpersonal relations; and (3) improved understanding and diagnostic awareness of self, others, and interactive processes in groups.

Burke and Bennis tried to determine whether sensitivity training brought about changes in a person's perception of himself.[18] Eighty-four participants from several different encounter groups made up the sample in this study. The researchers found that during the course of a three-week training period two changes in self-perception took place. First, greater agreement between the subjects' actual and ideal self-descriptions was reached: people became more self-accepting and more realistic in their expectations of themselves. Second, agreement between self-descriptions and descriptions by others also increased after training: people were better able to see themselves as they were seen by others.

These three studies are representative of those that report positive results from sensitivity training. They have been faulted for their methodological weaknesses, but even their critics admit that it is difficult to measure the kinds of changes that are the goal of this kind of training.

Negative Opinions

On the negative side of the ledger, several criticisms have been leveled at sensitivity training. It has been argued, for example, that as a management training technique, it is not worth the money because it does not show sufficient improvement in job effectiveness. In an extensive review of the literature, Campbell and Dunette conclude that though behavior changes occur as a result of sensitivity training, they do not have any specific value to a person in performing his job.[19] Others with less pragmatic inclinations might be less critical of the research findings. Those interested in personal growth, for example, might still be satisfied with their experience within the group.

A second objection to sensitivity training is that its effects are not permanent. This criticism is valid in several respects, and it is one that advocates of encounter group experience are aware of. In our discussion of personal change, we observed that new behaviors and attitudes are refrozen only if they are integrated into one's personality and significant ongoing relationships. But as Schein and Bennis point out, there are some forces at work in organizations that provide obstacles to change, because

> . . . change in one person generally involves change in a whole network of relationships. Organizations are patterns of shared and interlocking

expectations. Often, it is easier for a group to continue to use ineffective but stable patterns of relationships than to go through the painful process of building new patterns while trying to get the job done.[20]

In general, what determines how permanent changes through training will be is how effective they are in the back-home setting and whether it provides a supportive atmosphere for them. Training labs for married couples would seem to offer an excellent opportunity for personal development that is long-lasting.

A third and very serious criticism of sensitivity training is that it may cause significant psychological damage. It is common knowledge that the encounter group can bring about a relatively high level of emotional arousal, which in turn seems to make one more open to learning but also more vulnerable to conflict. Yet one group of researchers has shown that the level of emotional arousal during training experiences is not significantly higher than it is in other experiences, including sensory deprivation experiments.[21] They conclude that though the level of arousal during training is relatively high, it is not high enough to be harmful to the participant.

One study was conducted specifically to determine the "casualty rate" from encounter groups, with a "casualty" defined as a person who "as a result of his encounter-group experience, suffered considerable and persistent psychological distress."[22] One hundred and seventy students at Stanford University were studied after they had participated in eighteen different encounter groups representing ten different group styles; these ranged from the Esalen sensory awareness approach to the leaderless program using tape-recorded instructions. All the group experiences lasted a total of thirty hours. Out of the 170 people 16 were identified as casualties. Apparently the type of group attended had less to do with the casualty rate than the style of the group leader. Four leaders had seven of the sixteen casualties. The "poor" leaders were described as "aggressive," "confrontive," "challenging," "charismatic," and "authoritarian." It was also observed that they focused on the individual rather than the group. The casualties resulted from attacks or rejection by either the leader or the group. The authors conclude that people who are psychologically vulnerable (that is, those with low self-esteem) are more likely to become casualties. Perhaps these people should be especially cautious about encounter group experiences.

Guidelines for Choosing a Group

The information on sensitivity training is available. It is up to each of you to decide whether encounter groups are 90 percent safe or 10 percent dangerous. If you are interested in participating in an encounter group, we strongly recommend that you choose it carefully. A number of reputable organizations conduct encounter groups.

250   Among these is the Institute for Applied Behavioral Science in Bethel, Maine, a division of the National Training Laboratory (NTL), which has headquarters in Washington, D.C.[23]

Before you decide on a group, you might wish to consider this summary of the seven guidelines proposed by Shostrom, a consultant in sensitivity training:[24]

1. Do not respond to newspaper advertisements or other public announcements. Trained professionals are not permitted to advertise directly.
2. Do not participate in a group that has less than six members. Candor in a group that is too small can give rise to scapegoating and ganging up. A group that has more than sixteen members, on the other hand, usually cannot be handled effectively, no matter how skilled the trainer.
3. Give careful thought to your decision to participate in a group; do not join on impulse. And do not remain in a group in which everyone talks jargon.
4. Do not participate in a group with people you know well, either socially or professionally, unless the group is designed for people with such relationships.
5. Do not let yourself be influenced by the physical surroundings in which the meetings take place or by the status or appearance of various members. A good group session can be held in a ghetto classroom, and all good groups will include people and life styles you do not identify with closely.
6. Stay away from a group that has a "behavioral ax to grind"—that requires every member to espouse a particular doctrine.
7. Be sure that the group you join is formally connected with a professional you can check on. A good many people who conduct encounter groups have little or no training in this field. If a group leader does not have some professional degree in the behavioral or social sciences, his group should be avoided.

SENSITIVITY TRAINING AND INTERPERSONAL COMMUNICATION: SOME PARALLEL GOALS

How different is sensitivity training from other forms of human interaction? One writer comments eloquently on the criticism of the training group situation as "artificial":

> [This] accusation . . . is not only absurd but ironic, for in fact it is a rather precise analogue of life itself. What differentiates training groups from "natural" task groups is their mortality, their confusion, and their

leadership structure. Most groups formed to accomplish some purpose are potentially immortal, have a more or less clear goal or at least a plan of action or an agenda, and a clearly defined leadership. Training groups are born knowing they must die; they do not know, aside from some ill-formulated notions about self-understanding, growth, and knowledge of group processes, why they are there or what they are going to do; and [they] struggle perpetually with the fact that the object whom they fantasy to be powerful and omniscient in fact does nothing, fails to protect them or tell them what to do, and hardly seems to be there at all. Is this unlifelike?[25]

In this text our interest in sensitivity training focuses primarily on its goals, many of which parallel those of less formal attempts to improve interpersonal communication. Communication is the process through which we develop or destroy human relationships, and the overall objective of sensitivity training is, of course, to increase competence in human relationships. Within that framework there are a number of specific goals, which the trainer may or may not make explicit for the group. We shall discuss four that we believe have broad implications for improving all interpersonal communication.

The first goal of all sensitivity training, as the word "sensitivity" implies, is to increase **awareness** of oneself and others. Unlike many other types of interpersonal communication, the training experience attempts to be a totally conscious one. People are encouraged to become more aware not only of their own thoughts and feelings but of what others are thinking and feeling. A great part of this derives from sensitivity to the motivations for behavior. For example, aggressiveness on the part of a group member may be prompted by his need for assurance; if so, a supportive response may be more effective in reducing his need to act aggressively than a response in kind. Another common cause of discord both within and outside the group setting is resistance to change, which we often interpret as personal rejection if we do not see its motivation. In general, greater awareness of our own behavior and the behavior of others increases our effectiveness in many interpersonal situations.

A second desired objective of sensitivity training is to give and receive **open feedback** so that our own and others' behaviors and responses become more appropriate to the situation at hand. One writer graphically describes the difference between our intended and unintended cues as the **arc of distortion** (see Figure 19, page 252). Sensitivity training is designed to help us learn to minimize distortion in both sending and receiving messages, primarily through more open feedback.

Through open feedback we begin to find out which behaviors, both verbal and nonverbal, are effective in communicating with others and which need to be improved. This assumes, however, that the feedback we are receiving is of a high quality. Miles suggests that to be effective feedback must "(1) be clear and undistorted; (2) come from a trusted,

Figure 19

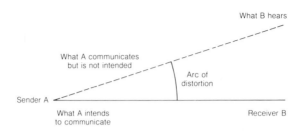

The Arc of Distortion

SOURCE: Warren G. Bennis, "Interpersonal Communication," in Warren G. Bennis, Kenneth Benne, and R. Chin, *The Planning of Change* (New York: Holt, Rinehart and Winston, 1961), p. 409.

non-threatening source; (3) follow as closely as possible the behavior to which it is a reaction."[26]

Another goal of sensitivity training is to improve our **perception and understanding of group dynamics**. Both the encounter group and the class in group discussion often enable their members to increase their knowledge of group dynamics by learning (either through readings or brief lectures) what behavioral scientists have been able to determine about small group behavior. The discussion class, however, usually stresses solving specific problems outside the group—how best to conduct a fund-raising drive, for example. The encounter group is more interested in the interpersonal relationships within its group—how to help Paul accept affection from the other participants, for example. Greater understanding of group processes allows us to reevaluate our common-sense notions of how to cope with emotions, conflicts, and decision making; it also offers us an excellent opportunity to experiment with new, potentially better group behaviors.

The fourth goal of sensitivity training that seems particularly relevant to interpersonal communication is **acceptance** of both self and others. As we saw in Chapter 5, people like those who resemble themselves. They find it reinforcing to have their ideas met with approval. Encounter groups are based on a different principle. They do not reinforce personal traits, beliefs, attitudes, or values. Instead they derive much of their strength from helping people acknowledge and allow differences.

How do encounter groups foster acceptance? Communication scholars and psychologists have known for some time that the more uneasy the psychological climate between two people, the more distortions and misinterpretations will occur. Encounter groups attempt to create a psychological atmosphere that is supportive rather than threatening, an atmosphere in which differences of all sorts—in attitude, dress, behavior, life style—are tolerated. Harrison explains why this new environment is necessary:

> . . . the destruction of defenses does not serve learning; instead, it increases the anxiety of the person that he will lose the more or less effective conceptual systems he has with which to understand and relate to the world, and he drops back to an even more desperate and perhaps unrealistic defense than the one destroyed.[27]

The application to all interpersonal communication is clear. Abruptly stripping someone of his defenses only increases his distance from other people. Acceptance of others permits more open communication.

Acceptance of others often brings with it a greater acceptance of self. At first glance, self-acceptance might seem an undesirable goal for anyone interested in personal growth. In many instances, however, it is the beginning of change. Argyris explains how an increase in self-acceptance can bring about a host of other positive changes:

> a. The greater the sense of self-acceptance, the greater the probability that one will be one's self and will *"own"* one's ideas, values, and feelings and permit others to do the same should they wish to do so.
> b. As the conditions in (a) above increase, the probability increases that the individual will be *open* to considering new ideas, values, and feelings.
> c. As the conditions in (a) and (b) increase, the probability increases that the individual will tend to *experiment* and *take risks* with new ideas, values, and feelings, and permit others to do so.
> d. As the conditions in (a) and (b) and (c) increase, the probability *decreases* that the opposite conditions will tend to occur.[28]

There is evidence that the conditions just described contribute to personal adjustment. Our assumption is that better adjustment will be both the result and the source of more effective interpersonal communication. This is not to say that self-acceptance or any of the other goals we have discussed can be achieved only through sensitivity training. We simply point out that it offers an interesting if somewhat controversial approach to improving communication skills.[29]

Summary

In our study of the sensitivity training group as one context of interpersonal communication, we first tried to re-create the development of a typical encounter group, discussing the focus on the here and now, the emphasis on personality rather than role, open feedback, and focal conflict. Two representative theories that we examined both conceptualized the life of the encounter group as moving through phases toward greater interdependence and affection among members.

Excerpts from the log of an encounter group participant showed some aspects of individual development within the group. The log illustrated some recurring conflicts experienced by all group members as well as the personal change that often takes place as a result of training. We saw how such growth could be explained either by learning theory or by Lewin's conception of the process of change: unfreezing, changing, and refreezing. We then considered some reasons for the increasing interest and participation in sensitivity training. A review of research on the outcomes of training presented both favorable and unfavorable opinions and listed guidelines for those considering a training experience.

We concluded the chapter by discussing four goals of sensitivity training and how they might be helpful in our efforts to improve interpersonal communication: awareness of self and others, open feedback, knowledge of group dynamics, and acceptance of self and others.

Review Questions

1. What is a focused exercise and what purpose(s) does it serve in an encounter group?
2. What is meant by the "here and now" as it relates to encounter groups?
3. Outline the six stages of Bennis and Shepard's theory of group development. What are the characteristics of each stage?
4. How does Schutz's theory explain the development of encounter groups?
5. How do the principles of reinforcement and extinction operate in encounter groups to produce learning? Give specific examples if you can.
6. Specify three ways in which the encounter group setting leads to unfreezing.
7. Discuss four possible reasons why people seek encounter group experiences.
8. What are at least two positive and two negative aspects of sensitivity training?
9. What are four goals of sensitivity training? Describe how each goal may be achieved.

Exercises

1. Pair yourself with a classmate, preferably a person you do not know very well. Write down five adjectives that you feel describe yourself and have the other person describe himself in the same way. Taking turns, reveal the five adjectives to the other and tell him why you think the adjectives describe yourself.
2. Place yourself and eleven other members of the class in two lines

that face each other. Have each person in one line stand close to the person across from him and communicate only by facial expression and eye contact, trying to express feelings in this manner. Then have each person shift one place to the right (or left) and conduct another "eyealogue" until each of you has experienced this with every other person in the opposite line. Then discuss the experience as a group.

3. Have a group of six people sit in a circle and observe a period of silence. Then discuss the experience. What did you notice about people's behavior? What did you notice about your own?

4. Have each person in a group of four write a paragraph on "What I am feeling about the group right now." These may be feelings that are particularly difficult for you to talk about. The papers should be collected, shuffled, and read aloud by the group leader. A discussion of these papers should then be conducted.

5. Using either the Bennis and Shepard or the Schutz theory of group development as a basis for examining an encounter group, write a paper comparing and contrasting encounter group development with other types of group development discussed in Chapter 9.

6. Refer to the model of interpersonal communication presented in Chapter 2. Discuss how each component of the model is related to communication within the encounter group. How does this type of interpersonal communication differ from others discussed in the book?

Suggested Readings

Bennis, Warren G., and others. *Interpersonal Dynamics: Essays and Readings on Human Interaction,* 3rd ed. Homewood, Ill.: Dorsey, 1973. This collection of essays and readings offers a good explanation of the rationale behind sensitivity training. The book is readable and contains a wide variety of viewpoints.

Bindrim, Paul. "Nudity." *Psychology Today* (June 1969), 3:24–28. The author presents an argument in favor of nude encounter groups. He suggests that nude marathon participants are more unified and open to each other; that nudity gives participants a sense of self-confidence, self-expression, and an overall acceptance of other persons; and finally that it enables participants to be more honest and more determined to struggle with their emotional problems. This article will undoubtedly be controversial enough to begin a discussion of the pros and cons of sensitivity training.

Murphy, Michael. "Esalen: Where It's At." *Psychology Today* (December 1967), 1:34–39. Esalen Institute, at Big Sur, California, is the first of many institutes like it all over the country, with well over four thousand people a year attending. The Institute does not endorse any one philosophy or doctrine; leaders ranging from clergymen to advocates of LSD have conducted seminars there. "No approach," says author Murphy, "is too far out to be tried here."

Notes

1 Carl Rogers, "Community: The Group Comes of Age," *Psychology Today*, 3 (December 1969), 30.

2 R. Whitman, "Psychodynamic Principles Underlying the T-Group Process," in Leland Bradford, Jack Gibb, and Kenneth Benne (eds.), *T-Group Theory and Laboratory Method* (New York: Wiley, 1964), pp. 310–335.

3 Carl Goldberg, *Encounter: Group Sensitivity Training Experiences* (New York: Science House, 1970), pp. 140–141.

4 Warren G. Bennis and Herbert A. Shepard, "A Theory of Group Development," *Human Relations*, 9 (1956), 415–457.

5 Bennis and Shepard, p. 422.

6 Bennis and Shepard, p. 426.

7 Philip E. Slater, *Microcosm: Structural, Psychological and Religious Evolution in Groups* (New York: Wiley, 1966), p. 256.

8 William D. Schutz, *The Interpersonal Underworld* (Palo Alto, Calif.: Science and Behavior Books, 1966), pp. 168–188; and *Joy: Expanding Human Awareness* (New York: Grove, 1967), pp. 117–187.

9 Schutz, *Joy*, p. 118.

10 Quoted in Richard Mann, Graham Gibbard, and John Hartman, *Interpersonal Styles and Group Development* (New York: Wiley, 1967), p. 25.

11 Edgar H. Schein, "Personal Change Through Interpersonal Relationships," in Warren G. Bennis and others (eds.), *Interpersonal Dynamics: Essays and Readings on Human Interaction*, rev. ed. (Homewood, Ill.: Dorsey, 1968), p. 363.

12 Quoted in "Human Potential: The Revolution in Feeling," *Time*, November 9, 1970, p. 56.

13 Charles Reich, *The Greening of America* (New York: Random House, 1970), Chap. IX.

14 Alfred Toffler, *Future Shock* (New York: Random House, 1970), p. 100.

15 Matthew B. Miles, "Human Relations Training: Processes and Outcomes," *Journal of Counseling Psychology*, 7 (1960), 301–306.

16 Matthew B. Miles, "Changes During and Following Laboratory Training: A Clinical-Experimental Study," *Journal of Applied Behavioral Science*, 1 (1965), 218, 240.

17 Douglas Bunker, "The Effect of Laboratory Education upon Individual Behavior," in Edgar H. Schein and Warren G. Bennis, *Personal and Organizational Change Through Group Methods* (New York: Wiley, 1965), pp. 255–267.

[18] H. Burke and Warren G. Bennis, "Changes in Perception of Self and Others During Human Relations Training," *Human Relations,* 14 (1961), 165–182.

[19] John P. Campbell and Marvin D. Dunette, "Effectiveness of T-Group Experiences in Managerial Training and Development," *Psychological Bulletin,* 70 (1968), 73–104.

[20] Schein and Bennis, p. 282.

[21] Bernard Lubin and Marvin Zuckerman, "Level of Emotional Arousal in Laboratory Training," *Journal of Applied Behavioral Science,* 5 (1969), 483–490.

[22] Morton Lieberman, Irvin Yalom, and Matthew B. Miles, "Casualty Lists from Group Encounters," cited in *Psychology Today,* 5 (July 1971), 28.

[23] For an extensive list of organizations that offer sensitivity training, see Jane Howard, *Please Touch: A Guided Tour of the Human Potential Movement* (New York: McGraw-Hill, 1970), pp. 258–262.

[24] Everett L. Shostrom, "Group Therapy: Let the Buyer Beware," *Psychology Today,* 2 (May 1969), 36–39.

[25] Slater, p. 12.

[26] Matthew B. Miles, *Learning to Work in Groups* (New York: Teachers College Press, Columbia University, 1967), p. 43.

[27] Roger Harrison, "Defenses and the Need to Know," in Robert Golembiewski and Arthur Blumberg (eds.), *Sensitivity Training and the Laboratory Approach* (Itasca, Ill.: Peacock, 1970), p. 85.

[28] Chris Argyris, *Interpersonal Competence and Organizational Effectiveness* (Homewood, Ill.: Dorsey, 1962), p. 25.

[29] See Stewart L. Tubbs, "Reactions to Sensitivity Training from the Standpoint of a Participant and Trainer," *Michigan Speech Journal,* 8 (1973), 32–35.

Chapter 11
Public Communication

OBJECTIVES

After reading this chapter the student should be able to:

1. Distinguish public communication from other forms of interpersonal communication.
2. Identify three purposes of public communication.
3. Define two major dimensions of source credibility.
4. Distinguish between extrinsic and intrinsic credibility.
5. State the general research finding regarding the relationship between source credibility and audience attitude change.
6. Describe the sleeper effect.
7. Describe four modes of delivery.
8. Outline six steps that may be used in organizing messages.
9. State the conditions under which one-sided and two-sided messages are most effective.
10. State the general research finding regarding the relative effectiveness of messages containing stated versus implied conclusions.
11. Describe the relationship between level of fear in a message and persuasive effect.
12. State the conditions under which climax and anticlimax order messages are most effective.
13. Distinguish between the assimilation effect and the contrast effect and describe the relevance of these concepts to the problem of how much change a speaker should advocate.
14. Distinguish between demographic audience analysis and purpose-oriented audience analysis.
15. State the general research finding about the relationship between sex and persuasibility.
16. State the general research finding about the relationship between self-esteem and persuasibility.
17. Distinguish between pleasurable listening, discriminative listening, and critical listening.
18. Define four methods of support and explain how each can be used as a propaganda device.

11

Speaking at Kansas State University in 1970, Richard M. Nixon was interrupted a number of times by antiwar chants and constantly harassed by a group of hecklers standing at the rear of the audience. He continued, but added special vocal emphasis and some unplanned comments as a way of responding to these attacks. He also seemed to become more enthusiastic in speaking after most of the audience responded with applause for his words. When participating in situations such as this one, we experience the most formal mode of interpersonal communication we shall ever encounter: public, or person-to-group, communication.

In Chapter 1 we defined interpersonal communication as face-to-face, two-way communication. We have already examined three contexts in which it occurs: dyads, problem-solving small groups, and therapeutic groups. Two-person interaction comes closest to an equal exchange between communicators. Theoretically each person is responsible for half of all the verbal and nonverbal messages transmitted; each is both speaker and listener. When we become members of problem-solving or therapeutic groups, the balance shifts and the communication process changes. We speak for shorter periods of time; we listen longer. Yet we still think of ourselves as speakers and listeners, senders and receivers of messages.

In public communication, however, one person is designated the speaker, and the rest are cast in the role of listeners, or audience members. Participants are still face to face and are still sending and receiving communicative stimuli. But the balance of message sending is quite uneven—the speaker initiates most of the verbal messages, and though audience members often send nonverbal messages, they are usually not expected to contribute verbal messages, except in a question-and-answer period following the speech. Despite this imbalance, public communication is still interpersonal communication, and we frequently find ourselves participating in it as either a speaker or a listener.

In addressing an audience a speaker ordinarily has one of two purposes: to inform or to persuade his listeners. A third purpose is to entertain, but more often than not entertaining speeches are designed to inform or to persuade the audience. When his purpose is to inform, the speaker is concerned primarily with information gain, one of the communication outcomes we referred to in Chapter 1. When his purpose is to persuade, he is interested in influencing attitude—in establishing an attitude not previously held by the listeners, or in strengthening or changing one they already hold. Of course, these purposes need not be mutually exclusive. A persuasive speech about this country's diplomatic relations with China may also be informative. Yet if the audience assimilates all the facts but fails to be persuaded by the speaker's arguments, he has not accomplished his primary objective. Similarly an informative lecture on marine biology may be delivered in an entertaining and appealing style. But if the audience laughs heartily at all the jokes and comes away with no knowledge of marine biology, the speaker can hardly think of himself as successful.

Most of the public communication situations in which you find yourself as both a speaker and a listener will involve some persuasion— usually in addition to information gain. Therefore, this chapter will give more emphasis to public communication that attempts to be persuasive. We begin with a consideration of the speaker himself, apart from his message.

THE SPEAKER

During Lyndon Johnson's administrations, the term "credibility gap" became a popular way of expressing the belief that the President was not always telling the American people the whole truth about the internal workings of our government. That belief was further reinforced during Richard Nixon's tenure. In its broadest sense, **credibility** refers to *our willingness to trust what a person says and does*. It is undoubtedly the single most important influence on our judgment of a speaker.

Source Credibility

Credibility is not a new concept. Aristotle and other classical writers spoke about it as ethos: the intelligence, good character, and good will of the speaker. During this century considerable research has been conducted on the subject of source credibility. Notice our use of the word "source." Although a speaker is usually perceived as the source of his message, this is not always the case. When a United Nations delegate addresses the General Assembly, he may not be considered the source of his message. Similarly, when an executive of a large oil company discusses Middle Eastern affairs, he may be seen not as the originator of his message but simply as a spokesman for his firm. In most instances, however, the source of the message will be viewed as the speaker.

Using a statistical procedure known as factor analysis, researchers have identified authoritativeness and character as two of the major dimensions by which we rate a source's credibility.[1] **Authoritativeness**, or expertness, refers to the speaker's perceived command of a given subject—to *how intelligent, informed, competent, and prestigious we think the speaker is.* **Character**, a vaguer but no less important dimension, refers to the speaker's perceived intentions and trustworthiness— to *how objective, reliable, well motivated, and likable the speaker seems to be.*

Both elements enter into our judgments of credibility. If a physician who also holds a doctorate in chemistry argues that preservatives in baby food have no adverse effects, most audiences will regard him as a high-credibility source. If it is then disclosed that he is a consultant to one of the largest producers of baby food in this country, his credibility may suffer a sharp decline. While the audience may not question his expertise, it will question his motives as well as his ability to be objective about a position from which he stands to gain. In one study a convicted criminal produced no attitude change in arguing for greater personal freedom and less police power but significant attitude change when he argued for greater police power.[2] By supporting a position that seemed to be against his own interests, he increased his credibility considerably. **Source credibility**, then, refers to both *the speaker's authoritativeness on a given topic and his character as these are perceived by the receiver of the message.*

Throughout our discussion of credibility, let us remember the word "perceived." Credibility has to do not with what the speaker is but with how he is perceived. Regardless of his demonstrated expertise or good character, no speaker has high credibility for every audience. The vice president of an airline may be a high-credibility source when addressing his employees but not when speaking before the Federal Aviation Agency. In lecturing on the causes of World War II, a Harvard historian may be a high-credibility source to his students; to his colleagues his credibility may be considerably less.

Because it is linked to perception, a speaker's credibility is not a constant. It may vary not only from one audience to another but from the time he steps up to the podium to the time he finishes his speech.

Extrinsic Credibility. A speaker comes into a speaking situation with a certain credibility level. For example, if Billy Graham, Al Capp, or Edward Kennedy gives a speech on your campus, his reputation will undoubtedly influence your evaluation of that speech. If the top student in your class gives a speech, your previous impression of him affects your attitude toward his message. This is referred to as **extrinsic credibility**—*the image of the speaker as it exists before he delivers his speech.*

There has been ample research on the influence of extrinsic credibility. The typical study involves the delivery of the same speech (sometimes tape-recorded for greater consistency) to several audiences but with the speaker introduced differently to each. For example, a speech (supposedly a taped radio program) favoring lenient treatment of juvenile delinquents was presented to three groups of high-school students, but the speaker was identified in turn as a juvenile court judge, a presumably neutral member of the studio audience, and an audience member who had a criminal record and had been a juvenile delinquent himself.[3] When the three groups of students were asked to assess the fairness of the speech, they rated the speech by the judge, the high-credibility source, as much fairer than the speech by the ex-convict. The judge's speech also resulted in more attitude change than the ex-convict's.

A number of studies confirm that speakers with high credibility tend to have more influence on an audience's attitudes than do those with low credibility. One summary of the literature qualifies this statement with the observation that ". . . the perceived-competence aspect adds to persuasive impact more than the trustworthiness aspect does. By competence we mean the perceived expertness, status, intelligence, etc., of the attributed source; by trustworthiness, we refer to his perceived disinterestedness, objectivity, and lack of persuasive intent."[4] It is also interesting to note that the credibility of the speaker does not seem to have a significant effect on the level of the audience's comprehension.[5] Credibility appears to be a more important consideration when we are persuading an audience than when we are informing them.

Extrinsic credibility may have another, more subtle effect on persuasion. Suppose that Cesar Chavez comes to your campus and that in the middle of a discussion of how he organized the migrant farm workers' strikes in California, he goes off on a long digression about religion or sex or even African art, topics on which his views may be no more authoritative than those of the man in the street. How much of his extrinsic credibility would be generalized to areas in which his expertise has not been demonstrated? Consider this question the next time one of your professors expresses strong opinions about a subject far removed from his field of specialization.

Intrinsic Credibility. Extrinsic credibility is only one aspect of credibility. A speaker's total credibility consists of how he is perceived by the audience before his speech plus the impressions he makes while delivering it. In other words, he comes into a speaking situation with some level of credibility and adds to or detracts from it by what he says. **Intrinsic credibility** is the name often given to this *image that a speaker creates as a direct result of his speech.*

Each of us may be accomplished in some way or make certain claims about our good character. By and large, however, we are not perceived as high-credibility sources. Our major opportunities for increasing our credibility come during the actual presentation of the speech.

One way in which a speaker may increase his intrinsic credibility is by *establishing a common ground* between himself and his audience. This rhetorical technique has been successfully used for centuries and is still used today. For example, Daniel J. Boorstin, a well-known historian, opened a speech to an audience of Associated Press managing editors with these remarks:

> Gentlemen, it's a great pleasure and privilege to be allowed to take part in your meeting. It is especially a pleasure to come and have such a flattering introduction, the most flattering part of which was to be called a person who wrote like a newspaperman.
>
> The historians, you know, sometimes try to return the compliment by saying that the best newspapermen write like historians but I'm not sure how many of the people present would consider that a compliment.
>
> This afternoon I would like to talk briefly about the problems we share, we historians and newspapermen, and that we all share as Americans.[6]

Boorstin attempted to show his listeners that he was sympathetic to their point of view and that he and they shared certain things: they were writers, they had some of the same problems, they were Americans, and so on. As you may recall from Chapter 5, balance theory predicts that similarities tend to increase liking and that in general we tend to like those who agree with us on a substantial proportion of salient issues. Thus it is quite possible that a speaker will be able to increase his intrinsic credibility if he can convince his audience that a common ground exists between them.

Another influence on the character dimension of credibility is *humor*. Many speakers use humor as a means of ingratiating themselves with the audience. Bill Russell, former player-coach of the Boston Celtics, applied this approach to advantage in an address to members of a small college. He would like to say, he remarked, that it was a rare privilege to be in their town and he would like to say that this stop was one of the highlights of his travels. Then he paused. The laughter of the audience indicated that they knew this was not true. Russell then went on to say that he *could* honestly say that he was very happy to have the chance to meet and speak with the people in the audience.

Research on the use of humor in speeches indicates that though it may not increase the listeners' understanding or change their attitude toward the speaker's topic, it affects their perception of his character. In general, they like a speaker more when he uses humor.[7]

The Sleeper Effect. Despite its impact on an audience's receptivity, credibility does not appear to have a sustained influence on persuasion. Earlier we mentioned a study in which a speech favoring a lenient attitude toward juvenile delinquency produced maximum attitude change when presented by a high-credibility source. This influence was greatest immediately after the speech was delivered. Differences resulting from the speaker's credibility tended to diminish over time so that the attitude change produced by the high-credibility source decreased and the message from the low-credibility source gained ground, producing more attitude change. This trend is sometimes called **the sleeper effect.**

The sleeper effect seems to result from the listener's tendency to dissociate the source and the message—presumably because he forgets who the source is. In experiments during which the listener was reminded of the source of the message, the high-credibility source regained his significantly greater influence on attitude change over the low-credibility source.[8] Apparently the sleeper effect can be overcome if audience members are reminded of the source of the message. Nixon often uses this tactic in press conferences when he answers questions by referring to speeches he made in the past.

Delivery

Another significant influence on how we judge the speaker is his delivery. How many times have you heard someone speak who uses a lot of "ahs," "uhs," and "ums"? This annoying habit, along with the needless repetition of such words or phrases as "like," "well," and "you know," falls into the category of **nonfluencies.** As we saw in Chapter 7, nonfluent speakers tend to be irritating and boring to listen to because their rate of speech is slow. Each of us is nonfluent at times, and this is normal. Research on nonfluent and fluent speakers shows, however, that a fluent speaker not only improves his image in the eyes of his audience but also produces more attitude change when giving a persuasive speech.[9]

Good delivery obviously involves much more than just fluency. It involves the effective use of many of the visual and vocal cues we discussed in talking about nonverbal messages: eye contact, hand gestures, posture, and general physical appearance as well as vocal quality, pitch, volume, and rate of speech. It has been demonstrated that when a speaker's message is weak (that is, when he uses no evidence to support his assertions), good delivery has no significant effect on attitude. But when he uses good delivery in combination with a strong (that is, well-documented) message, he elicits significantly greater attitude change in his audience than a speaker who delivers the same message, but has poor delivery.[10] This finding is important because it confirms that the various aspects of speech making are interrelated. Delivery alone cannot produce attitude change. Nevertheless poor delivery distracts from an otherwise effective message whereas good delivery allows listeners to concentrate on the quality of the message, giving it optimum impact.

For years two guidelines for effective delivery have been naturalness and poise. The delivery should not draw attention away from the content of the message, as it might, for example, if it is overly dramatic or if it reflects lack of confidence. In our experience the two most common faults of the student speaker are that he relies too heavily on his notes or that he tries to memorize the entire speech and ends up sounding like a robot. In considering such problems, it is helpful to review the four modes of delivery that are commonly used in public communication.

The first mode, **impromptu** delivery, describes the speech presented with little preparation. In essence, the speaker stands before his audience and thinks out loud. This style has one advantage: maximum spontaneity. It suffers, however, from the lack of advance planning. Less formal kinds of interpersonal communication place a high premium on spontaneity, but public address usually requires a more formal style of delivery. We therefore advise you to avoid using an impromptu delivery—provided, of course, that you have a choice.

The second mode of delivery is called **extemporaneous** speaking. The person who uses this style speaks from minimal notes, which usually consist of phrases or key words that remind him of all the topics he plans to cover. These notes represent the final stage of message preparation, a procedure we shall discuss in the following section. Extemporaneous delivery combines the spontaneity of impromptu speaking with the precision afforded by advance planning.

Memorized speech is the third mode of delivery. Here the entire speech has been planned beforehand, written in manuscript, and then committed to memory. The speaker is therefore free to look at his audience instead of reading from notes or manuscript. Although memorized speech might sound like the most effective kind of delivery, it has two drawbacks. The first is that many of the natural qualities of human communication—vocal inflection, facial expression, gesture, and so on—may be lost. This is the problem of robotlike delivery, which we mentioned earlier. Second, human memory being what it is, the speaker runs the risk of forgetting part of his message. If this happens to you and you have to sit down before you have finished, you are unlikely to forget the experience for a long time.

The fourth and most formal mode of delivery is **reading from manuscript**. For broadcasters, politicians, and other people whose remarks are often quoted, this is a valuable technique. It allows the speaker to be extremely precise in phrasing his message and to minimize the possibility that his message will be misconstrued. The speech is delivered exactly as it has been prepared. For the average person, however, manuscript speaking requires an unnecessarily long preparation time. It has another limitation. It makes the speaker so reliant on reading from manuscript that he is unable to look up at the audience, except for very brief periods of time, which drastically reduces his ability to adapt his message to audience feedback.

268   Different speaking situations unquestionably require different modes of delivery. In situations that most of us will encou.ıter, however, extemporaneous delivery is recommended. It is a style that allows you to be well-prepared and yet flexible enough to respond to feedback from your audience.

We have tried to isolate two important aspects of public communication that relate primarily to the speaker. We saw in our discussion of the sleeper effect, however, that over time the influence of the source of the message seems to decline and the impact of the message itself gains ground. Sooner or later the message gets through. Let us look more carefully at how this message can be constructed.

THE MESSAGE

If the students of the late sixties and early seventies could be characterized by a single quality, it was their willingness to speak out on the political and social issues of their day. Theirs was a time of confrontation, a time in which young and old alike expressed their beliefs with great intensity. Yet many of those who spoke out were far less effective than they might have been because they had not fulfilled the demands of the public speaking situation, which are in some sense unique. Their deficiencies did not go unnoticed.

> Perhaps less noticeable to the rhetorically untrained eye and ear has been a subtle but unmistakable shift from what we have traditionally regarded to be "proper" modes for the arrangement of verbal discourse to formless or stream-of-consciousness patterns. Gone from such contemporary discourse are the familiar introduction, body, and conclusions; the statement and partition of issues; internal summaries; topical, spatial, chronological, or any other particular kind of order. More typically today the spokesmen for peace or war . . . or cracking down on marijuana, or the pros and cons of cohabitation of college coeds begin to talk with rambling personal experiences, sometimes rather dramatic, and finish about where they started, with a liberal sprinkling of "you knows" in between.[11]

In this section we shall be concerned with two specific ways in which a speaker might improve his public communication skills: by organizing the material well and by choosing the appropriate strategy, which involves what we call message variables. The first relates to the structure of the speech and the second to both structure and content.

Organizing the Message

How does one go about putting together a speech? Our discussion of message preparation will be put in very concrete terms. In the following pages we shall outline a procedure that might be especially helpful if you have rarely spoken before an audience.

Step 1. Determine the Purpose of the Speech. The first question to ask yourself when you are about to prepare a speech is, "Why am I speaking?" We have already referred to the two purposes of most speech making: informing and persuading. Efficient message organization depends largely on the clarification of purpose. If you want to transmit information to your audience, your first concern is to be as clear as possible. If you want to influence audience attitude, you may be concerned primarily with developing the strategy that is most persuasive, a subject we shall discuss when we speak about message variables. Should the purpose of your speech be to entertain, organization will probably be secondary. For example, Bob Hope, Johnny Carson, and many other professional entertainers are often able to hold their audience's attention with a string of unrelated anecdotes and comments.

Step 2. Decide on a Topic. If you have been invited to speak, selecting the subject can be difficult. A good principle to keep in mind is that personal experiences are often the best source of ideas for a speech. It is always easier to build from firsthand knowledge. In any case, once you know that you are to give a speech, you should begin to observe events with the thought that these might become speech materials. If you watch television news programs, for example, a current topic there may be fair game for you. Perhaps you have read a good book or article recently; these often make excellent sources of both topic ideas and supporting materials. Talking with others will also expose you to new ideas for topics. Or simply observing people can often be a good source of speech topics. One student gave a persuasive speech against smoking after observing all the inconveniences associated with smoking. Another way to arrive at a topic is to "brainstorm" with a pad and pencil all the topics that come into your head. When doing so, use free association: think of a word and then jot down any ideas that come to mind.

The suggestions for topics included in the exercises at the end of this chapter should give you some ideas or stimulate your own thinking about possible subjects. If you have volunteered to speak on a given issue, your decision has already been made. Nonetheless you still have to take into account the amount of time allowed for your speech. If you have offered to speak on Russia and you have only ten minutes, you will obviously have to limit your topic. Perhaps you will speak on education in Russia or Russian attitudes toward trial marriages or Russian drama during the nineteenth century. Tailoring the topic to the time available to you is a task to complete before you go any further.

Step 3. Write Your Central Idea. Once you have selected the subject of your speech, your third step is to crystallize your central idea, or theme, in the form of a thesis sentence. If you were to summarize the thrust of your argument in a single sentence, what would it be? One student preparing an informative speech about the human nervous system used this statement: "The human nervous system consists of an intricate network of interrelated structures." Here is another thesis sentence, this one from a student's persuasive speech: "The United States foreign aid policy is not meeting its objectives because American dollars have been helping spread communism."

Step 4. Develop Your Main and Subordinate Points. You are now ready to elaborate your central idea by laying out the main and subordinate points of your argument. One of the best ways to approach organizing this material, which constitutes the body of your speech, is to make a working outline. Jot down in any order all the ideas that come to mind relating to what you want to say. If you think of a quote, an anecdote, or an example, you might want to include it too. You may add to your list over a period of several days as your ideas begin to take shape. After completing the list, you can then organize the points you want to make in the form of a traditional outline, in which some ideas are subordinated to others. The student preparing the informative speech on the human nervous system developed this outline:

I. The central nervous system consists of the brain and the spinal cord.
   A. The brain has three distinct regions, each with a special function:
      1. Forebrain.
      2. Midbrain.
      3. Hindbrain.
   B. The spinal cord has two distinct functions:
      1. Sensory functions.
      2. Motor functions.

II. The peripheral nervous system connects the central nervous system to the rest of the body.
   A. Afferent nerves carry neurochemical impulses from the body to the brain.
      1. Somatic nerves (from the extremities).
      2. Visceral nerves (from the abdomen and chest).
   B. Efferent nerves carry neurochemical impulses from the brain to the body.
      1. Somatic nerves (to the extremities).
      2. Visceral nerves (to the abdomen and chest).

In the example above, the student used a *topical* method of arranging his ideas. That is, he moved from one topic (or category) to the next in a manner that showed clearly the relationship of one to another. Several other forms of idea arrangement are also available to you. The *chronological* method uses a time sequence to organize events. Richard Nixon in his August 15, 1973 speech on Watergate tried to document his knowledge of the break-in and subsequent "cover-up" by showing step by step through time his increasing knowledge of these incidents. A third method of arrangement is the *spatial* pattern. This pattern uses space or position as an organizer. In an effective speech about our solar system, for example, a student briefly described each planet by beginning with Mercury (closest to the sun) and moving in order away from the sun to conclude with the planet Pluto. Another popular method of arrangement is the *problem-solution* pattern. Most affirmative debate cases are built around the idea that a problem exists and that the speaker is presenting a plan that will improve the situation. In discussing the energy shortage, for example, the size and severity of the problem would first have to be established, after which corrective steps could be described. A fifth type of idea arrangement is the *causal* pattern. With this approach the speaker describes a situation and then shows how it leads to certain predictable effects. Alcoholism, for example, can be seen as an effect of other underlying causes (unhappiness, failure, and so forth). Once you have decided on the pattern of arrangement that best fits your topic, you are ready to gather your supporting materials.

Step 5. Gather Your Supporting Materials. After you have determined the main and subordinate points of your presentation, your next step is to use what are called **materials of support** or **methods of support**—various *forms of evidence* that develop or strengthen each of the points you want to make. The student arguing against foreign aid gave *examples* of specific countries that had worsening relations with the United States despite the fact that they were still receiving a substantial amount of foreign aid. He used *statistics* to show the increasing amount of aid to various countries over the years and the simultaneous rise of communism in some of the same countries. He also gave *quotations* from experts on foreign relations who argued that our foreign aid policy was ineffective. Finally, he drew an *analogy* between the United States giving foreign aid and a person playing the stock market: "When an investment does not pay off," he said, "it is wise to stop investing in a losing cause and reinvest in another, more profitable venture."

All these supporting materials—examples, statistics, quotations, analogies—may increase the listener's understanding or influence his attitudes. One study found that a low-credibility source who uses evidence seems more credible as he speaks and that a high-credibility source who does not use evidence tends to lose ground if he follows a speaker who has. Evidence also seems to have long-term effects on attitude change: when a speaker documents his argument, his listeners are more likely to resist efforts at counterpersuasion by a second speaker.

As aids in gathering supporting materials you may want to consult some of the standard reference works, such as *Reader's Guide to Periodical Literature, Education Index, Biography Index, The World Almanac,* any set of encyclopedias, *Who's Who, Psychological Abstracts, The Congressional Record* and many others available in the Reference section of your library. In most cases, reference works such as those mentioned will lead you to the books, magazines, and journals that will be most helpful to you. When doing research in the library, save yourself time and energy by taking careful notes the first time around, so that you will not have to recheck your sources.

Step 6. Write the Conclusion, Introduction, and Transitions. The last part of your work is to give your speech continuity. We suggest that you begin by writing the conclusion. Your next step—believe it or not—is to write the introduction. For most people the introduction seems particularly difficult to complete. If you wait until the other decisions about the speech have been made (steps 1–5), the introduction should be much easier to write. Although this procedure has not been tested in controlled experiments, it seems to work in practice.

You are now ready to write the transitions, or connecting statements, that will link the parts of your speech together. There are any number of ways of smoothly relating two concepts to each other. In discussing leadership one speaker moved from one part of his speech to another by saying, "Let us turn from the leadership of yesterday to my second concern, the leadership of tomorrow." Effective transitions add more than finishing touches to your speech; they clarify your train of thought for the listener, they help give your speech unity and coherence, and sometimes they help make your argument seem well reasoned. They are well worth the time and effort you will spend writing them.

It is important to emphasize that the six steps described above constitute the preparation of your speech, not the delivery. Delivery, of course, follows the traditional three-step pattern: introduction, body, and conclusion. The steps we have outlined concern the mechanics of speech preparation. Let us now look at some substantive issues that influence how you organize the content of your message.

Message Variables

For centuries students of public communication have speculated about ways of presenting messages that will ensure optimum acceptance. Only within the twentieth century, however, have experimental investigations allowed us to put some of these age-old notions to the test. In studying message variables we shall be looking at the results of research conducted over the past twenty years. This period has been one of the most fruitful in providing experimental clarification of some long-standing questions.

One Side or Two Sides. Suppose that you want to persuade a mixed (male and female) audience to be more sympathetic toward the Women's Liberation Movement. Should you present only your side of the issue, or should you also discuss the case against Women's Lib?

We now know that if audience members are initially receptive to a message and are unlikely to hear any arguments opposing it, then a one-sided approach will probably be more persuasive than a two-sided approach. In this case your effort would probably be directed toward reinforcing existing attitudes rather than changing values. If, on the other hand, the audience is likely to be skeptical or hostile to the speaker's point of view or will hear later arguments opposing it, a two-sided approach will probably be more effective. You can prepare a two-sided argument by listing the pros and cons of your subject and trying to anticipate the objections of the skeptical listener. If you are speaking on Women's Lib, your list might look something like this:

Pros	*Cons*
1. Women are paid less than men for comparable jobs.	1. Women are poorer job risks than men because women often leave work soon after they marry.
2. Women are denied some legal rights of ownership.	2. Women enjoy more legal protection than men do; they even receive alimony in the event of a divorce.
3. Women are always assumed to be responsible for child care and housework; these responsibilities should be shared by men.	3. Woman's natural role is in the home, and this is her highest fulfillment.

Once you have made such a list, you will find evidence that refutes or substantiates the arguments against you. As you speak you present the first points and acknowledge the extent to which the second are valid, showing at the same time why these objections do not negate your main arguments. You then go on to cite evidence supporting your side of the issue.

Why should a two-sided approach work when the listener is likely to hear opposing arguments later on? **Inoculation theory** suggests an explanation in the form of a medical analogy. There are two ways in which a doctor can help a patient resist disease: he can try to maintain the patient's state of health by prescribing a balanced diet, adequate rest, and so on, or he can inoculate the patient with a small amount of the disease so that he builds up antibodies. Now, imagine that your patient, the audience member, is about to be attacked by a disease— that is, a persuasive message discrepant with your own. When you use a one-sided approach, you offer him support: you give him arguments in favor of your position and try to make him strong enough to ward off attacks in this way. When you use a two-sided approach, you "inoculate" the listener: you expose him to a weak form of the disease —the counterargument—so that he can refute it and thus strengthen his defense against future attacks. Inoculation theory holds that inoculation is more effective than support in building up resistance because listeners exposed to a weak version of the counterarguments tend to develop an immunity to later arguments favoring that side. You might try this tactic to see whether your experience corroborates the predictions of inoculation theory. Remember though that an inoculation is a weak version of the disease.

A final point to be made is that the one-sided approach seems to work better if most of the members of your audience are poorly educated or of low intelligence. Perhaps in this case presenting both sides confuses the listener, leaving him uncertain which side you actually advocate.

Stated or Implied Conclusions. Have you ever tried to persuade by hinting at what you were getting at? Sometimes it works, but sometimes the other person doesn't get the hint at all. Public speakers have long wondered whether it is more persuasive to state the conclusion of a speech explicitly or to allow the listener to draw his own conclusion from the arguments presented.

One argument in favor of implicit conclusions is that if the speech is already comprehensible on its own, an explicit conclusion is unnecessary. It has also been proposed that listeners with a high level of interest or ego involvement are more likely to be persuaded by an implied than by an expressed deduction, which might offend them if they hold an opposing view.

Despite these considerations most studies confirm that you have a better chance of changing audience attitude if you state your conclusion than if you allow listeners to draw their own.[12] One reason for this seems to be that the listener in making his own summation of your argument may distort it; he may even find support for his own point of view in the new information you present.

To Scare or Not to Scare. You want to persuade your audience that driving without safety belts is dangerous, that smoking can cause cancer, that disarmament will be detrimental to national security. What should your strategy be? Is the audience more likely to be persuaded if you appeal to fear? And if you do, what level of fear is optimal?

There have been a number of studies of the relationship between fear and attitude change. The original research, on dental hygiene, found that the higher the level of fear arousal, the less attitude change took place.[13] This is an appealing conclusion; none of us wants to feel vulnerable to persuasive "attacks" based on fear. We like to think, for example, that we are immune to all the television commercials that promote a product by playing on our fear of being unpopular, unattractive, or even offensive to others.

But the question turns out to be more complex than it seems. Many researchers report a strong positive correlation between fear arousal and attitude change. For example, under high-fear conditions students urged to get tetanus inoculations showed significantly greater attitude change than those given the same advice under low-fear conditions. High-fear conditions resulted in more behavior change as well: 22 percent of these students did get tetanus shots whereas only 13 percent of the students who heard the low-fear message did.[14]

How do we reconcile these apparently contradictory results? One theory, supported by much recent evidence, suggests that the relationship between fear and attitude change takes the form of an inverted U curve.[15] According to this theory low fear arousal results in little attitude change, presumably because the level is so low that the listener gives the message no special attention. As the level increases to the intermediate range, attitude change also increases. This is the optimal range for persuasive communication. Once the level of fear becomes extremely high, attitude change declines sharply because the listener responds defensively to the message, which interferes with message reception. Differences between people and differences in situation also influence the optimal level of fear arousal so that it is difficult to predict how effective a given appeal to fear will be. The point to remember is that if you make the listener so anxious that he has to block out the message, your efforts at persuasion are bound to be self-defeating.

Climax or Anticlimax Order. If you had three arguments, one of which was clearly the strongest, would you use it first or save it for last? When the speaker uses **the climax order** of presentation, *he saves his strongest argument until last*; when he uses **the anticlimax order**, *he presents his strongest argument first* and then proceeds to the weaker arguments. Which order to use poses a serious question when you would like to change group opinion on an important issue.

Research evidence on this question does not clearly favor one approach over the other. Nevertheless, if we take into account the existing attitudes of our listeners, we are able to come up with some answers. If the audience is initially interested in your topic and favorable to your point of view, you can better afford to save your strongest argument for last. Presumably the audience will be willing to give you the benefit of the doubt. If, on the other hand, your listeners are initially opposed to your point of view, you may be more effective if you use your most persuasive argument first.[16]

Two important assumptions underlie the issue of climax versus anticlimax order. The first is that you are able to determine which of your arguments your listeners are likely to perceive as strongest or most persuasive. It is not always possible to know in advance how your audience will react to a given line of reasoning. Even seasoned public speakers have been surprised by audience response to a particular argument or for that matter a casual remark. The second assumption is that you can know in advance whether most of the audience will be for or against your stand on a particular subject. In almost all cases some audience members will favor your position and others will not. Thus you are forced to make your choices about climax or anticlimax strategy on the basis of what you know about the majority of your listeners, knowing full well that these choices will be the wrong ones for the remaining listeners. Any decision you make will win over some listeners and risk alienating others.

How Much Change to Attempt. Confrontation is a persuasive style that has come to dominate numerous public communication contexts. The use of this strategy brings up an important question: Assuming that the speaker is interested in maximum persuasion, how much change should he argue for in his speech?

Let us explain the question by giving an example. Suppose the issue under discussion is whether the federal government should provide welfare benefits for the unemployed. Let the continuum in Figure 20 represent the range of opinion on this issue, and let us assume that there are 100 possible attitudes. Suppose a listener's preferred position on welfare can be quantified at 65. Surrounding this point on the scale is a range of opinions that he also finds acceptable, sometimes referred to as his latitude of acceptance. Beyond this point is a latitude of noncommitment and finally a latitude of rejection, a range of opinions that he finds unacceptable. Imagine that our listener's latitude of acceptance goes from 50 to 75. If the speaker advocates a position within this range—55, for example—the discrepancy between his view and the

Figure 20

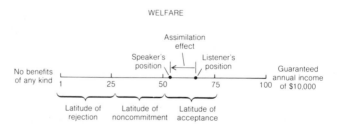

The Assimilation Effect: One Listener's Attitude Toward Welfare

listener's favored position is relatively small. Researchers have found that, other things being equal, such a moderate discrepancy will tend to shift the listener's attitude toward the position advocated by the speaker.[17] That is, the listener tends to perceive the speaker's position as closer to his preferred position than it really is; in fact, he tends to assimilate, or accept, the change in attitude urged by the speaker. This phenomenon is often referred to as an **assimilation effect**.

In the hope of bringing about maximum attitude change, the speaker may, of course, advocate a position that falls within the listener's latitude of rejection. This is the rationale behind confrontation tactics. But the results are often disappointing. Research has shown that when a message falls within the latitude of rejection, the listener tends to perceive the message as even more discrepant with his viewpoint than it actually is and therefore to reject it. Thus, instead of producing greater attitude change, the speaker elicits a negative reaction on the part of the listener that has variously been referred to as a **backlash**, **boomerang effect**, or **contrast effect**.

Bear in mind that the more deeply committed a person is to his system of beliefs or to a given position, the narrower his latitude of acceptance will be. Thus, in trying to persuade listeners whose minds are fairly well made up, a speaker should advocate a relatively moderate amount of change in order to produce the optimum reaction.

It is tempting to apply what we know about message variables to less formal kinds of communication. For example, if you want to persuade your parents to finance a new car for you, you might find yourself speculating about whether to hint or come right out and ask for it —and then whether to use a one-sided or two-sided approach. The research findings we have discussed, however, are based primarily on speaker-audience situations. Although they may indicate some trends in other kinds of communication, it is of doubtful value to generalize them to other contexts. At present the information about message variables is most relevant to person-to-group communication.

THE AUDIENCE

If delivering a speech is a new experience for you, the suggestion that you analyze your audience beforehand may come as something of a shock. When you stand before this group of people you may view them only as the proverbial sea of faces. Yet some common characteristics have brought them together in the first place. Are they parents, college students, liberals, Roman Catholics, businessmen, educators, anthropologists? Just about any group of listeners who gather in one place will do so for some of the same reasons. By establishing these reasons, you may find a strategy that allows you to appeal to the majority of your audience.

Audience Analysis

There are at least two traditional methods by which a speaker may determine how best to relate to his audience.[18] If he uses **demographic audience analysis** he first establishes some general characteristics of his listeners—age, sex, place of residence, occupation, socioeconomic level, education, religion, and so on. These known characteristics suggest inferences about the audience's knowledge, attitudes, and values, and these in turn allow him to gear his message to what he assumes to be its level and interests. If you are speaking in favor of more stringent antitrust laws and your audience consists primarily of well-educated corporation executives, you will probably choose a two-sided rather than a one-sided approach. If you are speaking to a group of farmers, you may decide on a one-sided approach and supply more information about violations of antitrust legislation.

An alternate method is the **purpose-oriented analysis**. Instead of analyzing audience characteristics, the speaker begins by asking himself what information about the audience is most important for his purposes. If you are an economist giving an informative speech about devaluation of currencies, you will want to know how much of an economics background the average listener has. Sometimes this information is easy to establish; sometimes you will have to make inferences. In any case you begin with a general idea of audience level and constantly refer back to it as you prepare your speech. Can you assume that the listener will know what the gold standard is, or will you have to explain the concept in some detail? Will a quote from John Kenneth Galbraith be recognized as evidence from a high-credibility source? In contrast to demographic analysis, in which you gather information about the audience before preparing your speech, purpose-oriented analysis will be an ongoing part of your message preparation.

Both these approaches are concerned with audience variability, with adapting a message to a specific audience. One interesting question we might ask in this connection is whether audiences are equally persuasible.

Listener Persuasibility

Persuasibility, as the term implies, refers to *a listener's susceptibility to persuasion*. A question that researchers and public speakers have often raised is whether there is a difference between men's and women's openness to persuasion. Research shows one consistent finding: women are more readily swayed than men. This pattern is not always borne out in studies of children, however, which suggests that willingness to be persuaded is learned as part of the female sex role.[19]

It is also possible that correlations between sex and persuasibility are specific to the issues that have been studied. Women may be more easily influenced than men, for example, on the question of compulsory arbitration of labor disputes but less persuasible on the subject of abortion. Whether women are more persuasible across all issues remains to be seen. If the female sex role in our society continues to undergo redefinition, as seems likely, it will be interesting to observe whether differences in persuasibility between the sexes become far less significant.

A second question that has been the object of much research concerns the correlation between personality and persuasibility. Is it true, for example, that some people are resistant to changing their minds in all situations whereas others tend to be yes men, going along with almost anything one says? Early research on this question looked for "those attitudes or personality factors leading to low or high resistance to *a wide variety of persuasive communication on many diverse topics.*"[20] College students were given a booklet with persuasive arguments on a number of topics: civil defense, cancer research, classical music, a new television comedian, and General Paul von Hindenburg. They were then given a second booklet containing arguments opposing the positions presented in the first booklet. The students filled out three attitude questionnaires: one before reading anything, one after reading the first booklet, and one after reading the second. The results were surprising: some participants tended to change their attitudes more than others on all five topics. In other words, some were more persuasible than others, regardless of the subject of the persuasive appeal. Furthermore these people tended to be more easily persuaded in either direction on a given topic—to be more in favor of or more opposed to cancer research, for example.

In another study the same research team tried to identify the personality characteristics linked to persuasibility.[21] Although they were unable to find correlations with specific traits, they did learn that people who are socially inhibited and show feelings of social inadequacy tend to be more persuasible. On the basis of these findings, it is generally agreed that the persuasible person tends to have low self-esteem, a perception he presumably extends to his opinions: he values those of others more than he does his own. By contrast, the person who resists persuasion is described as "likely to be little affected by external standards in other kinds of situations, to have a mature and strong self-image, to value subjective feelings and have a relatively rich inner life, to examine himself and his role in life to an extent that may include marked self-criticism, and to be independent without being rebellious."[22]

Although there is little the speaker can do to control for such variables as listener persuasibility, it is still of interest to know that sex differences and personality differences affect receptivity. This information might be especially useful in other communication settings, where the pattern of interaction is more balanced.

We have spoken of the audience from the speaker's vantage point. In most person-to-group situations, however, your time will be spent as a listener, not a speaker. All listening should be an active process involving your powers of attention, understanding, memory, and judgment. In concluding this chapter we shall try to demonstrate that the listener, like the speaker, can also make maximum use of his analytic powers.

THE CRITICAL LISTENER

Children marvel at how adults can sit around for hours just talking to each other at social gatherings. As an adult, much of your communication involves **pleasurable listening**, the aim of which is *enjoyment*. A second type of listening is **discriminative listening**, with the primary purpose of *understanding and remembering*. This is what you do while attending class, working, or receiving instructions. If you suspect that you are listening to a biased source of information, however, discriminative listening will not suffice. For example, if your family doctor is telling you about the drawbacks of Medicare, his personal feelings and interests might make it difficult for him to have a totally objective view of the subject. At such times you need **critical listening**—that is, *listening to discern whether, intentionally or unintentionally, a speaker distorts information for his own purposes*. As an audience member your ability to listen critically determines the extent to which you participate in what is taking place.

Evaluating Materials of Support

One of the greatest challenges to the critical listener is posed by assessing a speaker's materials or methods of support. When we discussed message preparation, we referred to four frequently used kinds of support: example, statistics, quotation, and analogy. This time we shall examine them from the listener's point of view. In doing so we shall refer to certain persuasive techniques that are probably as old as man but were identified and studied for the first time as propaganda devices during World War II by a number of federal agencies, as well as the Institute for Propaganda Analysis. Some are also legitimate means of presenting information. Once you become aware of them, you will notice their use not only in person-to-group contexts but also in many less formal encounters.

The Example. **The example** is an extremely popular method of support. Throughout this book we have used examples to illustrate many of the concepts discussed. Examples may be brief, or they may be as extended as the personal log reproduced in Chapter 10. Usually they clarify meaning for the listener, but they can also lead him into making unjustified inferences. Sometimes a speaker cites one or two examples and then proceeds to generalize from them. He may, for instance, mention two universities at which students taking tests under the honor system were caught cheating and then go on to argue that the honor system is not viable and should be abandoned at all schools. When he uses this propaganda device, **the hasty generalization**, the speaker *jumps to a conclusion on the basis of very limited evidence.* As a critical listener, it is your responsibility to decide first whether an example is appropriate to a speaker's point and second whether it is being used in lieu of an argument.

Statistics. Listeners sometimes find **statistics**, or *numerical data,* difficult to understand. When used in conjunction with other methods of support, however, they often clarify points considerably. In discussing the risks of teen-age marriages, for example, a speaker may point out that the divorce rate for people who marry in their teens is 100 percent higher than it is for those who marry at age twenty or above. Citing statistics may help the speaker prove that his is a valid conclusion, not a hasty generalization.

We tend to be impressed by figures, which is probably why the use of statistics is frequently abused. **Card stacking**—or *slanting facts to prove a point*—and **half-truths** often rely on a misleading use of statistics. In discussing the growing acceptance of birth control methods in India, a speaker may present statistics that show a declining birth rate in Delhi, Bombay, and Madras, three large Indian cities. His argument may sound convincing. Yet what of the statistics he has not cited? Perhaps the statistics from most of India's small towns and villages reflect a continuing increase in the birth rate.

Another propaganda device that sometimes makes use of statistics is **the bandwagon appeal**, *the argument that "Everybody's doing it."* Imagine that a survey reveals that 60 percent of all taxpayers cheat on their income tax returns. The speaker who argues that income tax fraud should not be punishable by law because it is such a common practice uses a bandwagon appeal.

Sometimes a speaker makes a statement that only seems to present a statistical fact. Consider the claim, "Skyhighs now relieve pain twice as fast." That sounds good. Why not switch to Skyhighs? Your inference may be that they act twice as fast as some competing product. But perhaps they only relieve pain twice as fast as they did two years ago and indeed take effect no faster than any of the competing products. We don't know. We would have to ask, "Twice as fast as what?" What are the terms of the comparison? Is this product being compared with itself or something else?

No blanket acceptance of statistics is possible in critical listening. You will have to decide on the relevance of the statistics to the speaker's point. You may have to question the source of the data or the unit of measurement. You will often have to consider whether the speaker should be supplying additional statistics. To paraphrase an old saying, statistics don't lie, but liars use statistics.

Quotation. The use of **quotation** or **testimony** is a third method of support. It is known that attitudes and beliefs become more acceptable to us if we think they have been accepted by others, especially if those others are prestigious or expert. In arguing about the effects of alcohol on the human body, for example, a speaker might support his position with quotations from medical authorities. Lawyers in court frequently call on or cite an expert witness to establish the validity of their cases: "Ladies and gentlemen of the jury, the coroner's report showed that the time of death was between midnight and 6 A.M. on May 16. We have established that my client was nowhere near the scene of the crime in that period on May 16. Therefore, my client could not have committed the murder."

Citing testimony can be an important and legitimate means of offering evidence in support of an argument. Yet even the testimony of a trusted and highly respected person has to be put in perspective. In discussing source credibility we mentioned that people with great expertise in one field may offer opinions about subjects in which their expertise has not been demonstrated. Quotations from Dr. Spock on baby care would probably be more expert than his views on military defense policies.

Testimony may be used to substantiate the speaker's personal credibility rather than the validity of his viewpoint, and in such cases it will often take the form of nonverbal cues that he himself gives rather than quotations from others. **The plain-folks approach** represents this sort of testimony. A middle-aged professor may try to identify with his student listeners by dressing like a student. A city-bred politician may take to milking cows and dressing casually in a rural area.

To a sophisticated audience these tactics may be quite transparent. Yet even an otherwise critical listener may be disarmed by a high-credibility source who uses this approach to establish common ground. Daniel Boorstin's remarks, which we reproduced earlier in the chapter, illustrate an effective and legitimate use of this technique.

Whether a speaker presents substantiation for his personal worth or for the worth of his opinion, make a conscious effort to ask yourself whether the evidence lends genuine or only apparent support to the issue.

Analogy. When we draw an **analogy**, we point out the *similarities between two different things.* An analogy may be the most concise and graphic way to get a complex idea or a point across. In a discussion of the increasing arrests of young people on drug charges, one student commented: "Relaxing the law would indeed reduce the number of arrests, but it would be like loosening your tie to relieve sweating. It is only a temporary measure that does nothing to eliminate the problem causing the arrests." As it stands, this analogy effectively conveyed the student's position. Suppose, however, that he had gone on to argue that laws, like ties and other articles of clothing, are unnatural constraints that should be discarded. He would then have been on very shaky ground.

The speaker may use an analogy to dramatize a point or to make it seem less significant. For example, he might compare dumping industrial wastes into the environment to adding a spoonful of dirt to each of our meals. Or he might say that the environment is so vast that these pollutants have no more effect than would adding a spoonful of dirt to an ocean.

Because an analogy draws parallels between two different things or situations, at some point it breaks down. If the objects of comparison are dissimilar enough to invalidate the attempt to juxtapose them, the analogy is a poor one. The critical listener must first determine the appropriateness of the speaker's analogy to the subject at hand and second the limits of its use.

Often listeners will recall the examples or analogies used by the speaker and miss the point the speaker intends to illustrate. In analyzing all materials of support, it is crucial first to identify the point the speaker is trying to make and then to evaluate the method of support he uses to prove it. Remember that materials of support do not in themselves constitute an argument.

Questioning the Speaker

In your role as a listener, another opportunity to maximize your participation in public communication is provided by the occasion to address questions or comments to the speaker, probably during a question-and-answer period. This is usually a brief period, and you will want to make the most of it. Therefore, it might be useful to keep the following suggestions in mind in formulating what you will say.

First and most obvious, be clear and audible. Speak loudly enough so that you can be heard not only by the speaker but by all the members of the audience. You know that poor delivery can affect one's view of the speaker. Poor delivery of your own remarks may also detract from your image.

Second, be concise in phrasing your questions. Other listeners will also want an opportunity to respond to the speaker.

Third, ask one question at a time. If you bombard the speaker with questions, it is likely that some will go unanswered.

Fourth, avoid loaded questions. Don't try to drive the speaker into a corner. Remember that listeners as well as speakers can be accused of card stacking.

And fifth, be aware of your own motives. Are you really asking a question? Or are you trying to make a point of your own—or perhaps simply call attention to yourself? Some people use a question-and-answer period for just these reasons. This remains your prerogative. Remember though that other members of the audience have come to hear the speaker and will be interested primarily in questions that clarify the meaning of his speech. Despite what you feel to be the subtlety of your comments, your motives quickly become apparent to others. Recall how easy it is to spot the student who asks questions in class just to impress everyone with his knowledge of the subject.

Summary

The most formal mode of interpersonal communication we shall ever encounter is public, or person-to-group, communication. We have tried to view it here in terms of both the speaker's and the listener's experience, giving special attention to persuasive rather than informative communication.

The single most important judgment we make about the speaker, apart from his message, concerns his credibility. Judgments about source credibility, as we saw, are not constant; they vary not only from audience to audience but from one time to another. In general, the high-credibility source has greater influence than the low-credibility source, but the impact of credibility on persuasion is greatest immediately after the message is received. Over time it tends to decline; this trend is known as the sleeper effect. Delivery is a second important speaker variable, and we discussed the advantages and disadvantages of four modes of delivery.

Our treatment of the message itself focused on structure rather than content. After outlining a six-step procedure for preparing a speech, we looked at some of the options open to the speaker in his efforts to be persuasive. Five message variables were discussed: one-sided versus two-sided messages, stated versus implied conclusions, appeals to fear, climax versus anticlimax order, and how much change to attempt.

Our last topic was the audience itself, which we viewed first from the speaker's vantage point. We described two methods—demographic and purpose-oriented analysis—that a speaker might use to adapt his message to his particular audience. Research findings on how listener persuasibility correlates with sex differences and personality traits were also examined. In closing we talked about the listener's role and suggested several ways in which he could make maximum use of his own critical abilities.

Review Questions

1. How does public communication differ from other forms of inter-personal communication? What are three purposes of public communication?
2. What are two major dimensions of source credibility? What is the difference between extrinsic and intrinsic credibility?
3. How does source credibility relate to attitude change?
4. What is the sleeper effect? What implications does it have for the would-be persuader?
5. Name the four modes of delivery. What are some advantages and disadvantages of each?
6. How can a message be organized using the six steps discussed in this chapter?
7. Under what conditions is a one-sided message most effective? Under what conditions is a two-sided message most effective?
8. What is the general research finding regarding the effectiveness of messages containing (1) stated conclusions, (2) implied conclusions?
9. How are different fear levels related to the persuasiveness of a message?
10. Under what conditions is a climax order message most effective? Under what conditions is an anticlimax order message most effective?
11. What is the difference between the assimilation effect and the contrast effect? How do these concepts relate to how much change a speaker should advocate?
12. Explain the difference between demographic audience analysis and purpose-oriented audience analysis.
13. What is the general research finding regarding sex and persuasibility?
14. How do pleasurable, discriminative, and critical listening differ?
15. What are four methods of support? How can each be used as a propaganda device?

Exercises

1. Select a speech from a newspaper or magazine like *Vital Speeches*. Analyze the speech by answering the following questions:

   a. What was the purpose of the speech?

   b. What was the most probable state of the speaker's extrinsic and intrinsic credibility in terms of two major dimensions of source credibility? What factors in the message and context of the message lead you to your conclusions?

   c. What method (s) of organization does the speech illustrate?

   d. What forms of support were used? How effective were they?

   e. Was the message one-sided or two-sided? Was it appropriate given the conditions of the speech?

   f. Were fear appeals used? If so, were they used appropriately (that is, according to research findings)?

   g. Was the conclusion stated or implied? Which was most appropriate for the situation in which the message was given?

   h. Was a climax or anticlimax order used? Which was most appropriate for the situation in which the message was given?

2. If you were asked to present a speech to the audience that heard the speech used in Exercise 1, how would you go about analyzing the audience?

3. Using the six steps for preparing a speech, write a three- to four-minute extemporaneous speech to inform, and present it to your class. Remember to aim for clarity and to make your presentation relevant to your listeners' interests. You may wish to choose a topic from the list that follows these exercises.

4. Give a one-minute impromptu speech on a topic assigned to you by a classmate or by the instructor. Try to determine your purpose and organization in the short time available.

5. Take your identity and membership cards out of your wallet or purse, and conduct an audience analysis on the groups to which you belong. Write a short paper on different approaches that would be appropriate for the different groups.

6. Tape-record one of your speeches, and play it back for self-analysis. What changes would you make if you were to give it again?[23]

Speech Topics and Thought Starters

Water pollution	Birth control
American Indians	Boxing
Latin American relations	Censorship
Divorce	Cigarette smoking
Overcrowded universities	Conformity
Farm surpluses	Country music

Flood control
Care of the mentally ill
Alcoholism
Vandalism
Overcrowded airports
The high cost of dying
Involuntary sterilization
The Academy Awards
Personality—what is it?
Muslim beliefs
Causes of earthquakes
Ethnocentrism
Why the Great Lakes tilt
The continental drift theory
Hazards in the home
What makes people buy
Social stratification
Interpreting dreams
The scientific lie detector
Improving your memory
Learning to listen
Wedding customs
Plastic surgery
Trick photography
Sky diving
Taxidermy
Baseball in America
Music education
Writing good letters
The importance of friendship
The honor system
The Nobel Prize
Buying a car
Benjamin Spock
Anarchy
Atheism
Capitalism
Culture
Empathy
Illiteracy
Libel
Morality
Prejudice
Slander
Abortion

Cryogenics
Jeane Dixon
Driver education
Drunk drivers
Narcotics
Euthanasia
The FBI
Firearms regulation
Foreign aid
Forest fires
Fraternities
Free college education
Grading systems
Hell's Angels
The John Birch Society
The Ku Klux Klan
Lecture classes
LSD
The metric system
Communism
Football for the spectator
Nuclear testing
Symbolism in *Peanuts*
Revision of the penal system
Prayer in public schools
Prostitution
Public works for the unemployed
The overorganized society
The semester system
Sex education
Slaughterhouses
The space program
Speech pathology
Suicide
Tornadoes
Trade with China
The Strategic Air Command
Traffic safety
Trial marriages
Dieting fads
Communication gap
Watergate
Twentieth-century religion
Urban blight
Rationalizing

Abstract art	*Games People Play*
Misleading advertising	Siamese twins
Animal intelligence	The laser beam
The armed forces	Medical practices

Suggested Readings

Bettinghaus, Erwin. *Persuasive Communication.* New York: Holt, Rinehart and Winston, 1968. This book specializes in communication that is intended to alter the receiver's attitudes, beliefs, values, or behaviors. It is soundly based on empirical research while remaining understandable and useful. It includes persuasion in group and organizational contexts in addition to the traditional speaker-audience situations.

McCroskey, James C. *An Introduction to Rhetorical Communication.* 2nd ed. Englewood Cliffs, N.J.: Prentice-Hall, 1972. This book, more than most others, attempts to integrate modern theory and research with the tradition and teachings of the past. It is more than a basic text in public speaking. It sets public speaking within the broader category of human communication, synthesizing what is known from both fields of study.

Walter, Otis. *Speaking to Inform and to Persuade.* New York: Macmillan, 1966. This little paperback is a valuable resource for those who seek to improve their public speaking abilities, but who do not wish to spend much time reading about how to do it. Although it is brief, it does cover both informative and persuasive speaking.

Notes

[1] James C. McCroskey, "Scales for the Measurement of Ethos," *Speech Monographs,* 33 (1966), 65–72.

[2] Elaine Walster, Elliot Aronson, and Darcy Abrahams, "On Increasing the Persuasiveness of a Low Prestige Communicator," *Journal of Experimental Social Psychology,* 2 (1966), 325–342.

[3] Herbert Kelman and Carl Hovland, " 'Reinstatement' of the Communication in Delayed Measurement of Opinion Change," *Journal of Abnormal and Social Psychology,* 48 (1953), 327–335.

[4] William J. McGuire, "The Nature of Attitudes and Attitude Change," in Gardner Lindzey and Elliot Aronson (eds.), *The Handbook of Social Psychology,* 2nd ed. (Reading, Mass.: Addison-Wesley, 1969), Vol. III, *The Individual in a Social Context,* p. 187.

[5] Charles Petrie, "Informative Speaking: A Summary and Bibliography of Related Research," *Speech Monographs,* 30 (1963), 83.

[6] Daniel J. Boorstin, "Dissent, Dissension, and the News" (speech delivered at the annual meeting of the Associated Press Managing Editors Association, Chicago, October 18, 1967).

[7] Charles Gruner, "The Effect of Humor in Dull and Interesting Informative Speeches," *Central States Speech Journal,* 21 (1970), 160–166.

[8] Kelman and Hovland.

[9] James C. McCroskey and Robert Mehrley, "The Effects of Disorganization and Nonfluency on Attitude Change and Source Credibility," *Speech Monographs,* 36 (1969), 13–21.

[10] James C. McCroskey and William Arnold, unpublished study reported in James C. McCroskey, *An Introduction to Rhetorical Communication* (Englewood Cliffs, N.J.: Prentice-Hall, 1968), p. 207.

[11] Franklyn S. Haiman, "The Rhetoric of 1968: A Farewell to Rational Discourse," in W. Linkugel, R. Allen, and R. Johannesen (eds.), *Contemporary American Speeches* (Belmont, Calif.: Wadsworth, 1969), p. 157.

[12] Stewart L. Tubbs, "Explicit Versus Implicit Conclusions and Audience Commitment," *Speech Monographs,* 35 (1968), 14–19.

[13] Irving Janis and Seymour Feshbach, "Effects of Fear-Arousing Communications," *Journal of Abnormal and Social Psychology,* 48 (1953), 78–92.

[14] J. M. Dabbs, Jr., and H. Leventhal, "Effects of Varying the Recommendations of a Fear-Arousing Communication," *Journal of Personality and Social Psychology,* 4 (1966), 525–531.

[15] William J. McGuire, "Personality and Susceptibility to Social Influence," in Edgar F. Borgatta and William W. Lambert (eds.), *Handbook of Personality Theory and Research* (Chicago: Rand McNally, 1968), pp. 1130–1187.

[16] Marvin Karlins and Herbert Abelson, *Persuasion: How Opinions and Attitudes Are Changed,* 2nd ed. (New York: Springer, 1970), pp. 30–32.

[17] Carl Hovland, O. J. Harvey, and Muzafer Sherif, "Assimilation and Contrast Effects in Reactions to Communication and Attitude Change," *Journal of Abnormal and Social Psychology,* 55 (1957), 244–252.

[18] Theodore Clevenger, Jr., *Audience Analysis* (New York: Bobbs-Merrill, 1966), pp. 43–48.

[19] See Thomas Scheidel, "Sex and Persuasibility," *Speech Monographs,* 30 (1963), 333–339; and Robert Abelson and Gerald Lesser, "The Measurement of Personality in Children," in Carl Hovland and Irving Janis (eds.), *Personality and Persuasibility* (New Haven, Conn.: Yale University Press, 1959), pp. 141–166.

[20] Irving Janis and Peter Field, "A Behavioral Assessment of Persuasibility: Consistency of Individual Differences," in Hovland and Janis, pp. 29–54.

[21] Irving Janis and Peter Field, "Sex Differences and Personality Factors Related to Persuasibility," in Hovland and Janis, pp. 55–68.

[22] Harriet Linton and Elaine Graham, "Personality Correlates of Persuasibility," in Hovland and Janis, p. 96.

[23] See Otto F. Bauer and Stewart L. Tubbs, "Speech by Television: A Case Study," *Ohio Speech Journal,* 7 (1969), 25–28.

Conclusion

part five

Chapter 12

Enhancing Interpersonal Relationships

OBJECTIVES

After reading this chapter the student should be able to:

1. Distinguish between the content and relationship aspects of communication.

2. Distinguish between confirming and disconfirming response styles.

3. Describe the dyadic effect and give at least two examples of it.

4. Distinguish between supportive and defensive climates of communication.

5. State the relationship between trust, accuracy, and effectiveness in interpersonal communication.

6. State the most important implication of research on behavior attribution for students of communication.

7. Describe the four levels of awareness illustrated by the Johari Window.

8. Define metacommunication.

9. Describe the need for self-actualization.

10. List five characteristics of appropriate self-disclosure.

12

Throughout this book we have touched frequently on the notion that interpersonal communication is the vehicle for establishing, maintaining, and improving human relationships. Because relationships are such a significant feature of interpersonal communication, in this final chapter we shall discuss ways in which human relationships can be enhanced. We shall also review the communication outcomes as they relate to the specific communication contexts discussed in Part Four.

"One way to understand communication," writes Gibb, "is to view it as a people process rather than as a language process."[1] And certainly in studying interpersonal communication we must make a distinction between its *content* and *relationship* aspects.

It seems obvious that every message has content, whether the information is correct or incorrect, valid or invalid, or even undeterminable. It is less apparent, however, that every message also defines how it is to be interpreted and consequently something about the relationship between the people involved. (A mother who cautions her exuberant son by saying, "Please don't run around when we're in a department store," defines her relationship with her child quite differently from the mother who says, "Be sure to run around a lot here so that I get good and angry.") Even the most casual message exists on this second level. Thus Ruesch and Bateson have observed that ". . . every courtesy term between persons, every inflection of voice denoting respect or contempt, condescension or dependency, is a statement about the relationship between the two persons."[2] It is the relationship aspect of communication that concerns us in the present chapter.

CONFIRMATION AND DISCONFIRMATION

As we communicate we expect more than a simple exchange of verbal and nonverbal information. Each person conveys messages that tell how he perceives the other and their relationship, and each expects to receive responses in kind. Perhaps the most satisfying interpersonal response we can hope to receive is total **confirmation**, or as Sieburg and Larson define it, *"any behavior that causes another person to value himself more."*[3] Buber writes: "In human society, at all its levels, persons confirm one another in a practical way, to some extent or other, in their personal qualities and capacities, and a society may be termed human in the measure to which its members confirm one another."[4]

Let us illustrate by imagining two sportscasters, Howard and Don, announcing a football game. Howard makes the comment, "That was some touchdown drive. Wasn't it dandy, Don?" "That it was, Howard," replies Don. "Beautiful execution." Don responds to Howard and also agrees with the content of his statement, thus confirming Howard's very existence as a person. Suppose instead that Don answers, "Well, *you* might think so, but I've seen better drives by the ninth-graders in my neighborhood." Don responds, but in a way that rejects the content of Howard's statement and by implication rejects Howard himself to some extent. His limited recognition of Howard is confirming on one level but disconfirming on another. A third response is possible. Imagine that Don ignores Howard's question entirely by commenting, "The Rams will now be kicking off into a fifteen-mile-per-hour wind." This remark has the same impact as would a fourth possibility: complete silence. Both are totally **disconfirming**, or to paraphrase Sieburg and Larson, they are *behaviors that cause a person to value himself less*; they reject both the speaker and what he has to say.

The painful experience of being disconfirmed time after time, especially by someone important to us, is expressed in a letter that the novelist Franz Kafka once wrote (and never sent) to his father:

> Maddening also were those rebukes in which one was treated as a third person, in other words, considered not worthy even to be spoken to angrily; that is to say, when you would speak ostensibly to Mother but actually to me, who was sitting right there. For instance: "Of course, that's too much to expect of our worthy son," and the like.[5]

Disconfirmation seems to be one of the most damaging interpersonal responses. The psychotherapeutic literature suggests that a person who is continually disconfirmed by others may even come to question his own identity. Even discussions of pathological communication have some bearing on everyday transactions between people:

> There can be little doubt that such a situation [being completely unnoticed by others] would lead to "loss of self," which is but a translation of the term "alienation." Disconfirmation, as we find it in pathological communication, is no longer concerned with the truth or falsity . . . of P's definition of himself, but rather negates the reality of P as the source. . . . In other words, while rejection amounts to the message "you are wrong," disconfirmation says in effect "you do not exist."[6]

Given some awareness of the confirming-disconfirming dimension of human relationships, we must still ask the practical question: What kinds of responses are most confirming or disconfirming? We find part of the answer in the Sieburg and Larson study whose definitions we have already noted. Appropriately enough the subjects were members of the International Communication Association. They were asked to describe the behaviors of the person they most enjoyed communicating with and of the person they least enjoyed interacting with. As we look at the results of this survey, two distinct response styles emerge.

If we list the responses considered most confirming, describing them briefly in order of rank, first comes *direct acknowledgment*. The other person acknowledges what you have said and gives you a direct verbal response. Next is the expression of *positive feeling*. He conveys his own positive feeling about what you have just said. Then comes *the clarifying response*. Here the other person tries to get you to clarify the content of your message ("Could you expand on that a bit?"). When he gives an *agreeing response,* he reinforces or affirms what you have already said. *The supportive response* offers comfort, understanding, or reassurance ("I know just how you feel").

It seems that the response people find most disconfirming is *the tangential response*. Here the other person acknowledges your previous comment but quickly shifts the direction of the conversation ("Did he cover a lot in class today?" "Not much. Does this skirt look too long?"). Next in unpopularity comes *the impersonal response,* marked by intellectualized speech and avoidance of the first person ("One often finds oneself getting angry"). *An impervious response* disregards you completely, offering neither verbal nor nonverbal recognition. When the other person gives *an irrelevant response,* he changes the subject as he would with a tangential response, but this time he makes no attempt to relate his response to your previous comment ("I had a lousy day. I'm really ready to quit." "I wonder why Ann hasn't called. Do you think she forgot?"). *An interrupting response* cuts you off before you have made your point and does not let you finish. A person makes *an incoherent response* if he consistently speaks in sentences that are rambling, disorganized, or incomplete. *The incongruous response* gives you conflicting verbal and nonverbal messages ("Of course you are the one who should decide. It's up to you," said in an exasperated tone of voice).

These lists of behaviors are by no means exhaustive. Nevertheless they highlight the differences between a confirming response style, which generally acknowledges, supports, and accepts other human beings, and a disconfirming response style, which denies and undermines their personal sense of worth.

To counsel that all our responses to others be totally confirming would be unrealistic. There are times when we want to or must reject the communication of others, at least at the content level. But even in taking issue with others, we should keep in mind the importance of maintaining a confirming response style. In this connection a few simple rules might be helpful. First, whether you agree with him or not, try to respond when a person addresses a remark to you. (The response need not be verbal.) Second, avoid interrupting a person while he is speaking. Third, even if you are bored, try not to launch off abruptly into a completely different topic. And fourth, do something nice for a person occasionally that is unnecessary or unexpected. One professor we know brought a large urn of coffee for his class to enjoy while taking the final exam. A gratuitous gesture such as this often serves to renew a relationship.

INTERPERSONAL TRUST

The story is told of two Russian businessmen who accidentally met in a Moscow railroad station. "My dear Ivan, where are you off to?" asks the first. "Minsk," replies Ivan only to hear the retort, "What a liar you are, Ivan. You're just saying that you are going to Minsk because you want me to think you are going to Pinsk, but I know that you are going to Minsk." There seems to be a variant of this anecdote for almost every national group. In the Austrian version, for example, the second man is on his way to Budapest.[7]

Implicit in all jokes of this kind is the recognition that what two people say to each other and how each interprets what is said depends to a great extent on the level of **interpersonal trust** between them. Although the term has been used in a number of ways, Rotter sums up the important issues when he defines it as *"an expectancy . . . that the word, promise, verbal (oral) or written statement of another individual can be relied on."*[8]

Game Behavior

Frivolous as it may seem, we approach the subject of interpersonal trust by looking at game behavior. The strategies people choose when they play games or have observed others playing games give us some opportunity to examine the effects of varying levels of trust on face-to-face communication. Game theory distinguishes between zero-sum games, in which players must compete, and non-zero-sum games, in which players may either compete or cooperate and increase their total gains. Researchers who have attempted to quantify data about levels of trust have been most interested in non-zero-sum games. Among the most popular of these is Prisoner's Dilemma.[9]

To understand how Prisoner's Dilemma works, imagine that two prisoners, Nick and Pete, are being held incommunicado. Charged with the same crime, they are put in separate rooms so that one cannot know how the other will respond to the accusations leveled against them. Nick and Pete are both aware that they can be convicted only if the other one confesses. Each then has two alternatives, shown in Figure 21: to confess or not to confess. But their situation is not that

Figure 21

Pete

Not confess   Confess

Nick

Not confess   1,1*   -2,2

Confess   2,-2   -1,-1

*Payoff Matrix for Prisoner's Dilemma**

* The first digit in each box represents Nick's payoff; the second represents Pete's payoff.

Source: Anatol Rapoport and Albert Chammah, *Prisoner's Dilemma: A Study in Conflict and Cooperation* (Ann Arbor, Mich.: University of Michigan Press, 1965), p. 9. Copyright © 1965 by The University of Michigan Press. Reprinted by permission.

clear-cut. There are other conditions. If both confess they will both be convicted (−1 designates the payoff). If only one confesses, he is freed for turning state's evidence and also given a reward (2 designates the payoff); in this case the prisoner who holds out receives a more severe sentence than he will if he also confesses (−2). If neither prisoner confesses both are acquitted (1).

While it is in the interest of each partner to confess to whatever the other does, it is in their collective interest to hold out. Yet if Nick wants to hold out but distrusts Pete—that is, thinks he will confess— it seems to be in Nick's interest to act competitively by betraying him. If Nick thinks that Pete will not confess, Nick's confession can earn him his freedom as well as a reward—another competitive strategy. If Nick and Pete trust one another completely, they can both hold out and gain their freedom—a cooperative strategy.

What makes the game so compelling is that it places each player in a mixed-motive situation: should he cooperate with his partner (not confess and face a possible prison term) or compete for his own gain (confess, get the reward, and let his partner take the rap)? Although games such as Prisoner's Dilemma seem contrived, we face mixed-motive situations quite frequently. Should you study alone or with a friend who needs help in the subject when you know that

300   helping him may slow you down but may also help you learn the material better by having to teach it to him? Should you share your notes with a student who missed class when you know that the next exam will be marked on a curve and each lower grade raises your own?

One of the authors used Prisoner's Dilemma to study the influence of competitive and cooperative strategies on the choices of a third party observing the game.[10] The subjects were sixty undergraduate women enrolled in a psychology course at the University of Kansas. Seated alone in a viewing room, each subject observed a sequence of ten Prisoner's Dilemma games. Only one of the players—a confederate of the experimenter—was visible, and she had been instructed to play the games in a predetermined sequence. After the games were over, each subject was asked to rate the players on a questionnaire and to indicate how she would have played the game against the player she had just observed. Results showed that the observation of cooperative (trust-producing) strategies prompted cooperative choices from viewers and that of competitive (distrusting) strategies produced competitive choices.

The study illustrates a frequently found phenomenon—that a given type of behavior by one person tends to elicit a similar response from the other. With respect to self-disclosure, Jourard confirms this sequence of behavior: when one person discloses himself to another, he tends to elicit a reciprocal openness from the second person. This pattern is called the **dyadic effect**.[11]

There seems to be an important difference between source credibility and other forms of interpersonal trust. You may recall from the research on public communication that source credibility depends on the perception of both character and expertness. The findings from the observation experiment suggest that variables in the public speaking situation may not be valid in other settings, for viewers rated the cooperative player as having better character but the competitive player as having greater expertness. In other words, trust-inducing behavior was perceived as evidence of good character, but competitive, defense-inducing behavior was seen as evidence of expertness. This is validated outside the laboratory: a person who brags about himself and is highly competitive may threaten others so much that they run down his character, but his behavior may still increase their respect for his abilities.

There is some evidence that in playing non-zero-sum games such as Prisoner's Dilemma, people tend to compete even when it is to their advantage to cooperate. Remember though that in the version of Prisoner's Dilemma we described, the two players were not allowed to communicate. This is the procedure in many non-zero-sum games. When communication between players is permitted, we see a significant increase in the number of cooperative choices.[12] It seems then that other things being equal, communication in and of itself sometimes raises the level of interpersonal trust.

Some Effects of Distrust

A study of small-group interaction conducted by Leathers gives us some insight into the effects of distrust. Through cooperative game playing and other reinforcing behaviors, a member of the group (actually a confederate of Leathers) developed a high level of trust in one of the subjects. Suddenly during a group discussion he started to give the subject negative reinforcement by inserting these statements into the conversation:

1. That's a ridiculous statement. I disagree.
2. Are you serious in taking such an absurd position?
3. You are wrong. Dead wrong.
4. I don't understand why I ever agreed with you.
5. That's downright foolish.[13]

This succession of trust-destroying responses had three pronounced effects. First, the subject became tense: he kept rubbing his hands vigorously and opened his eyes very wide, and his neck muscles became constricted. (Other members of the group began to squirm in their seats and avert their eyes.) Second, he became inflexible: he held rigidly to his beliefs and would not allow himself to be swayed. Third, his comments became more personal, and they were often insulting. ("Man, are you a strange cat. Oh wow, you can't be real. Are you kidding me. You are nothing but a white racist.") While it remains to be seen whether lack of trust between members of a group affects their ability to achieve group goals (consensus, for example), it had some disastrous effects on their interaction.

The responses we have just described bear out Mellinger's observation that ". . . a primary goal of communication with a distrusted person becomes the reduction of one's own anxiety, rather than the accurate transmission of ideas."[14] Moreover defensive behavior tends to be circular—it generates defensiveness on the part of the other person and often cancels out some of the major outcomes of effective communication. For example, Mellinger has shown that when two people distrust each other, each will try to distort the other person's perception of his thoughts and feelings. In addition to distorting understanding, defensive behavior takes away from the pleasurable aspects of communication by creating tension. It may even interfere with efforts to introduce attitude change or motivate action.

Reducing Defensiveness

We said in Chapter 10 that if we strip someone of his defenses, we increase his distance from other human beings. If we arouse his defenses, we get the same results. In therapeutic groups a conscious effort is made to create an atmosphere that is supportive rather than threatening. We can be supportive in all our interpersonal relationships if we know more about the behaviors that reduce or arouse defensiveness.

In his highly influential article on interpersonal trust, Gibb contrasted two atmospheres that could be established through communication. He called them **supportive** and **defensive climates**, and he described them in terms of six sets of categories:

Supportive Climates	Defensive Climates
1. Description	1. Evaluation
2. Problem Orientation	2. Control
3. Spontaneity	3. Strategy
4. Empathy	4. Neutrality
5. Equality	5. Superiority
6. Provisionalism	6. Certainty[15]

At first glance categories 1 and 4 in the defensive climate seem contradictory: evaluative, or judgmental, behavior arouses defensiveness, but so does complete neutrality. We can reconcile this apparent contradiction if we recall that complete neutrality is disconfirming because it communicates a lack of concern. Gibb points out, for example, that if a person is troubled, attempts to reassure him by telling him that he is overanxious or should not feel bad can impress him as a lack of acceptance. It can be highly supportive, however, to show empathy with his emotions without attempting to change him. Pearce and Newton, who consider it "the basic mode of significant communication between adults," define **empathy** as "perception and communication by resonance, by identification, by *experiencing in ourselves some reflection of the emotional tone that is being experienced by the other person.*"[16]

In Chapter 11 we discussed pleasurable, discriminative, and critical listening. To these categories we add **empathic listening**, which in a therapeutic context Reik refers to as *"listening with the third ear."*[17] Empathic listening becomes particularly relevant when we want to improve interpersonal relationships. It implies sensitivity to nonverbal as well as verbal cues in addition to a willingness to withhold judgment and criticism.

From his survey Gibb concluded that when trust increases, efficiency and accuracy in communication also increase. To this we might add that while a supportive climate is important even in short-term relationships, in more permanent relationships (in marriage or on the job, for example) it has even greater possibilities for influencing all five communication outcomes.

AWARENESS OF SELF AND OTHERS

In Chapter 4 we stressed inaccurate perception of others as both a symptom and a cause of difficulties in interpersonal communication. It now seems likely that at least one qualitative difference exists between perception of self and perception of others, and that it may compound the problem. A recent series of studies suggests that while we see our own behavior as responses to the demands of a given *situation,* we view the same behavior in another person as generated by his *disposition,* that is, his stable traits and needs.

Even when we know others well, we seem to interpret their motivations in different terms. In one experiment male college students were asked to write a brief explanation of why they liked the girl they dated most regularly and another of why they had chosen their major.[18] Each also wrote explanations of his best friend's choices of girl friend and college major. While subjects tended to explain their own choices in terms of situation ("She's a relaxing person"; "Chemistry is a high-paying field"), they frequently saw the behavior of their friends in terms of personality traits or needs ("He needs someone he can relax with"; "He wants to make a lot of money").

Two reasons for these perceptual differences have been proposed. First, the information available to the actor (the one who performs the action) and the observer may be different. The observer sees the actor at a particular point in time. Generally he does not—he cannot—know firsthand the actor's history, experiences, motives, or present emotional state; he can only infer them. Thus if we see a man overreact to a mildly critical remark, as observers we may not know what events preceding this episode made it the straw that broke the camel's back. A second possibility is that even when the same information is available to both actor and observer, they process it differently because different aspects of it are salient to each of them.

Storms suggests that these information differences may exist in actor and observer because their points of view are literally quite different. You do not see yourself acting; under ordinary circumstances you cannot be an observer of your own behavior. And while as an actor you watch the situation in which you find yourself, the other person spends most of his time observing you, not the situation.

But suppose we reverse the viewpoints of actor and observer. Storms found that he could change the orientation of actor and observer by showing them videotapes of their own interaction.[19] Videotape offered the actor a new perspective, that of an observer, and often changed his inferences about why he had behaved as he did. After seeing himself on tape, he was much more likely to explain his behavior as a reflection of his personal disposition than as a response to the environment.

    While a change in visual orientation seems to heighten self-awareness, the prospect of viewing videotapes of all our behavior is neither appealing nor feasible. Nor is it perhaps desirable. Storms mentions, for example, that when videotape is used in therapy, the patient sometimes takes undue responsibility on himself for his behavior, overlooking genuine elements in his environment that have influenced his actions. Videotape is not the answer. What is needed is a more balanced view of oneself and of others, a view that enables us to interpret behavior in terms of both disposition and environment.

    Research on behavior attribution has several implications. The most important for our purposes is that by combining information about ourselves that is available only to us with an awareness of how other human beings perceive us, we may begin to see ourselves in sharper perspective.

The Johari Window

One of the most provocative models for conceptualizing levels of awareness in human behavior is the **Johari Window** ("Johari" derives from the first names of the two psychologists who developed it, Joseph Luft and Harry Ingham).[20] Essentially the model offers a way of looking at the interdependence of intrapersonal and interpersonal affairs. The illustration in Figure 22 represents the total person as he relates to other human beings by four quadrants—in effect, four panes of a single window. The size of each quadrant or pane is determined by

Figure 22

	Known to self	Not known to self
Known to others	Open 1	Blind 2
Not known to others	Hidden 3	Unknown 4

The Johari Window

Source: Reprinted from *Of Human Interaction* by Joseph Luft by permission of National Press Books. Copyright © 1969 by National Press Books.

awareness—awareness by himself and by others—of his behavior, feelings, and motivations. Unlike most windowpanes, those of the Johari Window sometimes change in size.

Each of you may be described by a Johari Window. Quadrant 1, the *open quadrant,* will reflect your general openness to the world, your willingness to be known. It comprises all aspects of yourself known to you and to others. This quadrant is the basis for most interpersonal communication.

By contrast quadrant 2, the *blind quadrant,* consists of all the things about yourself that other people perceive but that are not accessible to you. Perhaps you tend to monopolize conversation unwittingly, or you think of yourself as quite a wit but your friends find your humor heavy-handed. Then again you might feel quite confident and yet have several nervous mannerisms that others are aware of but you are not. The blind quadrant could contain any of the unintentional communicative stimuli mentioned in Chapter 2.

In quadrant 3, the *hidden quadrant,* you are the one who exercises discretion. This quadrant is made up of all the things you prefer not to disclose to someone else, whether they concern yourself or other people: your salary, your parents' divorce, your feelings about your roommate's closest friend, your overdue bills, and so on.

The last pane, quadrant 4, is the *unknown quadrant.* The blind quadrant is unknown to you though known to others. The hidden quadrant is unknown to others but known to you. Quadrant 4 is completely unknown. It represents everything about yourself that has never been explored, either by you or by other people. It contains all your untapped resources, all your potential for personal growth. You can only infer that it exists or confirm its existence in retrospect.

The four quadrants of the Johari Window are interdependent: a change in one quadrant will affect others. As you reveal something from the hidden quadrant, for example, you make it part of the open quadrant, thus enlarging it and reducing the size of the hidden quadrant. Should friends tell you about your nervous mannerisms, this information becomes part of the open quadrant, with a corresponding shrinkage of the blind quadrant. Such change is not always desirable. Sometimes, for example, telling a person that he seems nervous only makes him more ill at ease. Because inappropriate disclosure of a feeling or perception about another can be damaging, your friends will need to use some discretion in communicating with you about quadrant 2.

Basically, however, Luft proposes that it is rewarding and satisfying to enlarge the open quadrant—that is, not only to learn more about yourself but to reveal yourself to some degree so that others will know you better too. It is also his belief that greater knowledge of self in relation to others will result in greater self-esteem and self-acceptance.

If you can learn more about yourself and others—through metacommunication, for example—you can change the shape of your own Johari Window. An improved window might look something like the one in Figure 23.

Figure 23

	Known to self	Not known to self
Known to others	Open 1	Blind 2
Not known to others	Hidden 3	Unknown 4

An Improved Johari Window

Metacommunication

Metacommunication, or *communication that is about communication,* is a concept closely linked to the relationship level of human encounters. For example, if you say to your mother, "Tell him to mind his own damned business," and she replies, "I wish you wouldn't swear so much. You do it more and more, and I don't like it," she is responding not to the content of your remark but to your method of getting your point across. The content of her communication is communication itself.

Any comment directed at the way in which a person communicates is an example of metacommunication. For years the procedure in public speaking classes has been for students to give practice speeches and then have the instructor and class members give their reactions to the speaker and the speech. Comments such as "I thought you had excellent examples," "You could have brought out your central idea more explicitly," and "Try to be a little more enthusiastic" are all instances of metacommunication.

Metacommunication is not always so explicit. Sometimes discussions that begin at the content level become forms of metacommunication. We can best illustrate with an anecdote. A young man and woman, dressed for a night on the town, have just stepped out of a cab. As they stand at the corner waiting for the light to change, they rapidly become involved in a heated argument:

WIFE: Next time try to get home earlier so we can be on time.
HUSBAND: It's only a party. Next time tell me beforehand if you think it's so important to be there at 8 sharp. And don't sound so annoyed.
WIFE: But you're always late.
HUSBAND: I'm not *always* late. Don't generalize like that.
WIFE: Well, you're late a lot of the time. Why do you always put me down when I say something about you?
HUSBAND: I don't "always" put you down. There you go again, generalizing.

Although they may well remember it simply as a quarrel about lateness, this couple is arguing about how they communicate with each other. The husband tells the wife not to sound so annoyed, the husband informs her that she makes too many generalizations, she counters that he puts her down, and so on. As they make these disclosures, they bring information from the blind quadrant into the open quadrant. But disclosures about the blind quadrant have to be made with some discretion. Moreover, because these disclosures take place in a defensive atmosphere, there is little chance that they will improve the relationship between husband and wife.

In a more supportive climate, we can use metacommunication to help each other become aware of ineffective communication practices. It is sometimes awkward to provide such feedback, but when it is done in a kindly rather than a malicious way, it can give valuable impetus to self-improvement.

Self-Disclosure

Some years ago Lewin, a German-born psychologist, made a comparison between the personality structures of Americans and Germans.[21] Americans, he observed, start conversations more easily, are more willing to help strangers, and form friendships more readily than Germans. Superficially Americans are less resistant to communicating than Germans, but their openness is restricted to the more peripheral aspects of personality. While Germans seem more aloof in casual encounters, Lewin felt, once they make friends they are more open about the central, or core, levels of their personalities, and the friendships they do form tend to be deeper and last longer.

Whatever the reasons for these differences, in Johari terms the Americans seem to suffer by comparison because they interact on a relatively shallow level, leaving the most central areas of their personality inaccessible to others. We can be more specific about American patterns of self-disclosure if we look at the work of Jourard and his associates.

They find, for example, that married people typically disclose themselves more to their spouses than to anyone else. Unmarried college students usually reveal more to their best friend of the same sex than to any friend of the opposite sex; they also reveal less to their fathers than to people in any of their other close relationships. Females are more open about themselves than males, and Jewish college males disclose significantly more about themselves than do Catholics, Methodists, or Baptists. Self-disclosure also decreases with advancing age. And as we might expect, certain categories of personal information are disclosed more readily than others: people seem to be much freer in talking about their tastes and interests, attitudes, and opinions than they are in answering questions about money, personality, or anything to do with their bodies.[22] (See Appendix for an exercise in self-disclosure.)

Jourard's work with the mentally disturbed has led him to the conclusion that we often expend a great deal of energy trying to keep others from knowing us for fear that if our true selves were known we would be rejected. He believes that this very act of concealment keeps us from sustaining healthy human relationships:

> Self-disclosure, or should I say "real" self-disclosure, is both a symptom of personality health . . . and at the same time a means of ultimately achieving healthy personality. . . . I have known people who would rather die than become known. . . . When I say that self-disclosure is a symptom of personality health, what I mean really is that a person who displays many of the other characteristics that betoken healthy personality . . . *will also display the ability to make himself fully known to at least one other significant human being.*[23]

Jourard is not suggesting indiscriminate self-disclosure. He acknowledges that efforts at revelation can be damaging or even faintly comic. In the movie *Bob and Carol and Ted and Alice*, Natalie Wood played the part of a young woman who could not turn off the openness she had learned to express in an encounter group. When a waiter in a restaurant asked her how she was, she replied in some detail. Then she asked the waiter how he was, and he replied—briefly. Not satisfied with his response, she left her dinner companions and followed him into the kitchen, saying emphatically that she really did want to know how he was. The waiter was very embarrassed by her behavior.

Self-disclosure is an attempt to let authenticity enter our social relationships. At times it is an attempt to emphasize enacted rather than expected roles. It may even be an attempt to step out of a role entirely. When does it work? When does it improve interpersonal relationships? Luft describes several characteristics of appropriate self-disclosure, five of the most salient being these:

1. It is a function of the ongoing relationship.
2. It occurs reciprocally.
3. It is timed to fit what is happening.
4. It concerns what is going on within and between persons present.
5. It moves by small increments.[24]

Apply these standards to the restaurant scene just described or to any of your own attempts at self-disclosure that didn't come off and you may be able to determine what went wrong.

Appropriate self-disclosure is not one-sided. It is an exchange process. It can and often does prompt greater disclosure from the other person. It also results in more positive feelings between two people. Jourard reports a high correlation between the disclosure output to a given person and the disclosure input from that person, and, as we mentioned, he refers to this phenomenon as the dyadic effect. He goes even further when on the basis of his experience as a therapist he suggests that ". . . the capacity to disclose authentically, *in response* that is appropriate to the setting, to the authentic disclosure of the other person in a dyad is probably one of the best indicants of healthy personality."[25]

The Need for Self-Actualization

Throughout this book we have taken the view that it is possible for each of us to improve our ability to communicate. In some cases the desire to perfect communication skills arises out of the need to correct some deficiency or shortcoming. But it may be prompted by a sense of creativity and curiosity, or what the late Abraham Maslow popularized as the need for **self-actualization**. He explains this need as the desire for *self-fulfillment,* the need for *realization of one's human potential* by becoming "everything that one is capable of becoming."[26]

According to Maslow man has certain basic needs that are structured hierarchically and that he satisfies level by level, beginning with the most basic: the physiological needs such as hunger, thirst, and sex. After these are fulfilled, needs for safety become more salient. Then in turn come the needs for love and belonging, esteem, and finally self-actualization.

Self-actualization takes many forms: developing one's talents as a pianist, pursuing a difficult career, learning to ski, running for public office, or even improving one's competence in interpersonal relations. In any of its forms, self-actualization is a way of changing the shape of the Johari Window. As we actualize our potential, our untapped resources, we decrease the size of the unknown quadrant and enlarge either the open or the hidden quadrant. Whether or not this new information about oneself is available to others, it increases self-awareness.

Today we are witnessing a growing interest in all methods of self-development, but particularly in those directed at interpersonal relationships. Much of this interest is formalized in sensitivity training, which we have already discussed, and in other kinds of therapeutic communication. But old patterns are comfortable, and when they are reinforced they tend to be repeated. Maslow warns that we sometimes resist personal growth, talking ourselves out of attempts to self-actualize:

> In my own notes I had first labeled this defense the "fear of one's own greatness" or the "evasion of one's destiny" or the "running away from one's own best talents." . . . Often we run away from the responsibilities dictated (or rather suggested) by nature, by fate, even sometimes by accident, just as Jonah [in the Bible] tried—in vain—to run away from his fate.[27]

Despite these self-imposed obstacles, we know from our study of social learning that it is possible and often desirable to change communication behaviors. As you complete this course, we encourage you in your efforts to reevaluate and improve your interpersonal skills as part of a continuing process of self-actualization.

A REVIEW OF COMMUNICATION OUTCOMES

We spoke in Chapter 1 of five possible outcomes of effective interpersonal communication—understanding, pleasure, attitude influence, improved relationships, and action—and at different points in this book we have given special attention to each of them. For example, the concepts of status (Chapter 8), social influence and consensus (Chapter 9), acceptance of self and others (Chapter 10), and persuasion and attitude change (Chapter 11) all have some bearing on attitude influence. Similarly the concepts of cohesiveness (Chapter 9), interpersonal relations (Chapter 10), source credibility (Chapter 11), and interpersonal trust (the present chapter) are all relevant to improved relationships.

These five outcomes are neither exhaustive nor mutually exclusive. For example, a look at the relationship aspects of communication illustrates that defensive behaviors distort understanding, that disconfirming responses are not pleasurable, that negative feedback makes for resistance to attitude influence—in short, that communication outcomes are often interdependent. In Figure 24 we attempt to review all the outcomes and communication contexts we have been studying in a form that shows their interrelationships. We hope that this grid offers a helpful synthesis of the concepts we have been discussing throughout the book.[28]

Figure 24

Social Contexts

Outcomes	Dyad	Problem-solving small group	Therapeutic group	Public communication
Understanding	Understanding	Understanding	Understanding of others / Understanding of self	Understanding and/or information gain
Pleasure	Pleasure	Pleasure	Social acceptance	Entertainment
Attitude influence	Social influence	Consensus	Acceptance of others / Acceptance of self	Persuasion and attitude change
Improved relationships	Interpersonal trust	Cohesiveness	Interpersonal relations	Source credibility
Action	Behavioral response	Behavioral response	Behavioral response	Behavioral response

Outcomes of Effective Communication in Four Social Contexts

312 ## Summary

In Chapter 1 the improvement of human relationships was seen as a mediating outcome. We proposed then that the more satisfying the relationship between two communicators, the more likely it was that the other outcomes of effective interpersonal communication would occur. As we discussed the relationship aspects of communication, we tried to demonstrate why this should be the case. We spoke of the differences between confirming and disconfirming response styles and of the specific behaviors that increase or diminish self-esteem.

We approached our second subject, interpersonal trust, by looking at how people behave when they play games or observe others playing them, particularly in mixed-motive situations. We looked at some of the effects of trust-destroying behavior and discussed the supportive and defensive climates that could be established through communication.

Awareness of self, as the next section demonstrated, differs from awareness of others because the perspectives of the actor and the observer differ. We then turned to the Johari model for a way of conceptualizing the effects of various levels of awareness on human interaction. Metacommunication, self-disclosure, and self-actualization were discussed as means of improving the Johari Window.

In closing we reviewed the communication outcomes and contexts that have drawn our attention throughout the book and summarized their interrelationships in Figure 24.

Review Questions

1. How do the content and relationship aspects of communication differ? Provide examples of each.
2. What are some major differences between confirming and disconfirming response styles? Give examples of each.
3. What is the dyadic effect? Give at least two examples.
4. How do supportive and defensive climates of communication differ?
5. What is the relationship between trust, accuracy, and effectiveness in interpersonal communication?
6. State the most important implication of research on behavior attribution for students of communication.
7. What are four levels of awareness illustrated by the Johari Window? How do these different levels affect interpersonal communication?
8. What is metacommunication? Give some examples of metacommunication.
9. What is the need for self-actualization? How does it relate to interpersonal communication?
10. What are five characteristics of appropriate self-disclosure? How does self-disclosure relate to interpersonal communication?

Exercises

1. The next time you observe a disagreement between two people, try to determine whether they are disagreeing on the content level, the relationship level, or both. Relate your observations to two other disagreements that you have experienced, and analyze those disagreements in the same way.

2. Observe five communication events that illustrate five different outcomes of interpersonal communication. Analyze the events in terms of the following questions:

   a. What were the relative frequencies of confirming and disconfirming response styles for each communication event? Does there appear to be any relationship between the type of interpersonal communication outcome and the predominant response style? If so, why do you think this is the case and what implications does this have for your own communication behavior?

   b. In which communication events were trust and self-disclosure most apparent? Why do you think this was so?

3. Write a paragraph describing someone whom you trust very much. Then write a description of someone you do not trust. Finally, elaborate the behaviors that you want to develop and avoid in building a trusting relationship with someone in the future.

4. In a small group—five people or so—have each person attempt to increase his awareness of self and others by telling each of the others one positive and one negative impression he has formed about him. If time permits, have a free discussion in which group members go into greater depth, asking for and giving further impressions.

5. Have each person in a group of five write down anonymously three or four of his most fulfilling experiences. Then exchange papers at random, and have the responses read aloud. Let one member of the group write some of the common themes on the board to represent the types of experiences that seem representative of self-actualization.

Suggested Readings

Johnson, David. *Reaching Out: Interpersonal Effectiveness and Self-Actualization.* Englewood Cliffs, N.J.: Prentice-Hall, 1972. This book offers an insight into the relationship between the development of interpersonal communication skills and the attainment of self-actualization. It complements what you have studied in the present book, including such topics as listening, acceptance of self and others, constructive confrontation, modeling, and reinforcing interpersonal skills.

Luft, Joseph. *Of Human Interaction.* Palo Alto, Calif.: National Press, 1969. This book elaborates on the rationale behind and the application of the Johari Window and explains more fully the value of self-

314 disclosure. It is understandable to the undergraduate student and provocative to the graduate student.

Maslow, Abraham H. *Toward a Psychology of Being.* Princeton, N.J.: Van Nostrand, 1962. The late Abraham Maslow offered a great deal to the understanding of man through this book. His concept of self-actualization is among the most interesting of those explained in the book. It is excellent reading for those who want to explore one man's ideas about learning to become more fully human.

Notes

[1] Jack R. Gibb, "Defensive Communication," *Journal of Communication,* 11 (1961), 141.

[2] Jurgen Ruesch and Gregory Bateson, *Communication: The Social Matrix of Psychiatry* (New York: Norton, 1968), p. 213. For an extensive discussion of content and relationship levels of communication, see Paul Watzlawick, Janet Helmick Beavin, and Don D. Jackson, *Pragmatics of Human Communication* (New York: Norton, 1967), pp. 51–54.

[3] Evelyn Sieburg and Carl Larson, "Dimensions of Interpersonal Response" (paper delivered at the annual conference of the International Communication Association, Phoenix, April 1971), pp. 2–5. Italics added.

[4] Martin Buber, "Distance and Relation," *Psychiatry,* 20 (1957), 101.

[5] Franz Kafka, *Letter to His Father,* tr. by Ernst Kaiser and Eithne Wilkins (New York: Schocken, 1966), pp. 37, 39.

[6] Watzlawick, Beavin, and Jackson, p. 86.

[7] Joseph Luft, *Of Human Interaction* (Palo Alto, Calif.: National Press, 1969), pp. 52–53.

[8] Julian Rotter, "Generalized Expectancies for Interpersonal Trust," *American Psychologist,* 26 (1971), 444. Italics added.

[9] Anatol Rapoport and Albert Chammah, *Prisoner's Dilemma: A Study in Conflict and Cooperation* (Ann Arbor, Mich.: University of Michigan Press, 1965), pp. 24–25.

[10] Stewart L. Tubbs, "Two Person Game Behavior, Conformity-Inducing Messages and Interpersonal Trust," *Journal of Communication,* 21 (1971), 326–341.

[11] Sidney M. Jourard, *Self-Disclosure: An Experimental Analysis of the Transparent Self* (New York: Wiley, 1971), p. 105.

[12] Morton Deutsch, "The Effect of Motivational Orientation upon Trust and Suspicion," *Human Relations,* 13 (1960), 123–137; and Morton Deutsch and Robert M. Krauss, "The Effect of Threat on Interpersonal Bargaining," *Journal of Abnormal and Social Psychology,* 61 (1960), 181–189.

[13] Dale Leathers, "The Process Effects of Trust-Destroying Behavior," *Speech Monographs,* 37 (1970), 184.

[14] Glen D. Mellinger, "Interpersonal Trust as a Factor in Communication," *Journal of Abnormal and Social Psychology*, 52 (1956), 304.

[15] Gibb, p. 147.

[16] L. Pearce and S. Newton, *The Conditions of Human Growth* (New York: Citadel, 1963), p. 52. Italics added.

[17] Theodore Reik, *Listening with the Third Ear* (New York: Grove, 1948), p. 125. Italics added.

[18] Richard E. Nisbett and others, "Behavior as Seen by the Actor," *Journal of Personality and Social Psychology*, 27 (1973), 154–164.

[19] Michael D. Storms, "Videotape and the Attribution Process: Reversing Actors' and Observers' Points of View," *Journal of Personality and Social Psychology*, 27 (1973), 165–175.

[20] Luft, p. 6.

[21] Kurt Lewin, *Resolving Social Conflicts* (New York: Harper & Brothers, 1948), pp. 18–25.

[22] Jourard, p. 105.

[23] Sidney M. Jourard, *The Transparent Self: Self-Disclosure and Well-Being* (Princeton, N.J.: Van Nostrand, 1964), p. 24.

[24] Luft, pp. 132–133.

[25] Jourard, *The Transparent Self*, p. 179.

[26] Abraham H. Maslow, *Motivation and Personality* (New York: Harper & Brothers, 1954), p. 92.

[27] Abraham H. Maslow, "The Jonah Complex," in Warren G. Bennis and others (eds.), *Interpersonal Dynamics: Essays and Readings on Human Interaction*, rev. ed. (Homewood, Ill.: Dorsey, 1968), p. 715.

[28] For further material on these topics, see Stewart L. Tubbs (ed.), *New Directions in Communication* (Flint, Mich.: International Communication Association, 1972).

Supplementary Exercises
appendix

Anyone who has ever taught a course in speech communication realizes that there is often a major gap between the theory and the application of that theory. This appendix includes some supplementary exercises which may be used to help bridge the above-mentioned gap. For maximum benefit, however, the behaviors stimulated by these exercises should be discussed to show their relationship to the conceptual material presented in this text and to class lectures. It is important to keep in mind that the exercises are a *means* of increasing student learning and are not an end in themselves.

ROLE-PLAY EXERCISES

TWO-PERSON ROLE-PLAY EXERCISES

1. Student-Professor Conference

JANE: You are a college sophomore in Dr. Patterson's speech communication class. You are dissatisfied with a grade for one of your class projects and are trying to persuade Dr. Patterson that you should have received a higher grade.

DR. PATTERSON: You have had ten students come to your office to complain about their low grades. Jane has been an uninterested student all semester long. Now she enters your office.

2. Parent-Son Episode

PARENT: You have been looking for a lost article of your son's clothing and you find some pornographic pictures in one of the drawers of his dresser.

NINETEEN-YEAR-OLD SON: You have just been out with some friends and you find your parent in your room.

3. Employer-Applicant Interview

EMPLOYER: You are looking for a man or woman to hire as a summertime sales person in your department store. You are primarily looking for someone who can relate to your young college customers.

APPLICANT: You are a twenty-year-old college student who desperately needs a summer job to help finance your way through school. You have had no sales experience but are popular and personable.

4. Employer-Employee Interview

EMPLOYER: You have noticed that one of your employees' work has been substandard lately. He has worked for you as a used car salesman for the past five years and has been a better than average salesman. You have just received a call from his wife that he has been drinking somewhat lately and that she suspects him of having spent several nights with another woman. She is completely against any drinking, and she gets upset when he drinks even one beer or mixed drink. You call him in for a discussion.

EMPLOYEE: You have been disappointed about your level of pay lately and you would like to be considered for a promotion as a used car sales manager. You have been moonlighting at a second job lately to buy your wife a special birthday gift.

5. Counselor-Student Interview

STUDENT: You are a college student who has become involved in drug use to an extent that you feel it is becoming a problem. You go to the university counseling center to get some help.

COUNSELOR: You are employed by the university counseling center to give help to students who seem to have problems of various kinds. You are eager to help in any way you can. A student has just entered your office.

GROUP ROLE-PLAY EXERCISES

The Sinking Ship

You seven people are the only survivors of a passenger ship that was hit in the South Pacific by an old World War II mine. You are now trapped in the bottom of the ship's hold, with only a small, one-man air lock to let you return to the surface. It takes approximately three minutes to operate the air lock to allow one person to escape.

The hold is steadily filling with water, and judging by the list of the ship, you have at the most fifteen minutes before the ship sinks quickly to the bottom of the 37,000-foot-deep Mariana trench.

Your problem is one of survival. You are to determine as quickly as possible the most equitable way of deciding who will be saved in the fifteen minutes' time. Remember that it takes three minutes to save each person, so the very maximum number that can be saved is five.

As each person is "saved," he will separate from the group and sit in a chair. Both the amount of time taken by each person in the air lock and the remaining time left for the victims will be watched closely.

To impress the disaster victims with the seriousness of their situation, it is necessary to emphasize that those who are left in the hold will suffer a most hideous death—death by drowning.

Ability Grouping Meeting

The participation group members (group A) are to assume they represent the English teachers in a senior high school. The principal of the school has asked them to meet by themselves to formulate their recommendations pertaining to ability grouping in their classes for next year. ("Ability grouping" for this situation means the use of standardized test results as a basis of placement of students in class sections.) Two years ago the students were placed in classes on the following basis: Above Average Ability, Average Ability, and Below Average Ability. The following year students were not placed in classes on the basis of ability, but were randomly placed into class sections. The principal is aware of some dissatisfaction with the grouping of students in English classes; thus, he is asking for the recommendation of the teachers involved.

Procedure. The participation group (group A) will meet in the center of the room for a period of twenty minutes to discuss the situation presented above. They realize that they must reach a decision before they meet with the principal. The rest of the members (group B) will observe group A's activity during their meeting. Following this twenty-minute period, group B will meet in the center of the room to discuss what they observed from group A's activity. (They will meet for approximately twenty minutes.) Group A will observe group B's evaluation. At the end of this period group A and group B will combine for a general reaction and/or summary of the two group meetings.

CASE PROBLEMS

A clinical psychologist at a university feels that his interviews with a client should be recorded on tape and that the benefits to be derived from such recordings would be impaired if the client knew in advance that the recording was to be made. The psychologist sometimes uses these recordings in his classroom to illustrate his lectures, always without the knowledge of the client, though the client's name is not revealed to the class.

QUESTION: Should the psychologist use these tape recordings as class demonstrations without the permission of the client?

John and Mary are college students. John is nineteen years old and in his sophomore year in business administration; Mary is nearly nineteen and a sophomore in home economics. They met about a year and a half ago at school and have been dating steadily since that time. There is no question that they are really in love. Three months ago, with the consent of their parents, they became engaged, and they wish to be married within the next three months.

Neither John nor Mary is self-supporting. Their tuition and most of their expenses are paid by their parents, who in both cases are fairly well-to-do. It will take John two more full years, including summers, to complete his degree. Mary can complete her degree in about two years and should have no difficulty in getting a teaching position after graduation.

The parents, though not entirely happy about the marriage plans, have promised to continue giving the couple, until their education has been completed, the same financial support they now receive.

QUESTION: Should this couple marry now?

Jan Dorn is an attractive twenty-year-old college student majoring in art. She is a student in Dr. Thompson's small-group communication class. Jan and her husband, Jim, rent a home on the same block where Dr. Thompson lives. Jim and Dr. Thompson have met and become friends as well as neighbors. Jim is presently serving six months' duty in the army. With comfortable financial support from her parents, Jan is able to continue her education.

The first day of class Jan appears without her wedding ring, and in her self-introduction she does not reveal the fact that she is married. As the term progresses, Dr. Thompson learns that Jan has had a number of male members of the class spend the night at her house. On Easter Sunday Jan and Jim (home on leave) unexpectedly visit Dr. Thompson and his wife at their home.

QUESTION: How should Dr. Thompson react in this situation?

Two years ago Sandy (now twenty) became engaged to Thad against the wishes of her parents and the rest of her family as well. None of them liked him, especially Sandy's mother. However, since that was what Sandy wanted they all went along with it. Her parents never said she couldn't get married and were willing to pay for the wedding. After two years, Thad called Sandy and broke the engagement. Her whole family was angry and thought that Sandy had seen the light as well. She acted as if she had; in fact, she went out with some other boys and seemed to have a good time. Unknown to her family, though, she still loved Thad and, despite what he had done, still wanted to marry him. A few months later Thad met Sandy where she worked. She hadn't seen him for four weeks. Unexpectedly, they eloped. Her family had no idea he had come into town and didn't know what had happened until after the fact.

QUESTION: How can this couple improve the relationship between Thad and Sandy's families?

The problem lies with my communication. I don't say much in class or give much feedback. Whenever I am part of a group, whether in a class or in the fraternity, I don't feel a strong attraction toward the group. I am always putting myself in the background to observe. I feel firmly convinced that any communication on my part will not help the situation, and that by participating in the group I will lose some of my concentration on the conversation. I very rarely feel any rewards from being in a group. I can associate with a group and understand their beliefs and feelings, but I can't really become a part of it. If forced to participate or be a part of the group, I generally do a poor job and don't get much out of it. I don't like conforming with rules or goals that other people have set. There are many things that I don't wish to share with others.

QUESTION: How might this person overcome his difficulty?

324   My difficulty in communication isn't unusual in today's society. It is the communication gap between the young and old generations. That difficulty of communication happened between me and my parents, mainly my father.

Compared with other families we have more difficulties than usual because of his Japanese, and my Latin traditions.

When I was twelve years old I left my farm home in Brazil and went to attend high school; until then I had just a Japanese education due to the influences of my family and the Japanese colony I lived in. So, at twelve I started a complete new life far from home. I don't know if it is the peculiarity of this age, but I had no trouble in accepting changes—after one year I was completely absorbed by the Latin customs and education (that's why I don't act like a Japanese but like a Brazilian). Since then there has been a conflict between my father and me which is both a generation gap and a culture gap.

QUESTION: How might this person improve his relationship with his father?

DISCLOSURE GAMES

The disclosure game* is a structured way for two people to become acquainted with one another through mutual disclosure on assigned topics. The topics are roughly graded for intimacy. Participants in the game take turns disclosing themselves to their partner on each topic. The rules of the game are simple: first, complete honesty is called for, including an honest statement of unwillingness to disclose any given subject. Second, the listener must avoid pressuring and probing, unless the other person expresses a willingness to be pressured or probed.

The long version of the game is also designed in such a way that, in addition to the two partners' mutual self-disclosure, an investigator might gather useful data on the "depth" to which two players have permitted themselves to be known. I have also used a short version of the game, which eliminates the more complicated instructions and simply invites pairs of people to begin getting acquainted by disclosing themselves to one another on just five or ten topics, such as hobbies, attitudes toward their own bodies, problems and satisfactions in work, and personal satisfactions and problems with members of their own family. What nearly always happens is that, after initial embarrassment at the artificiality of the situation, the partners become intensely involved in mutual disclosure, spending sometimes as much as seven hours at it.

I include the game in this book so that others may play it or use it as a research tool. If it is employed in research, the investigator is advised to pretest the items, so that they may be assigned an intimacy value appropriate for the groups or individuals whom he is testing.

I have observed that many people do not know how to become acquainted with others. On large campuses, in dormitories, and other places where crowds of people reside, they live in mutual ignorance and misunderstanding. The disclosure game could be a step in the direction of increased mutual understanding.

A DISCLOSURE GAME FOR TWO PLAYERS

I am asking you to play this "game" both for serious scientific purposes and to give you an illuminating experience. You will participate in a kind of "dialogue" with a stranger.

*Found in Sidney M. Jourard, *Self-Disclosure: An Experimental Analysis of the Transparent Self* (New York: Wiley, 1971), pp. 173–178 (slightly adapted). Reprinted by permission of John Wiley & Sons, Inc.

Procedure

1. Record your name, age, occupation, religious denomination, and your partner's name.
2. Read the thirty-five topics listed below in Part 1. Check those topics that you have disclosed fully to *somebody* in your life. If there is nobody to whom you have *fully* revealed that aspect of your self, leave the space blank.
3. In Part 2 check the topics you are willing to discuss *fully* with the partner to whom you have just been introduced, when once the dialogue between you begins. If you are reluctant for any reason to discuss a topic fully, leave that space blank.
4. After you have completed the above procedure, go through the fuller acquaintance process as instructed by the investigator. He may ask you to give each other back rubs, engage in ordinary conversation, or participate in some other activity.
5. After the acquaintance process, turn to Part 3 and check on the left side of the page the topics you feel willing to disclose to your partner.
6. Now, flip a coin with your partner. Whoever wins the toss asks the first question. The other person answers or declines, according to his intent. He then asks the same question of the other, who answers or not, as he wishes. If the other person has answered the question you asked, place a check mark on the right-hand side of the page. Otherwise do not check. Take turns asking each question first, throughout the entire list.

    At any time during the dialogue you can change your mind. If you intended to speak on a topic and in the course of the interview find you would rather not, then simply decline that topic. And if you intended not to disclose on a topic but decided you will, go ahead and do so. Circle the items on which you changed your mind.

Part 1

Check those topics on which you have disclosed yourself *fully* to *somebody*.

1. Your hobbies; how you like best to spend your spare time.
2. Your favorite foods and beverages, and chief dislikes in food and drink.
3. Your preferences and dislikes in music.
4. The places in the world you have traveled and your reaction to these places.
5. Your educational background and your feelings about it.
6. Your personal views on politics, the presidency, foreign and domestic policy.
7. The aspects of your body you are most pleased with.
8. Aspects of your daily work that satisfy and that bother you.

9. The educational and family background of your parents.
10. What your personal goals are for the next ten years or so.
11. Your personal religious views; nature of religious participation if any.
12. Your views on the way a husband and wife should live their marriage.
13. The names of the people who helped you significantly in your life.
14. Your present financial position: income, debts, savings, sources of income.
15. The occasions in your life when you were happiest, in detail.
16. The worries and difficulties you experience now, or have experienced in the past, with your health.
17. Habits and reactions of yours that bother you at present.
18. Your usual ways of dealing with depression, anxiety, and anger.
19. The features of your appearance you are most displeased with and wish you could alter.
20. Your favorite forms of erotic play and sexual lovemaking.
21. Your most common sexual fantasies and reveries.
22. The names of the persons you have significantly helped and the ways in which you helped them.
23. Characteristics of yourself that give you cause for pride and satisfaction.
24. The unhappiest moments in your life, in detail.
25. The circumstances under which you become depressed, and when your feelings are hurt.
26. The ways in which you feel you are most maladjusted or immature.
27. The actions you have most regretted doing in your life, and why.
28. The main unfulfilled wishes and dreams and the failures in your life.
29. Your guiltiest secrets.
30. What you regard as the mistakes and failures your parents made in raising you.
31. How you see and evaluate your parents' relationship with one another.
32. What you do to stay fit, if anything.
33. The sources of strain and dissatisfaction in your marriage (or relationship with the opposite sex).
34. The people with whom you have been sexually intimate; the circumstances of your relationship with each.
35. The persons in your life whom you most resent; the reasons why.

Part 2

Check those topics you are willing to reveal to your partner.
1. Your hobbies; how you like best to spend your spare time.

2. Your favorite foods and beverages, and chief dislikes in food and drink.
3. Your preferences and dislikes in music.
4. The places in the world you have traveled and your reactions to these places.
5. Aspects of your daily work that satisfy and that bother you.
6. Your educational background and your feelings about it.
7. The educational and family background of your parents.
8. Your personal views on politics, the presidency, foreign and domestic policy.
9. Your personal religious views; nature of religious participation if any.
10. What your personal goals are for the next ten years or so.
11. Your present financial position: income, debts, savings, sources of income.
12. Habits and reactions of yours that bother you at present.
13. Characteristics of yourself that give you cause for pride and satisfaction.
14. Your usual ways of dealing with depression, anxiety, and anger.
15. The unhappiest moments in your life, in detail.
16. The occasions in your life when you were happiest, in detail.
17. The circumstances under which you become depressed, and when your feelings are hurt.
18. The ways in which you feel you are most maladjusted or immature.
19. The actions you have most regretted doing in your life, and why.
20. The main unfulfilled wishes and dreams and the failures in your life.
21. Your guiltiest secrets.
22. What you regard as the mistakes and failures your parents made in raising you.
23. How you see and evaluate your parents' relationship with one another.
24. Your views on the way a husband and wife should live their marriage.
25. The worries and difficulties you experience now, or have experienced in the past, with your health.
26. What you do to stay fit, if anything.
27. The aspects of your body you are most pleased with.
28. The features of your appearance you are most displeased with and wish you could alter.
29. The sources of strain and dissatisfaction in your marriage (or relationship with the opposite sex).
30. Your favorite forms of erotic play and sexual lovemaking.
31. Your most common sexual fantasies and reveries.
32. The people with whom you have been sexually intimate; the circumstances of your relationship with each.

33. The persons in your life whom you most resent; the reasons why.
34. The names of the persons you have significantly helped and the ways in which you helped them.
35. The names of the people who helped you significantly in your life.

Part 3

Check the topics you *intend to reveal* to your partner on the *left* side of page. On the right side, check those topics your partner fully discussed.

1. Your hobbies; how you like best to spend your spare time.
2. Your favorite foods and beverages, and chief dislikes in food and drink.
3. Your preferences and dislikes in music.
4. The places in the world you have traveled and your reactions to these places.
5. Aspects of your daily work that satisfy and that bother you.
6. Your educational background and your feelings about it.
7. The educational and family background of your parents.
8. Your personal views on politics, the presidency, foreign and domestic policy.
9. Your personal religious views; nature of religious participation if any.
10. What your personal goals are for the next ten years or so.
11. Your present financial position: income, debts, savings, sources of income.
12. Habits and reactions of yours that bother you at present.
13. Characteristics of yourself that give you cause for pride and satisfaction.
14. Your usual ways of dealing with depression, anxiety, and anger.
15. The unhappiest moments in your life, in detail.
16. The occasions in your life when you were happiest, in detail.
17. The circumstances under which you become depressed, and when your feelings are hurt.
18. The ways in which you feel you are most maladjusted or immature.
19. The actions you have most regretted doing in your life, and why.
20. The main unfulfilled wishes and dreams and the failures in your life.
21. Your guiltiest secrets.
22. What you regard as the mistakes and failures your parents made in raising you.
23. How you see and evaluate your parents' relationship with one another.
24. Your views on the way a husband and wife should live their marriage.
25. The worries and difficulties you experience now, or have experienced in the past, with your health.

26. What you do to stay fit, if anything.
27. The aspects of your body you are most pleased with.
28. The features of your appearance you are most displeased with and wish you could alter.
29. The sources of strain and dissatisfaction in your marriage (or relationship with the opposite sex).
30. Your favorite forms of erotic play and sexual lovemaking.
31. Your most common sexual fantasies and reveries.
32. The people with whom you have been sexually intimate; the circumstances of your relationship with each.
33. The persons in your life whom you most resent; the reasons why.
34. The names of the persons you have significantly helped and the ways in which you helped them.
35. The names of people who helped you significantly in your life.

A SHORTER DISCLOSURE GAME

Interpersonal Yoga

The immediate object of Hatha Yoga is to master the various *asanas*. Each of these is a specific position which one's body assumes. A novice begins to assume one of these positions and finds that his muscles "protest." The means by which one fully enters an *asana* is to enter it up to one's limit and then to press gently at that limit. There can be no forcing, no cheating. The novice enters a position no further than he has "earned."

One can view authentic dialogue as a kind of interpersonal *asana*. The ultimate in dialogue is unpremeditated, uncontrived, spontaneous disclosure in response to the disclosure of the other. The following is an exercise aimed at helping a person discover his limits in ongoing dialogue. The first person discloses himself on the first topic until he and his partner are satisfied there is no more to be said. Then, the other person does likewise. Then, on to the next *asana*, or topic. The rule is complete honesty, respect for one's own limits (as they are experienced in the form of embarrassment, anxiety, and so forth). As soon as this point is reached, the person declares he is at a limit. The partners can then discuss reasons for the reserve, and the person may overcome it.

Part 1: Disclosure

1. My hobbies, interests, and favorite leisure pursuits.
2. What I like and dislike about my body—appearance, health, and so forth.
3. My work—satisfactions, frustrations.

4. My financial situation: income, savings, debts, investments, and so forth.
5. Aspects of my parents I like and dislike; family problems encountered in growing up.
6. Religious views, philosophy of life, what gives meaning to my life.
7. My love life, past and present.
8. Problems in my marriage or in my dealings with the opposite sex at present.
9. What I like and dislike about my partner on the basis of this encounter.

Part 2: Physical Contact

The same rules of respect for one's own limits, and one's partner's, apply.
1. Massage the head and neck of the partner.
2. Massage the shoulders of the partner.
3. Give a back rub.
4. Rub the stomach of the partner.
5. Massage the partner's feet.

Name Index

Subject Index

About the Authors

STEWART L. TUBBS is Associate Professor of Communication at General Motors Institute, the residential, coeducational college in Flint, Michigan, established by General Motors Corporation in 1919 to provide an undergraduate work-study curriculum in engineering and management. Its Department of Communication and Organizational Behavior, with which Dr. Tubbs is associated, offers courses integrating communication theory and research with organizational development.

Dr. Tubbs received his doctorate jointly from the Departments of Speech and Psychology at The University of Kansas. His masters and bachelors degrees are in speech, from Bowling Green State University.

He has twice been named an Outstanding Teacher: by The University of Kansas for the Department of Speech and Drama in 1968 and by the Central States Speech Association in 1973. The editor of International Communication Association's *New Directions in Communication* (1972), he is a member of the Speech Communication Association, the International Communication Association, and the American Psychological Association, and is listed in *Outstanding Young Men of America* and *American Men and Women of Science*. A frequent contributor to professional journals in speech-communication, psychology, and education, Dr. Tubbs lives in Flint with his wife and their son.

SYLVIA MOSS is a professional writer whose major interest is the behavioral sciences. Following her undergraduate work at Barnard (where she recalls "being appalled at first hearing a tape recording of my voice in an introductory speech course") and at The University of Wisconsin at Madison, she received a masters degree from Columbia University and pursued further graduate studies in psychology at New York University and The New School.

In addition to the social sciences, Ms. Moss follows developments in modern poetry and translates literature in several languages. She lives in Larchmont, New York, with her husband, who is in airline management, and their four-year-old son.